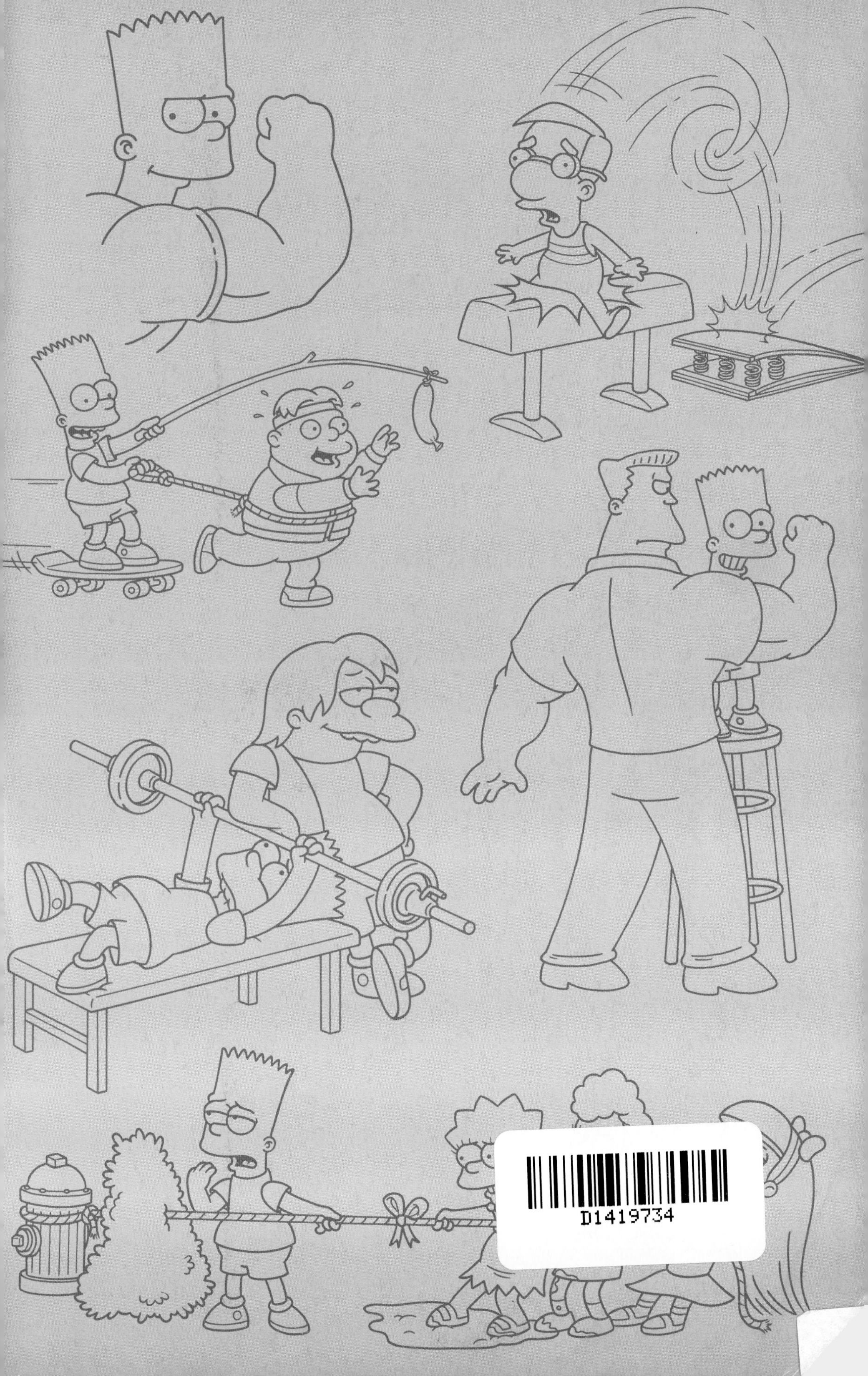

BIG BEEFY BOOK OF
BART SIMPSON ™

TITAN BOOKS

BIG BEEFY BOOK OF BART SIMPSON

Copyright © 1999, 2003, 2004 & 2005 by
Bongo Entertainment, Inc. All rights reserved.
No part of this book may be used or reproduced in any manner whatsoever
without written permission except in the case of brief quotations
embodied in critical articles and reviews. For information address
Bongo Comics Group c/o Titan Books
P.O. Box 1963, Santa Monica, CA 90406-1963

Published in the UK by Titan Books, a division of Titan Publishing Group,
144 Southwark St., London SE1 0UP, under licence from Bongo Entertainment, Inc.

FIRST EDITION: APRIL 2005
ISBN 10: 1-84576-057-3
ISBN 13: 978-1-84576-057-1
2 4 6 8 10 9 7 5 3

Publisher: MATT GROENING
Creative Director: BILL MORRISON
Managing Editor: TERRY DELEGEANE
Director of Operations: ROBERT ZAUGH
Art Director: NATHAN KANE
Art Director Special Projects: SERBAN CRISTESCU
Production Manager: CHRISTOPHER UNGAR
Legal Guardian: SUSAN A. GRODE

Trade Paperback Concepts and Design: SERBAN CRISTESCU

Contributing Artists:
KAREN BATES, JOHN COSTANZA, LUIS ESCOBAR, TIM HARKINS, JASON HO,
BRIAN ILES, NATHAN KANE, JAMES LLOYD, ISTVAN MAJOROS, JOEY MASON,
BILL MORRISON, KEVIN M. NEWMAN, JOEY NILGES, PHYLLIS NOVIN, PHIL ORTIZ,
PATRICK OWSLEY, RICK REESE, RYAN RIVETTE, MIKE ROTE,
HOWARD SHUM, CHRIS UNGAR, ART VILLANUEVA, MIKE WORLEY

Contributing Writers:
JAMES BATES, TERRY DELEGEANE, ABBY DENSON, TONY DIGEROLAMO,
GEORGE GLADIR, EVAN GORE, EARL KRESS, AMANDA McCANN,
JESSE LEON McCANN, MICHAEL NOBORI, DAVID RAZOWSKY,
JEFF ROSENTHAL, ERIC ROGERS, GAIL SIMONE, BRYAN UHLENBROCK,
SERAN WILLIAMS, CHRIS YAMBAR

PRINTED IN ITALY

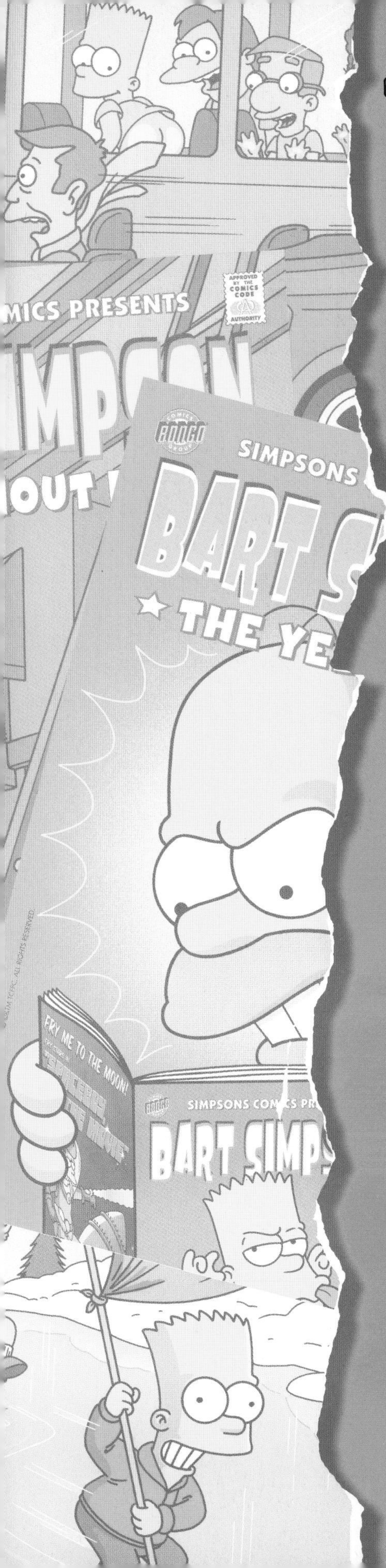
MICS PRESENTS
SIMPSONS
FRY ME TO THE MOON!
SIMPSONS COMICS PR

TABLE OF CONTENTS

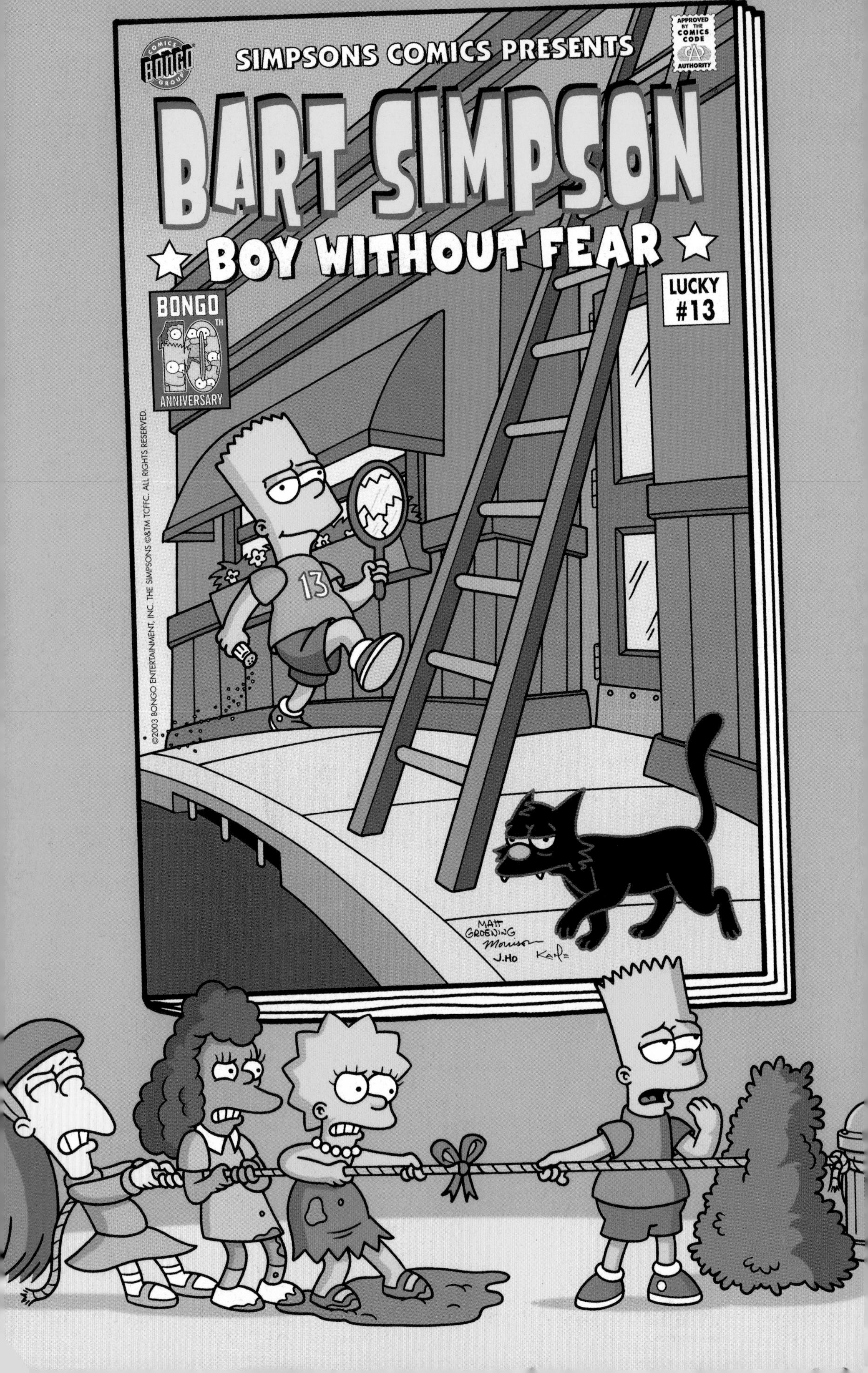
SIMPSONS COMICS PRESENTS
BART SIMPSON
BOY WITHOUT FEAR
LUCKY #13
BONGO 10TH ANNIVERSARY
APPROVED BY THE COMICS CODE AUTHORITY
©2003 BONGO ENTERTAINMENT, INC. THE SIMPSONS ©&TM TCFFC. ALL RIGHTS RESERVED.
MATT GROENING
J.HO
13

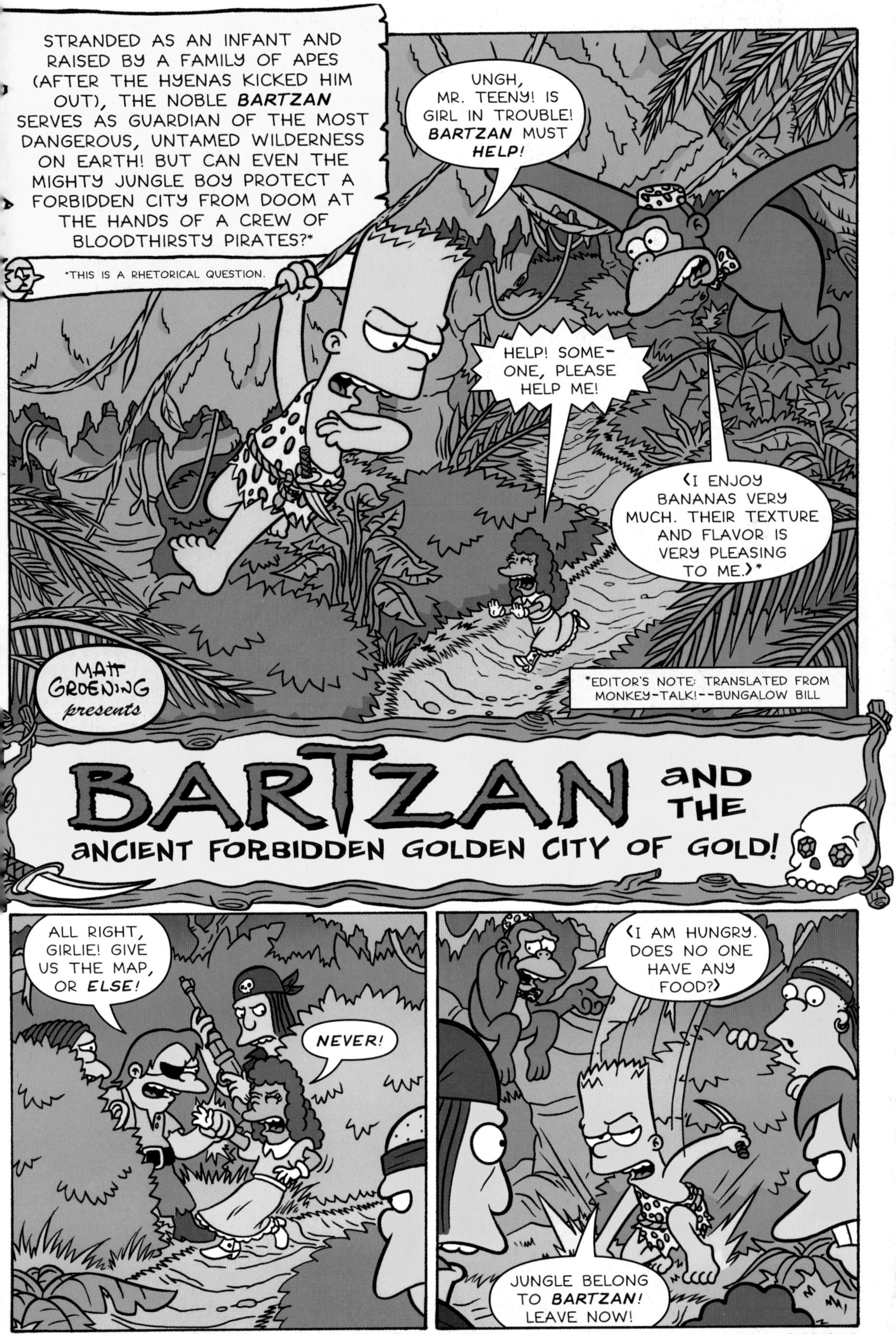
STRANDED AS AN INFANT AND RAISED BY A FAMILY OF APES (AFTER THE HYENAS KICKED HIM OUT), THE NOBLE ***BARTZAN*** SERVES AS GUARDIAN OF THE MOST DANGEROUS, UNTAMED WILDERNESS ON EARTH! BUT CAN EVEN THE MIGHTY JUNGLE BOY PROTECT A FORBIDDEN CITY FROM DOOM AT THE HANDS OF A CREW OF BLOODTHIRSTY PIRATES?*
*THIS IS A RHETORICAL QUESTION.
UNGH, MR. TEENY! IS GIRL IN TROUBLE! ***BARTZAN*** MUST ***HELP!***
HELP! SOME-ONE, PLEASE HELP ME!
‹I ENJOY BANANAS VERY MUCH. THEIR TEXTURE AND FLAVOR IS VERY PLEASING TO ME.›*
MATT GROENING *presents*
*EDITOR'S NOTE: TRANSLATED FROM MONKEY-TALK!--BUNGALOW BILL
BARTZAN and THE ancient FORBIDDEN GOLDEN CITY OF GOLD!
ALL RIGHT, GIRLIE! GIVE US THE MAP, OR ***ELSE!***
NEVER!
‹I AM HUNGRY. DOES NO ONE HAVE ANY FOOD?›
JUNGLE BELONG TO ***BARTZAN!*** LEAVE NOW!

GAIL SIMONE *SCRIPT* **JASON HO** *PENCILS* **HOWARD SHUM** *INKS* **JOEY MASON** *COLORS* **KAREN BATES** *LETTERS* **BILL MORRISON** *EDITOR*

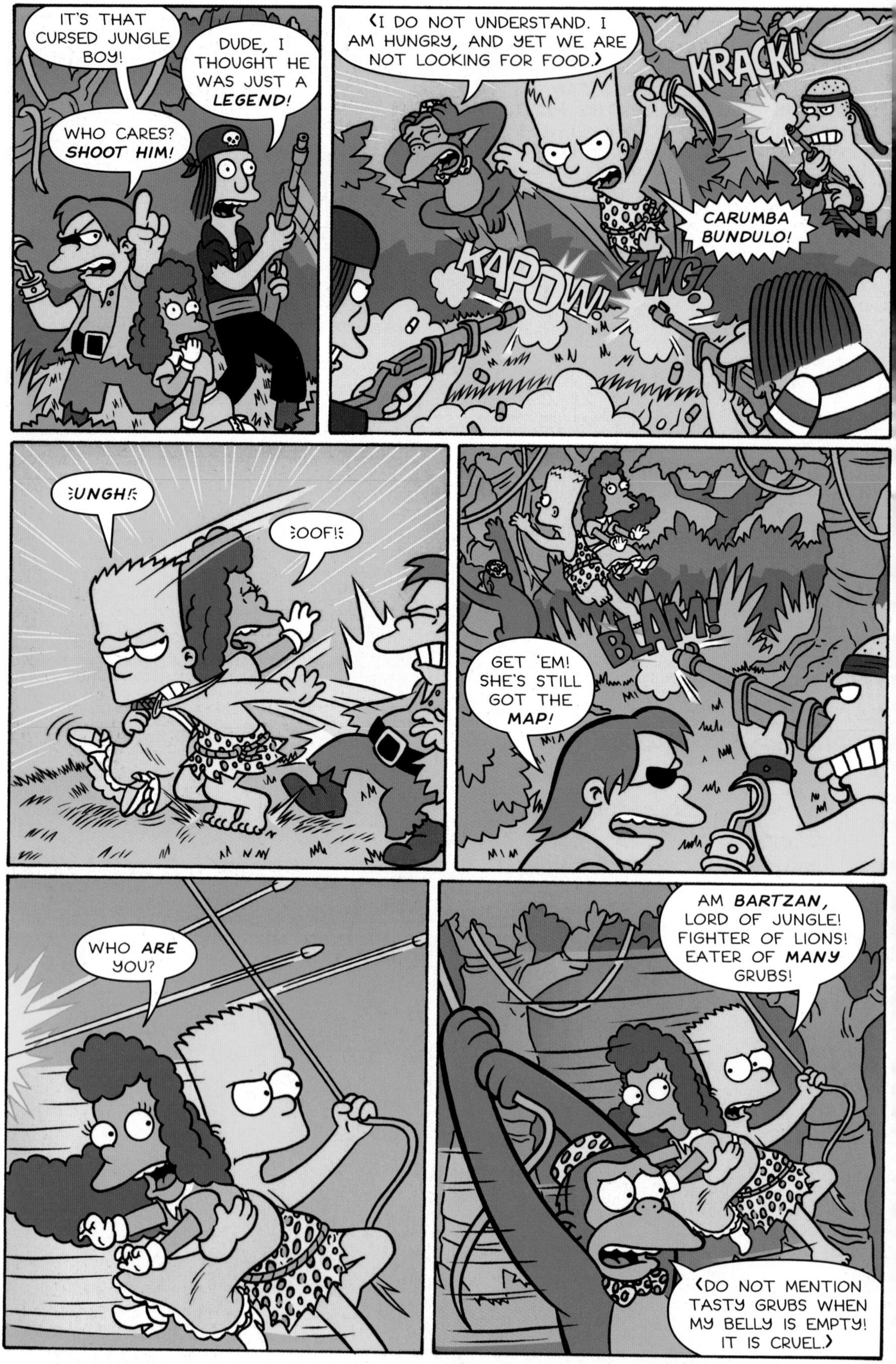
IT'S THAT CURSED JUNGLE BOY!
DUDE, I THOUGHT HE WAS JUST A LEGEND!
WHO CARES? SHOOT HIM!
‹I DO NOT UNDERSTAND. I AM HUNGRY, AND YET WE ARE NOT LOOKING FOR FOOD.›
KRACK!
CARUMBA BUNDULO!
KAPOW!
ZING!
UNGH!
OOF!
BLAM!
GET 'EM! SHE'S STILL GOT THE MAP!
WHO ARE YOU?
AM BARTZAN, LORD OF JUNGLE! FIGHTER OF LIONS! EATER OF MANY GRUBS!
‹DO NOT MENTION TASTY GRUBS WHEN MY BELLY IS EMPTY! IT IS CRUEL.›

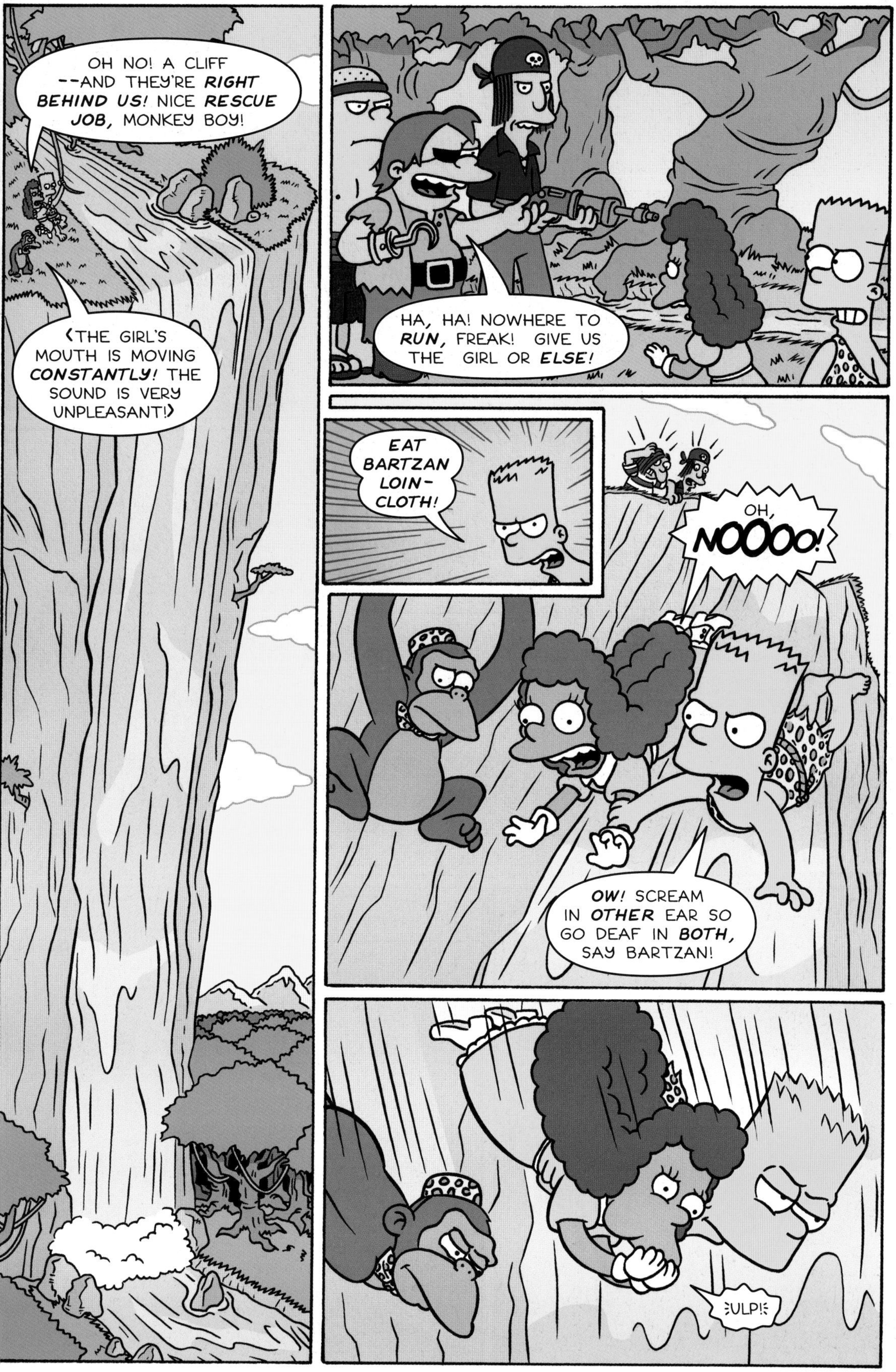

OH NO! A CLIFF --AND THEY'RE RIGHT BEHIND US! NICE RESCUE JOB, MONKEY BOY!
‹THE GIRL'S MOUTH IS MOVING CONSTANTLY! THE SOUND IS VERY UNPLEASANT!›
HA, HA! NOWHERE TO RUN, FREAK! GIVE US THE GIRL OR ELSE!
EAT BARTZAN LOIN-CLOTH!
OH, NOOOO!
OW! SCREAM IN OTHER EAR SO GO DEAF IN BOTH, SAY BARTZAN!
ULP!

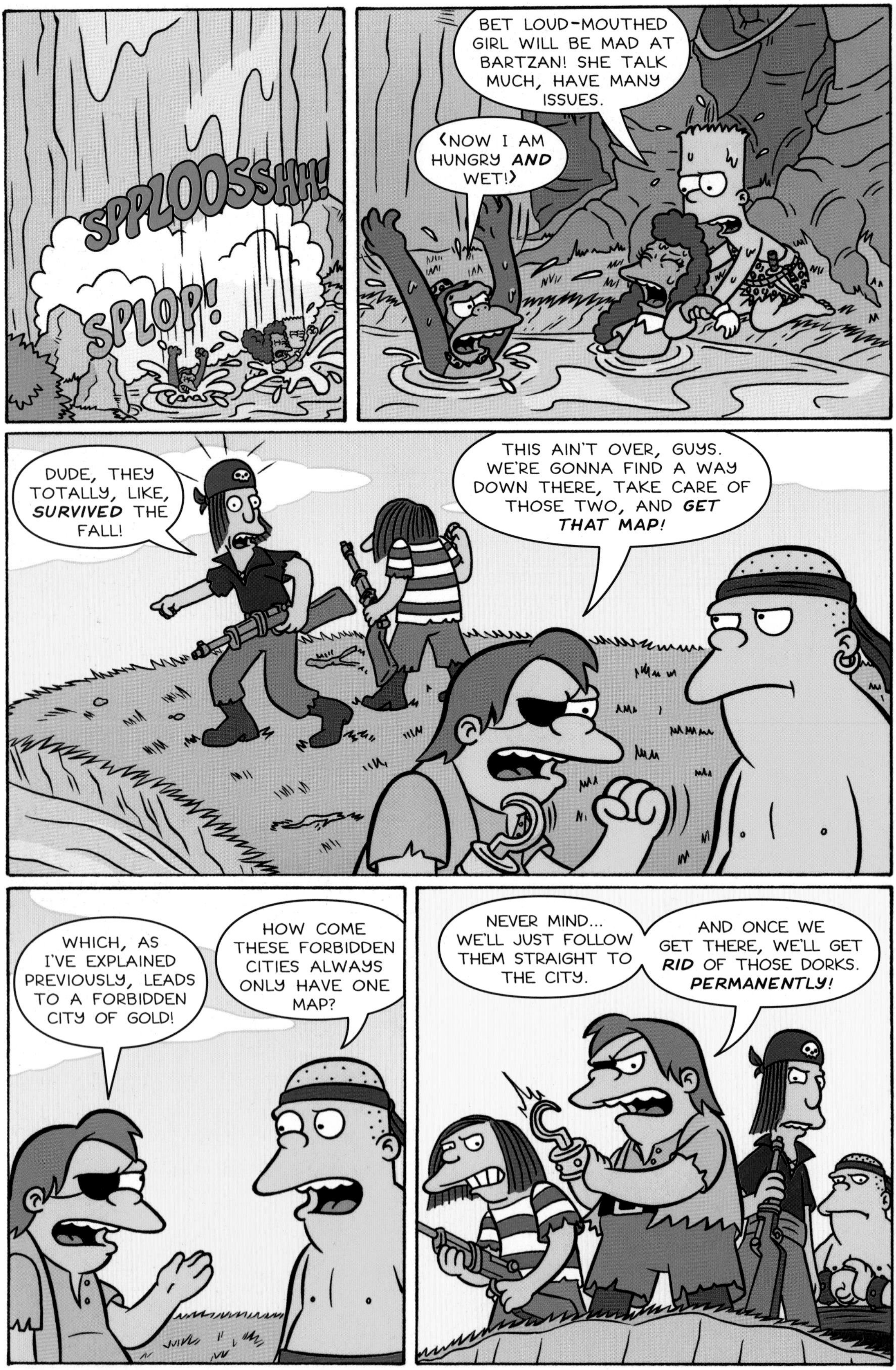
SPPLOOSSHH!
SPLOP!
BET LOUD-MOUTHED GIRL WILL BE MAD AT BARTZAN! SHE TALK MUCH, HAVE MANY ISSUES.
‹NOW I AM HUNGRY AND WET!›
DUDE, THEY TOTALLY, LIKE, SURVIVED THE FALL!
THIS AIN'T OVER, GUYS. WE'RE GONNA FIND A WAY DOWN THERE, TAKE CARE OF THOSE TWO, AND GET THAT MAP!
WHICH, AS I'VE EXPLAINED PREVIOUSLY, LEADS TO A FORBIDDEN CITY OF GOLD!
HOW COME THESE FORBIDDEN CITIES ALWAYS ONLY HAVE ONE MAP?
NEVER MIND... WE'LL JUST FOLLOW THEM STRAIGHT TO THE CITY.
AND ONCE WE GET THERE, WE'LL GET RID OF THOSE DORKS. PERMANENTLY!

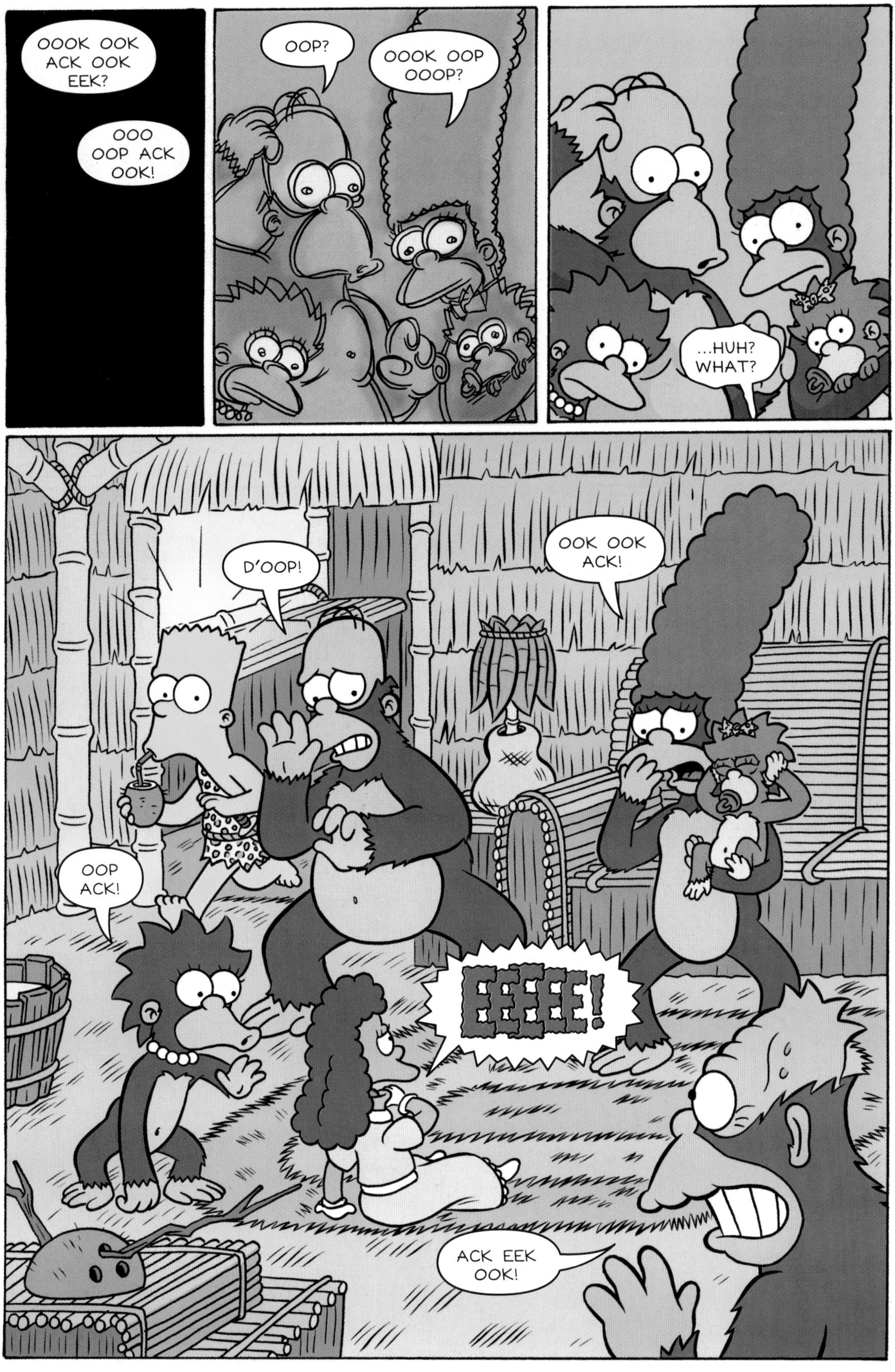
OOOK OOK
ACK OOK
EEK?
OOO
OOP ACK
OOK!
OOP?
OOOK OOP
OOOP?
...HUH?
WHAT?
D'OOP!
OOK OOK
ACK!
OOP
ACK!
EEEEE!
ACK EEK
OOK!

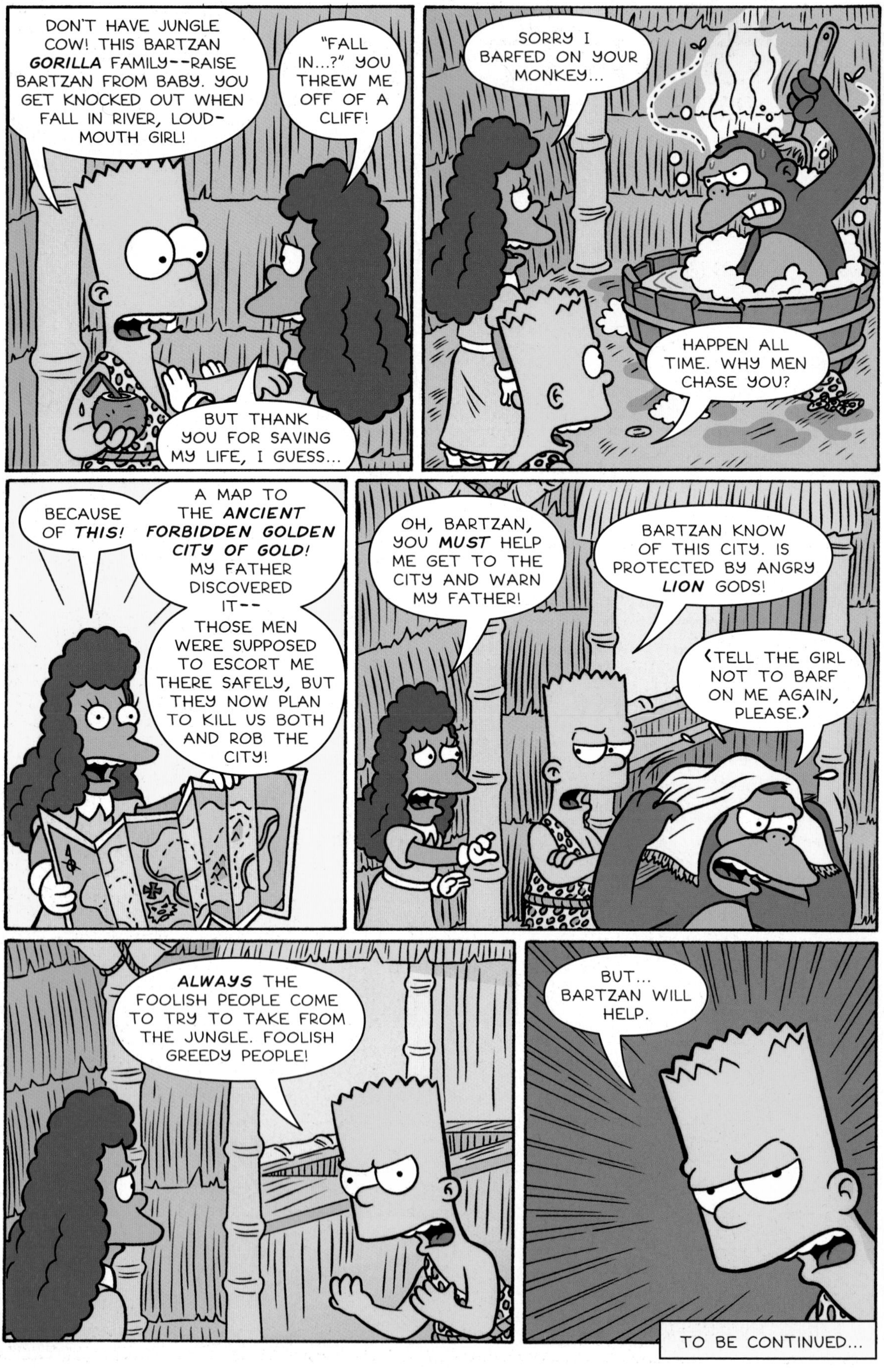
DON'T HAVE JUNGLE COW! THIS BARTZAN GORILLA FAMILY--RAISE BARTZAN FROM BABY. YOU GET KNOCKED OUT WHEN FALL IN RIVER, LOUD-MOUTH GIRL!
"FALL IN...?" YOU THREW ME OFF OF A CLIFF!
BUT THANK YOU FOR SAVING MY LIFE, I GUESS...
SORRY I BARFED ON YOUR MONKEY...
HAPPEN ALL TIME. WHY MEN CHASE YOU?
BECAUSE OF THIS!
A MAP TO THE ANCIENT FORBIDDEN GOLDEN CITY OF GOLD! MY FATHER DISCOVERED IT--
THOSE MEN WERE SUPPOSED TO ESCORT ME THERE SAFELY, BUT THEY NOW PLAN TO KILL US BOTH AND ROB THE CITY!
OH, BARTZAN, YOU MUST HELP ME GET TO THE CITY AND WARN MY FATHER!
BARTZAN KNOW OF THIS CITY. IS PROTECTED BY ANGRY LION GODS!
‹TELL THE GIRL NOT TO BARF ON ME AGAIN, PLEASE.›
ALWAYS THE FOOLISH PEOPLE COME TO TRY TO TAKE FROM THE JUNGLE. FOOLISH GREEDY PEOPLE!
BUT... BARTZAN WILL HELP.
TO BE CONTINUED...

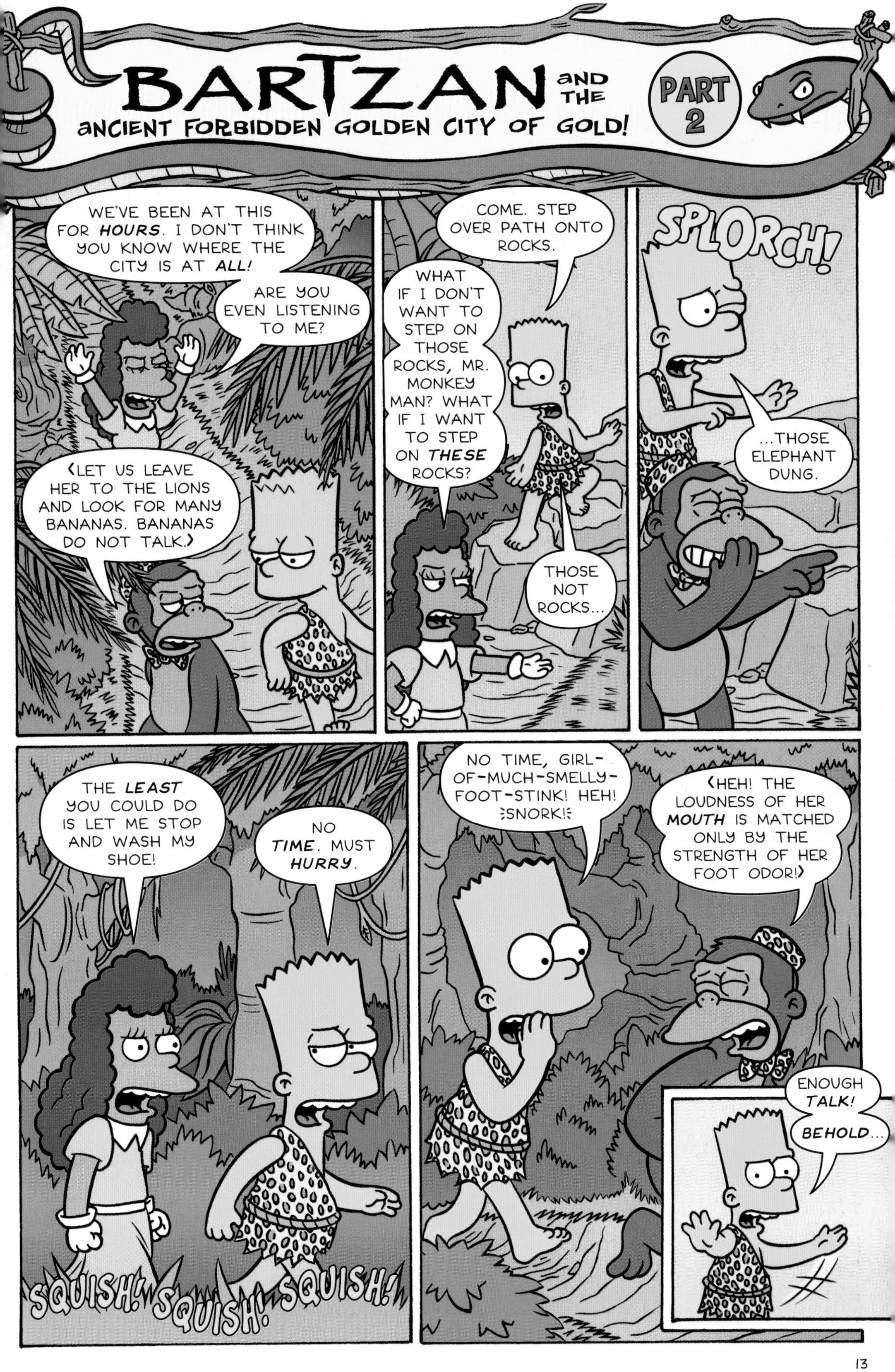
BARTZAN AND THE ANCIENT FORBIDDEN GOLDEN CITY OF GOLD!
PART 2
WE'VE BEEN AT THIS FOR HOURS. I DON'T THINK YOU KNOW WHERE THE CITY IS AT ALL!
ARE YOU EVEN LISTENING TO ME?
‹LET US LEAVE HER TO THE LIONS AND LOOK FOR MANY BANANAS. BANANAS DO NOT TALK.›
COME. STEP OVER PATH ONTO ROCKS.
WHAT IF I DON'T WANT TO STEP ON THOSE ROCKS, MR. MONKEY MAN? WHAT IF I WANT TO STEP ON THESE ROCKS?
THOSE NOT ROCKS...
SPLORCH!
...THOSE ELEPHANT DUNG.
THE LEAST YOU COULD DO IS LET ME STOP AND WASH MY SHOE!
NO TIME. MUST HURRY.
SQUISH! SQUISH! SQUISH!
NO TIME, GIRL-OF-MUCH-SMELLY-FOOT-STINK! HEH! SNORK!
‹HEH! THE LOUDNESS OF HER MOUTH IS MATCHED ONLY BY THE STRENGTH OF HER FOOT ODOR!›
ENOUGH TALK!
BEHOLD...

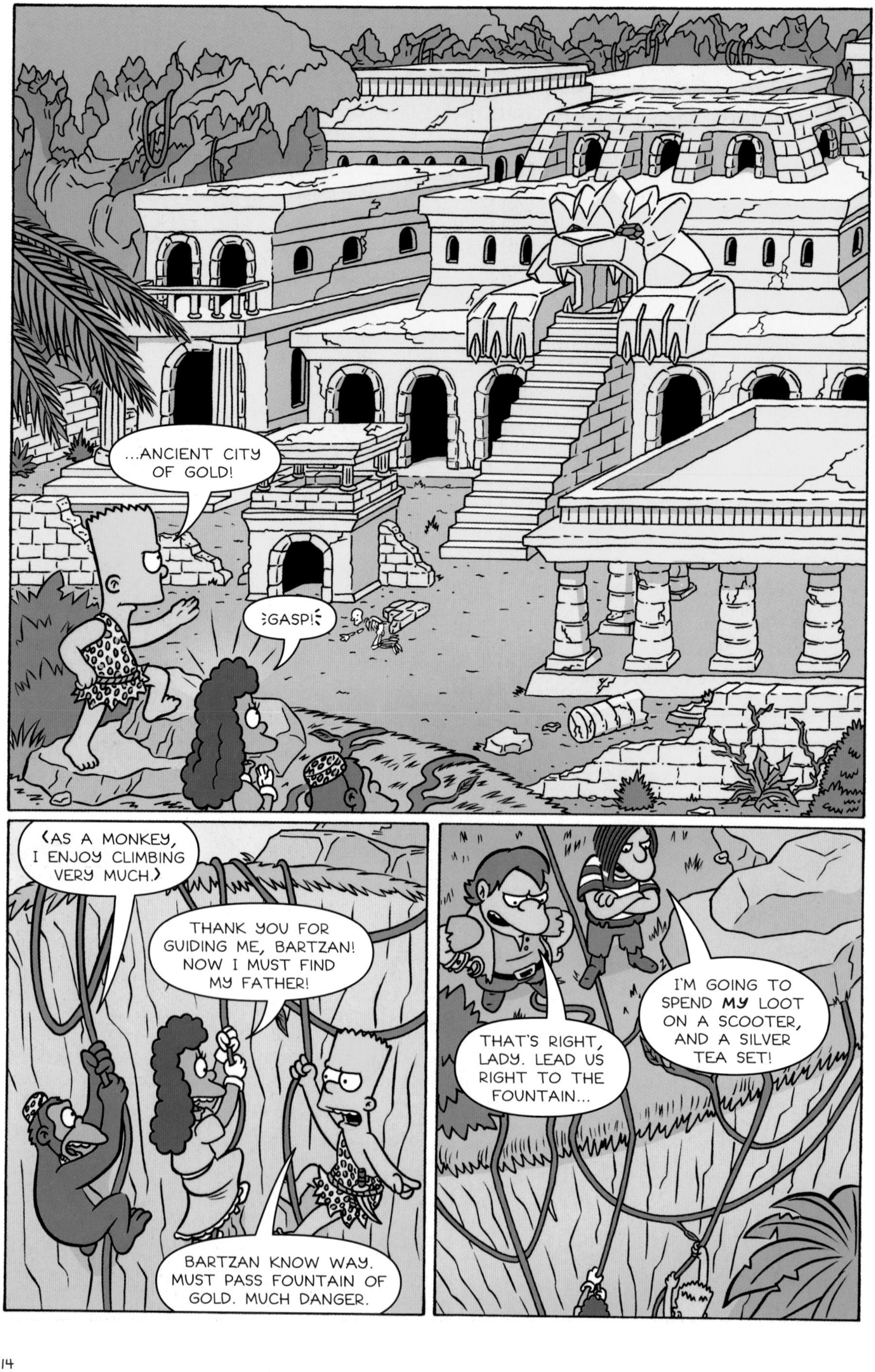
...ANCIENT CITY OF GOLD!
GASP!
‹AS A MONKEY, I ENJOY CLIMBING VERY MUCH.›
THANK YOU FOR GUIDING ME, BARTZAN! NOW I MUST FIND MY FATHER!
BARTZAN KNOW WAY. MUST PASS FOUNTAIN OF GOLD. MUCH DANGER.
THAT'S RIGHT, LADY. LEAD US RIGHT TO THE FOUNTAIN...
I'M GOING TO SPEND **MY** LOOT ON A SCOOTER, AND A SILVER TEA SET!

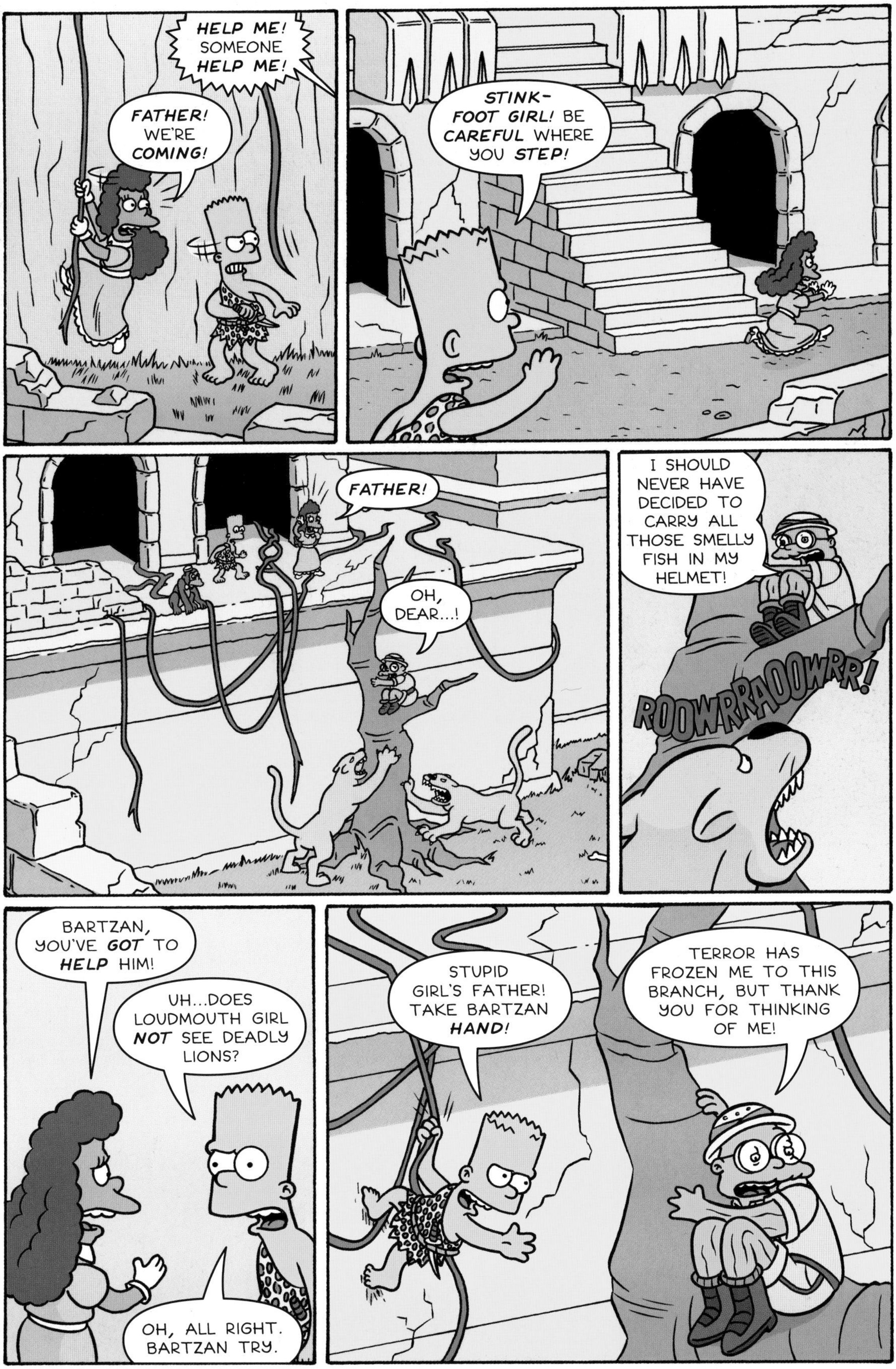
HELP ME! SOMEONE HELP ME!
FATHER! WE'RE COMING!
STINK-FOOT GIRL! BE CAREFUL WHERE YOU STEP!
FATHER!
OH, DEAR...!
I SHOULD NEVER HAVE DECIDED TO CARRY ALL THOSE SMELLY FISH IN MY HELMET!
ROOWRRAOOWRR!
BARTZAN, YOU'VE GOT TO HELP HIM!
UH...DOES LOUDMOUTH GIRL NOT SEE DEADLY LIONS?
OH, ALL RIGHT. BARTZAN TRY.
STUPID GIRL'S FATHER! TAKE BARTZAN HAND!
TERROR HAS FROZEN ME TO THIS BRANCH, BUT THANK YOU FOR THINKING OF ME!

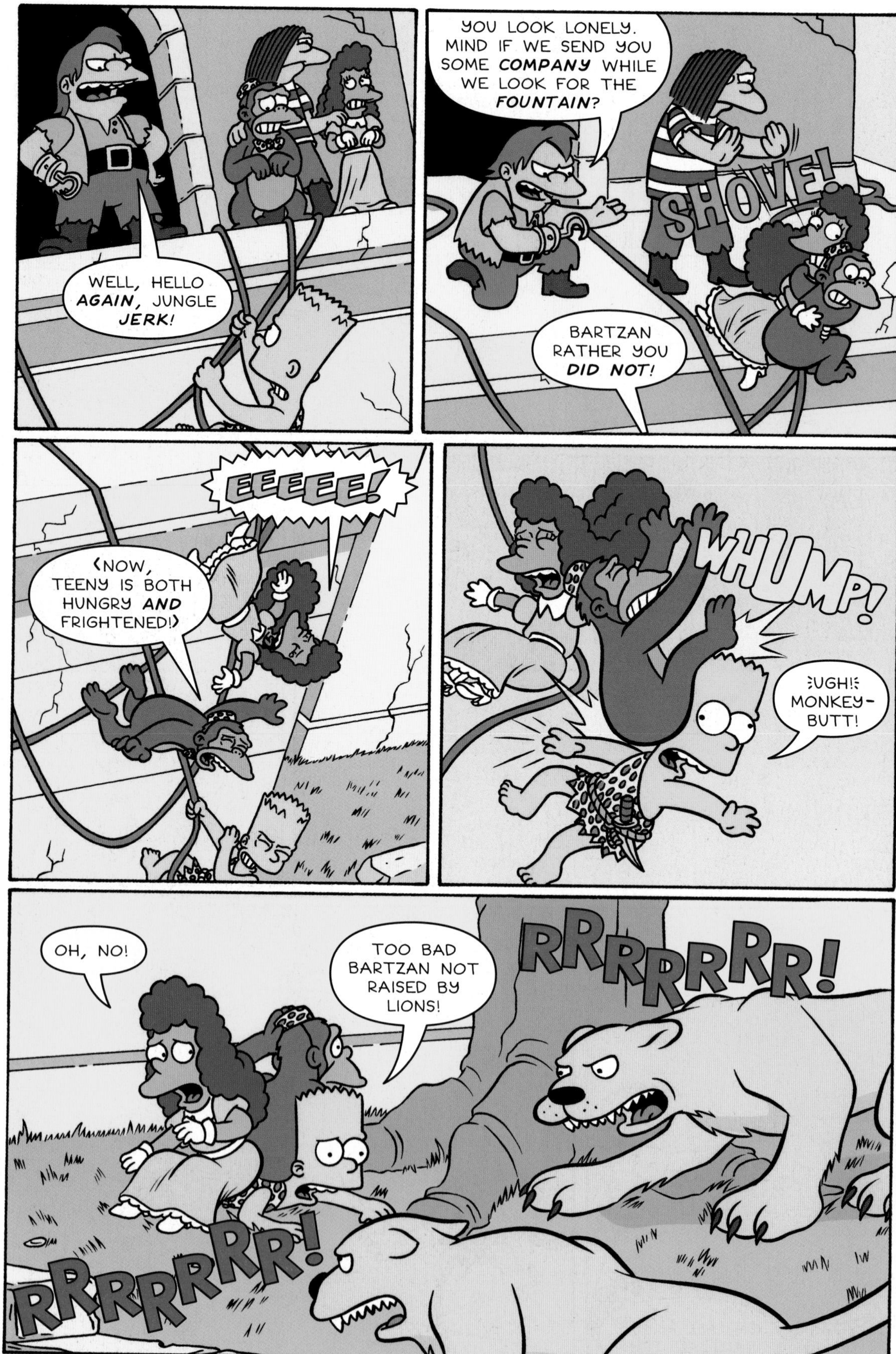

WELL, HELLO AGAIN, JUNGLE JERK!
YOU LOOK LONELY. MIND IF WE SEND YOU SOME COMPANY WHILE WE LOOK FOR THE FOUNTAIN?
SHOVE!
BARTZAN RATHER YOU DID NOT!
EEEEEE!
‹NOW, TEENY IS BOTH HUNGRY AND FRIGHTENED!›
WHUMP!
UGH! MONKEY-BUTT!
OH, NO!
TOO BAD BARTZAN NOT RAISED BY LIONS!
RRRRRRRR!
RRRRRRRR!

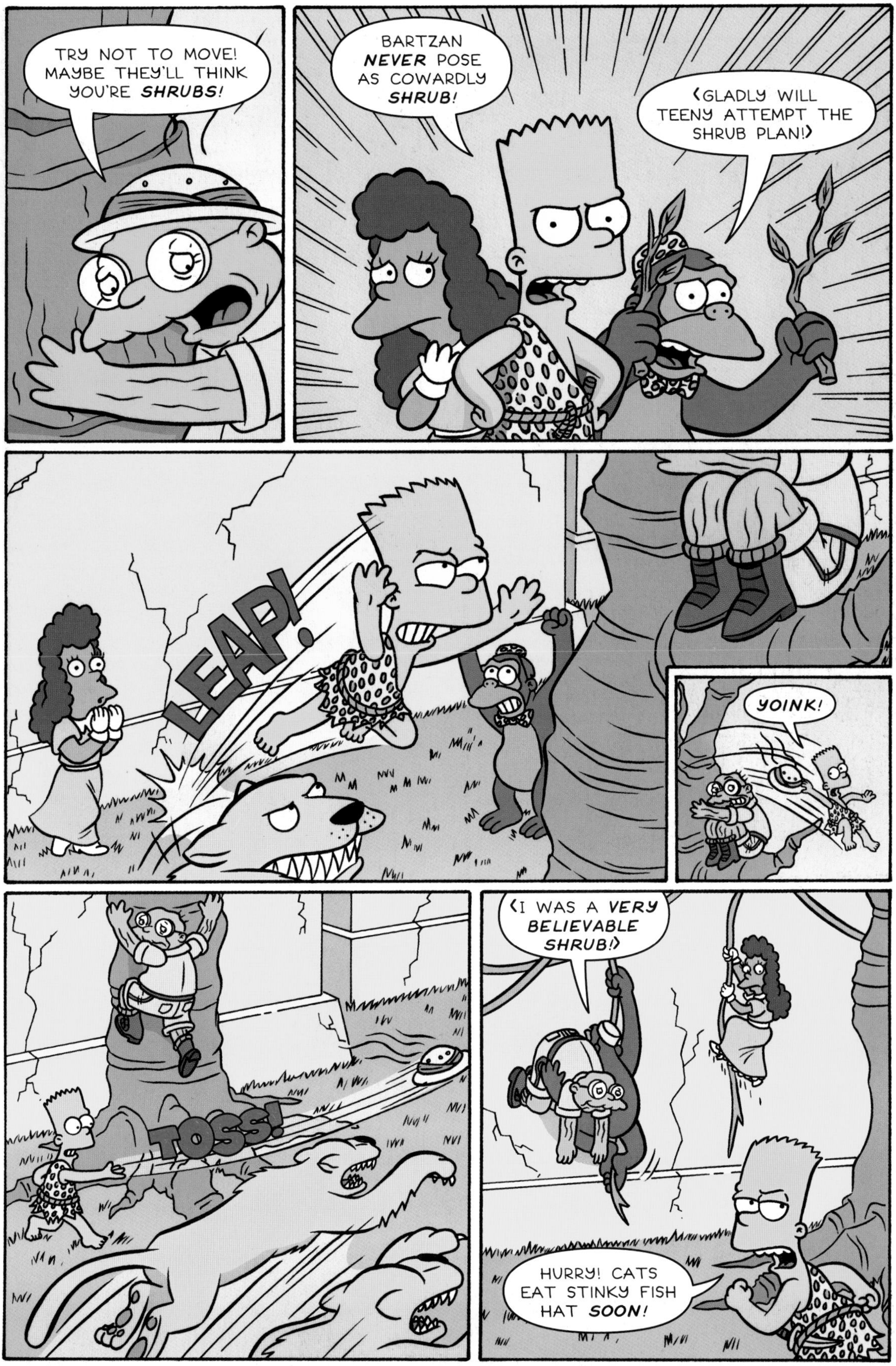
TRY NOT TO MOVE! MAYBE THEY'LL THINK YOU'RE SHRUBS!
BARTZAN NEVER POSE AS COWARDLY SHRUB!
‹GLADLY WILL TEENY ATTEMPT THE SHRUB PLAN!›
LEAP!
YOINK!
TOSS!
‹I WAS A VERY BELIEVABLE SHRUB!›
HURRY! CATS EAT STINKY FISH HAT SOON!

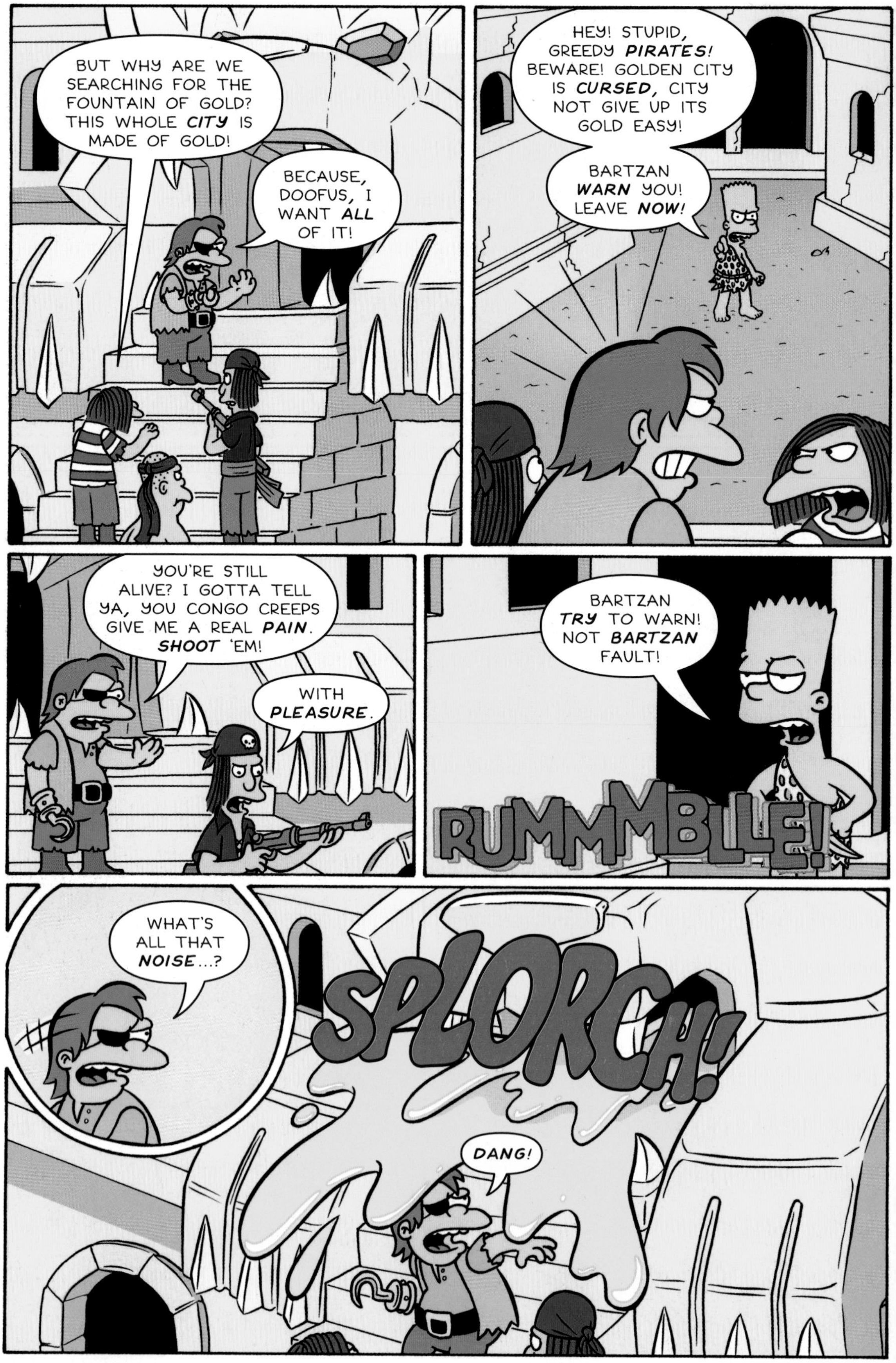
BUT WHY ARE WE SEARCHING FOR THE FOUNTAIN OF GOLD? THIS WHOLE CITY IS MADE OF GOLD!
BECAUSE, DOOFUS, I WANT ALL OF IT!
HEY! STUPID, GREEDY PIRATES! BEWARE! GOLDEN CITY IS CURSED, CITY NOT GIVE UP ITS GOLD EASY!
BARTZAN WARN YOU! LEAVE NOW!
YOU'RE STILL ALIVE? I GOTTA TELL YA, YOU CONGO CREEPS GIVE ME A REAL PAIN. SHOOT 'EM!
WITH PLEASURE.
BARTZAN TRY TO WARN! NOT BARTZAN FAULT!
RUMMMBLLE!
WHAT'S ALL THAT NOISE...?
SPLORCH!
DANG!

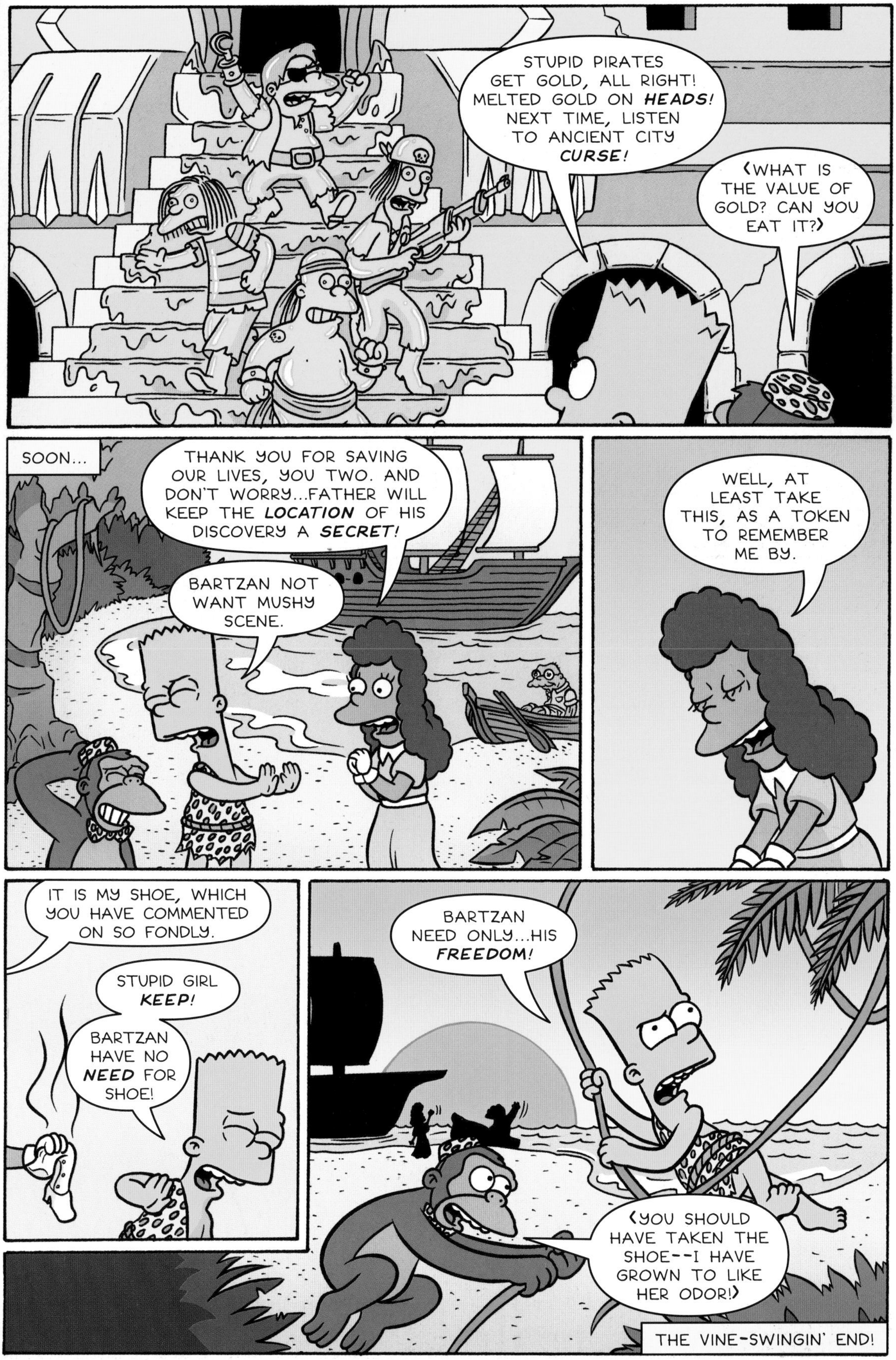
STUPID PIRATES GET GOLD, ALL RIGHT! MELTED GOLD ON HEADS! NEXT TIME, LISTEN TO ANCIENT CITY CURSE!
‹WHAT IS THE VALUE OF GOLD? CAN YOU EAT IT?›
SOON...
THANK YOU FOR SAVING OUR LIVES, YOU TWO. AND DON'T WORRY...FATHER WILL KEEP THE LOCATION OF HIS DISCOVERY A SECRET!
BARTZAN NOT WANT MUSHY SCENE.
WELL, AT LEAST TAKE THIS, AS A TOKEN TO REMEMBER ME BY.
IT IS MY SHOE, WHICH YOU HAVE COMMENTED ON SO FONDLY.
STUPID GIRL KEEP!
BARTZAN HAVE NO NEED FOR SHOE!
BARTZAN NEED ONLY...HIS FREEDOM!
‹YOU SHOULD HAVE TAKEN THE SHOE--I HAVE GROWN TO LIKE HER ODOR!›
THE VINE-SWINGIN' END!

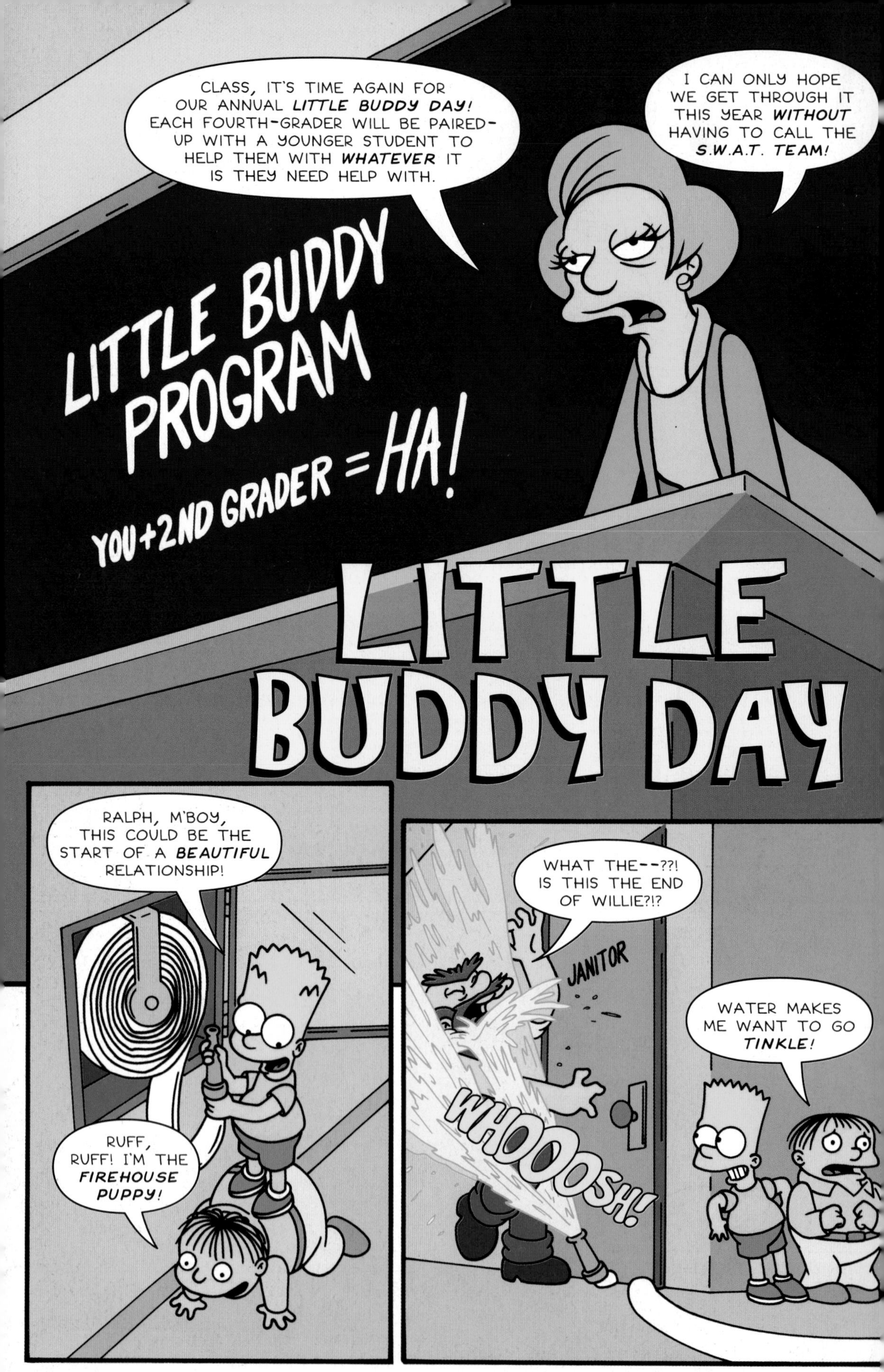
CLASS, IT'S TIME AGAIN FOR OUR ANNUAL LITTLE BUDDY DAY! EACH FOURTH-GRADER WILL BE PAIRED-UP WITH A YOUNGER STUDENT TO HELP THEM WITH WHATEVER IT IS THEY NEED HELP WITH.
I CAN ONLY HOPE WE GET THROUGH IT THIS YEAR WITHOUT HAVING TO CALL THE S.W.A.T. TEAM!
LITTLE BUDDY PROGRAM
YOU+2ND GRADER=HA!
LITTLE BUDDY DAY
RALPH, M'BOY, THIS COULD BE THE START OF A BEAUTIFUL RELATIONSHIP!
RUFF, RUFF! I'M THE FIREHOUSE PUPPY!
WHAT THE--??! IS THIS THE END OF WILLIE?!?
JANITOR
WHOOOOSH!
WATER MAKES ME WANT TO GO TINKLE!

JESSE MCCANN & AMANDA MCCANN SCRIPT · LUIS ESCOBAR PENCILS · PATRICK OWSLEY INKS · CHRIS UNGAR COLORS · KAREN BATES LETTERS · BILL MORRISON EDITOR

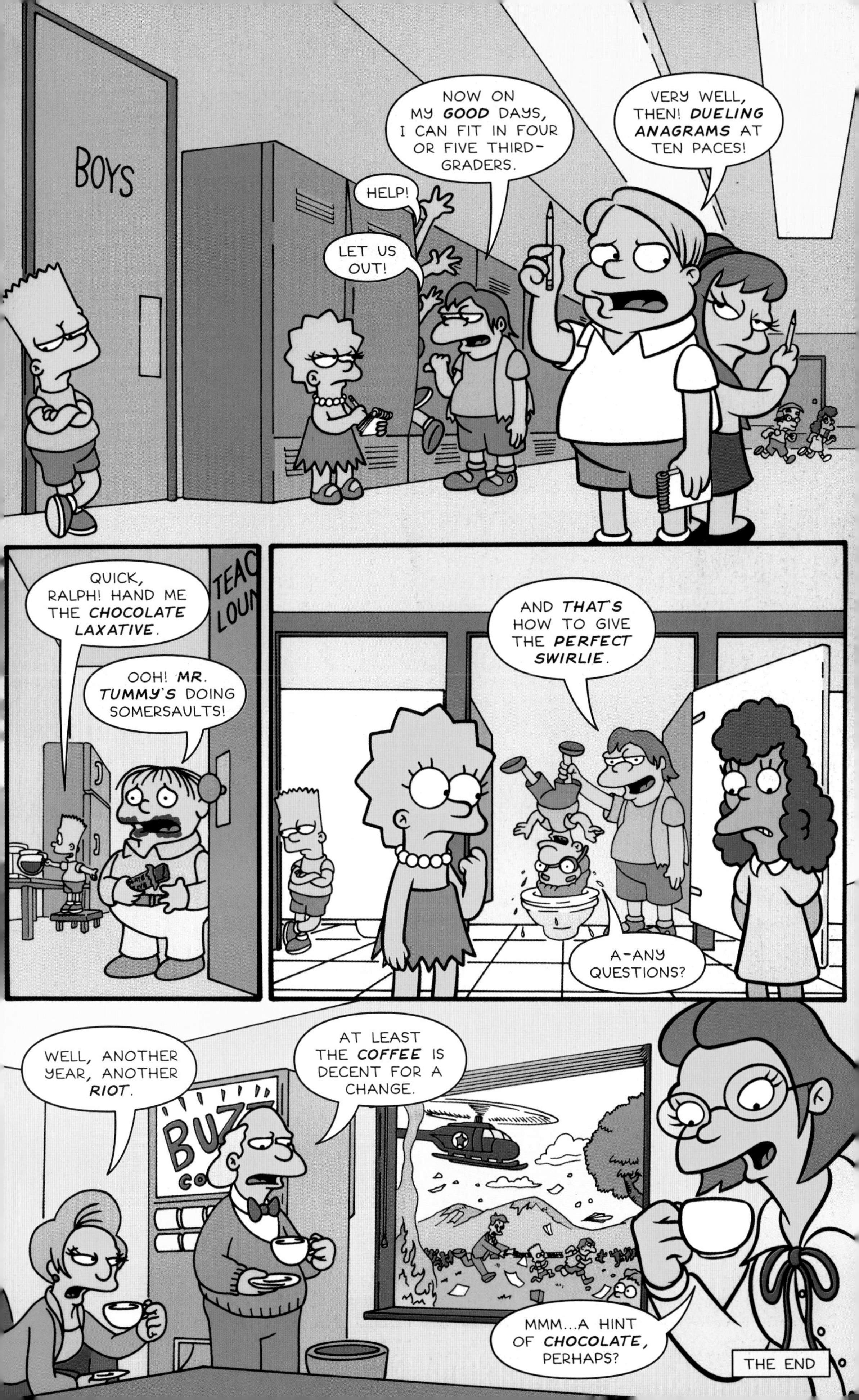
BOYS
HELP!
LET US OUT!
NOW ON MY GOOD DAYS, I CAN FIT IN FOUR OR FIVE THIRD-GRADERS.
VERY WELL, THEN! DUELING ANAGRAMS AT TEN PACES!
QUICK, RALPH! HAND ME THE CHOCOLATE LAXATIVE.
OOH! MR. TUMMY'S DOING SOMERSAULTS!
AND THAT'S HOW TO GIVE THE PERFECT SWIRLIE.
A-ANY QUESTIONS?
WELL, ANOTHER YEAR, ANOTHER RIOT.
AT LEAST THE COFFEE IS DECENT FOR A CHANGE.
MMM...A HINT OF CHOCOLATE, PERHAPS?
THE END

SCAREDY CATS

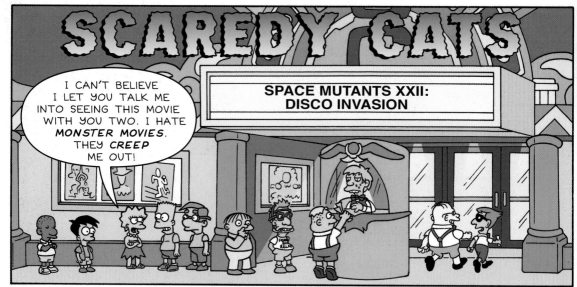

SPACE MUTANTS XXII: DISCO INVASION

I CAN'T BELIEVE I LET YOU TALK ME INTO SEEING THIS MOVIE WITH YOU TWO. I HATE *MONSTER MOVIES*. THEY *CREEP* ME OUT!

OH, COME ON, LISA! DON'T BE SUCH A *SCAREDY CAT*! IT'S *ONLY* A MOVIE.

LIGHTEN UP, LIS. ONLY A *BABY* BELIEVES THAT MONSTER MOVIES ARE *REAL*!

CHRIS YAMBAR
SCRIPT

JASON HO
PENCILS

HOWARD SHUM
INKS

ART VILLANUEVA
COLORS

KAREN BATES
LETTERS

BILL MORRISON
EDITOR

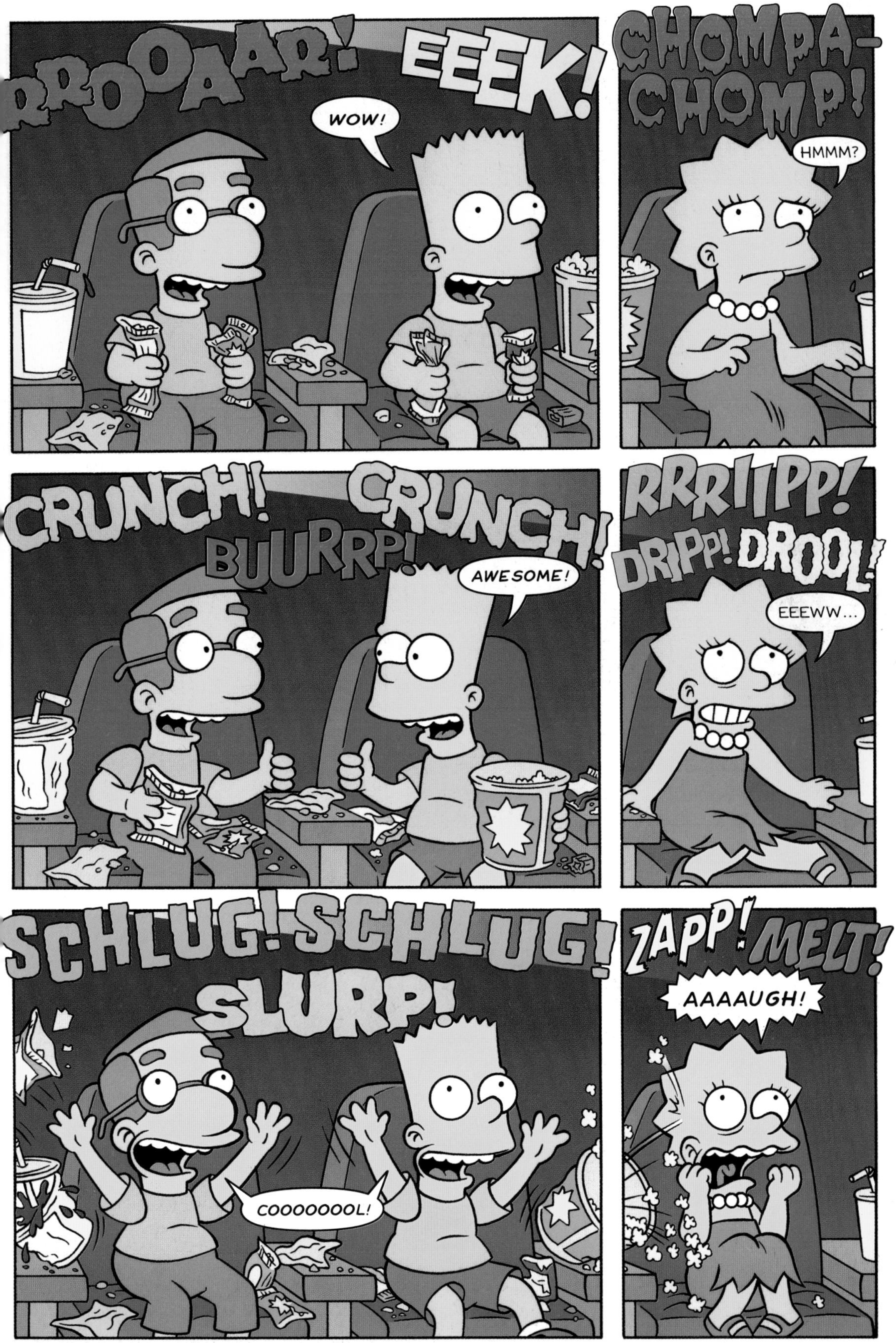
RROOAAR!
EEEK!
WOW!
CHOMPA-CHOMP!
HMMM?
CRUNCH! CRUNCH!
BUURRP!
AWESOME!
RRRIIPP!
DRIPP! DROOL!
EEEWW...
SCHLUG! SCHLUG!
SLURP!
COOOOOOOL!
ZAPP! MELT!
AAAAUGH!

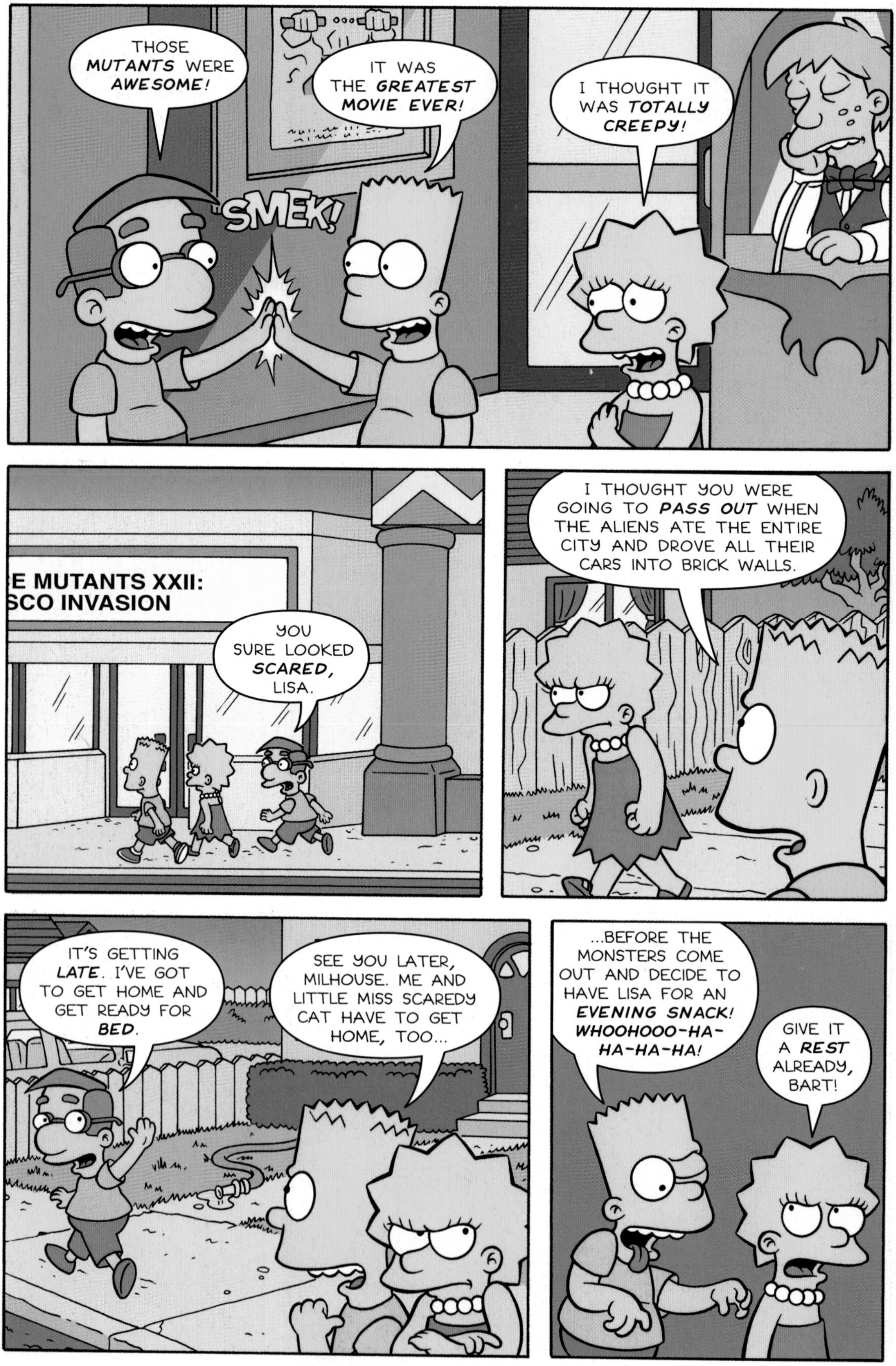
THOSE MUTANTS WERE AWESOME!
IT WAS THE GREATEST MOVIE EVER!
SMEK!
I THOUGHT IT WAS TOTALLY CREEPY!
E MUTANTS XXII:
SCO INVASION
YOU SURE LOOKED SCARED, LISA.
I THOUGHT YOU WERE GOING TO PASS OUT WHEN THE ALIENS ATE THE ENTIRE CITY AND DROVE ALL THEIR CARS INTO BRICK WALLS.
IT'S GETTING LATE. I'VE GOT TO GET HOME AND GET READY FOR BED.
SEE YOU LATER, MILHOUSE. ME AND LITTLE MISS SCAREDY CAT HAVE TO GET HOME, TOO...
...BEFORE THE MONSTERS COME OUT AND DECIDE TO HAVE LISA FOR AN EVENING SNACK! WHOOHOOO-HA-HA-HA-HA!
GIVE IT A REST ALREADY, BART!

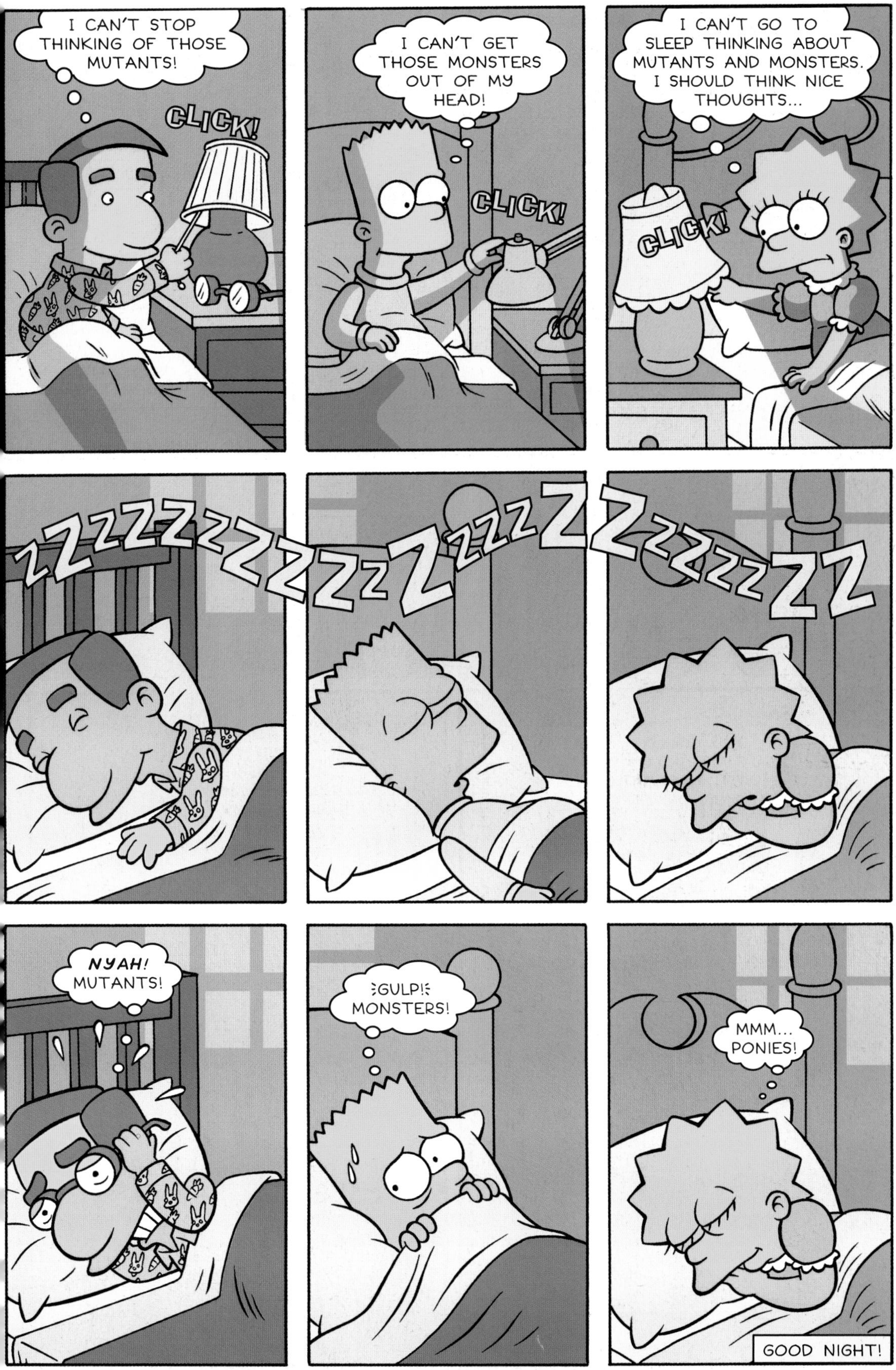
I CAN'T STOP THINKING OF THOSE MUTANTS!
CLICK!
I CAN'T GET THOSE MONSTERS OUT OF MY HEAD!
CLICK!
I CAN'T GO TO SLEEP THINKING ABOUT MUTANTS AND MONSTERS. I SHOULD THINK NICE THOUGHTS...
CLICK!
NYAH! MUTANTS!
GULP! MONSTERS!
MMM... PONIES!
GOOD NIGHT!

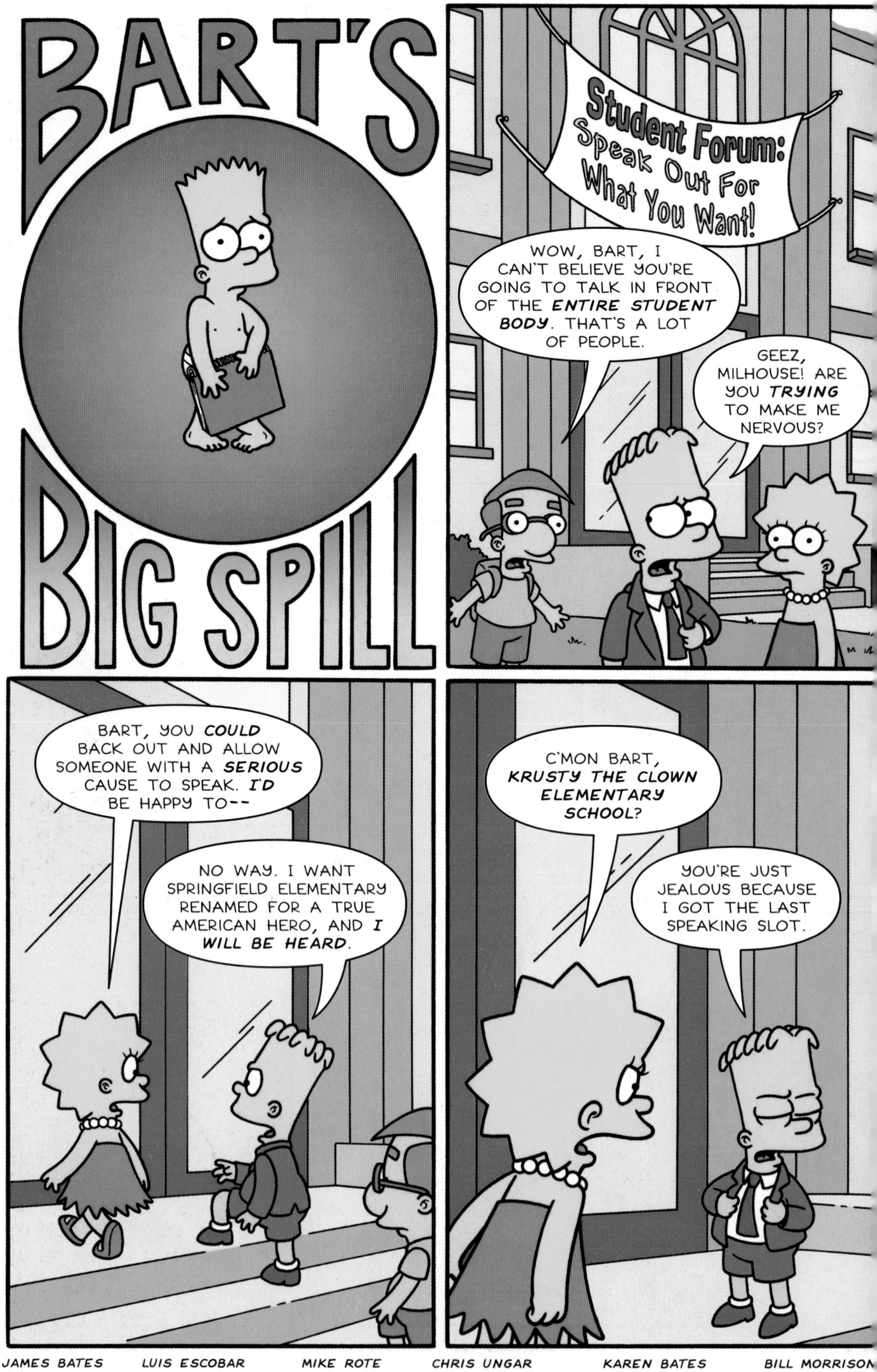
BART'S BIG SPILL
Student Forum: Speak Out For What You Want!
WOW, BART, I CAN'T BELIEVE YOU'RE GOING TO TALK IN FRONT OF THE ENTIRE STUDENT BODY. THAT'S A LOT OF PEOPLE.
GEEZ, MILHOUSE! ARE YOU TRYING TO MAKE ME NERVOUS?
BART, YOU COULD BACK OUT AND ALLOW SOMEONE WITH A SERIOUS CAUSE TO SPEAK. I'D BE HAPPY TO--
NO WAY. I WANT SPRINGFIELD ELEMENTARY RENAMED FOR A TRUE AMERICAN HERO, AND I WILL BE HEARD.
C'MON BART, KRUSTY THE CLOWN ELEMENTARY SCHOOL?
YOU'RE JUST JEALOUS BECAUSE I GOT THE LAST SPEAKING SLOT.

JAMES BATES	LUIS ESCOBAR	MIKE ROTE	CHRIS UNGAR	KAREN BATES	BILL MORRISON
SCRIPT	PENCILS	INKS	COLORS	LETTERS	EDITOR

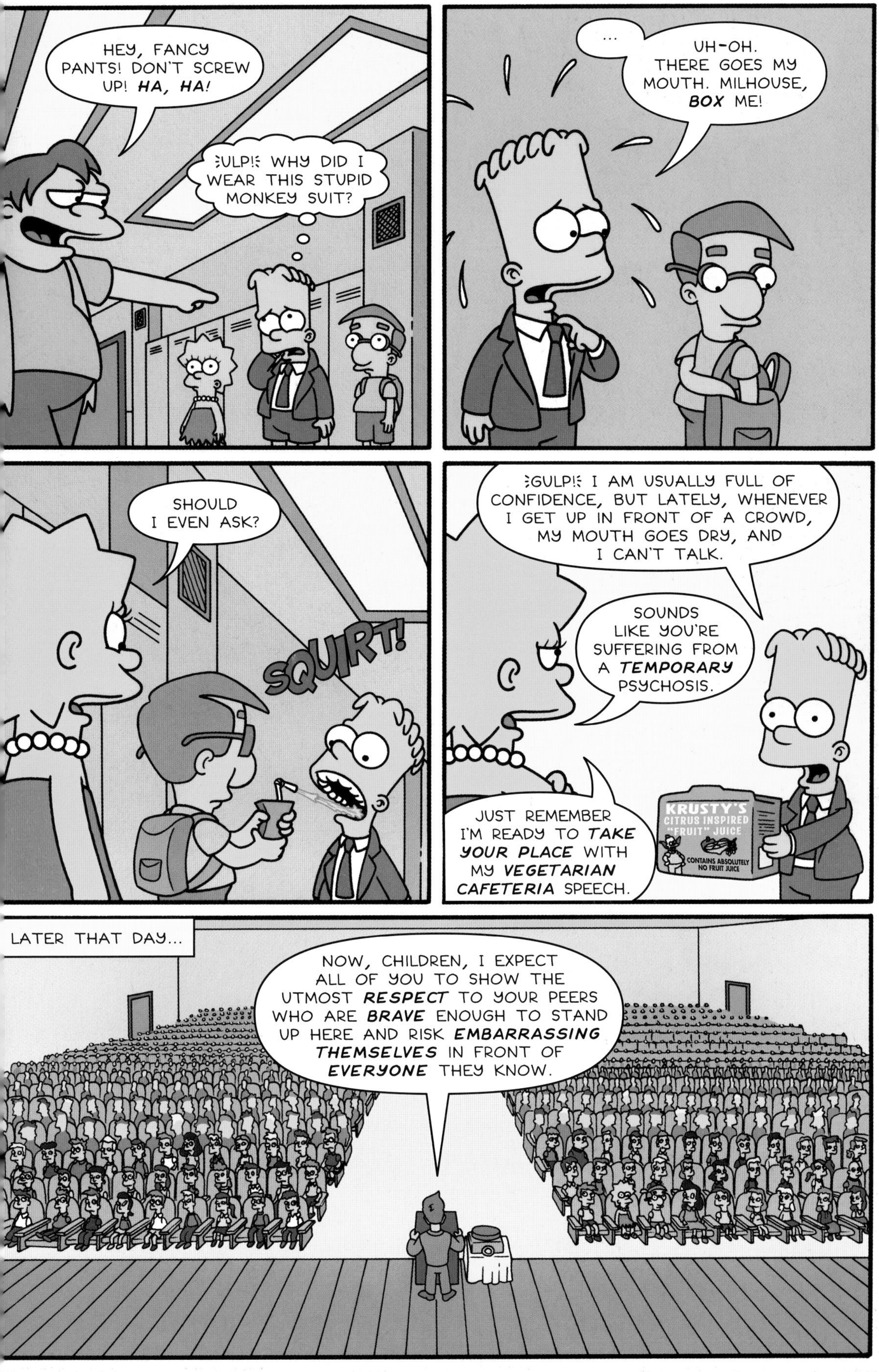
HEY, FANCY PANTS! DON'T SCREW UP! HA, HA!
GULP! WHY DID I WEAR THIS STUPID MONKEY SUIT?
...
UH-OH. THERE GOES MY MOUTH. MILHOUSE, BOX ME!
SHOULD I EVEN ASK?
SQUIRT!
GULP! I AM USUALLY FULL OF CONFIDENCE, BUT LATELY, WHENEVER I GET UP IN FRONT OF A CROWD, MY MOUTH GOES DRY, AND I CAN'T TALK.
SOUNDS LIKE YOU'RE SUFFERING FROM A TEMPORARY PSYCHOSIS.
JUST REMEMBER I'M READY TO TAKE YOUR PLACE WITH MY VEGETARIAN CAFETERIA SPEECH.
KRUSTY'S CITRUS INSPIRED "FRUIT" JUICE
CONTAINS ABSOLUTELY NO FRUIT JUICE
LATER THAT DAY...
NOW, CHILDREN, I EXPECT ALL OF YOU TO SHOW THE UTMOST RESPECT TO YOUR PEERS WHO ARE BRAVE ENOUGH TO STAND UP HERE AND RISK EMBARRASSING THEMSELVES IN FRONT OF EVERYONE THEY KNOW.

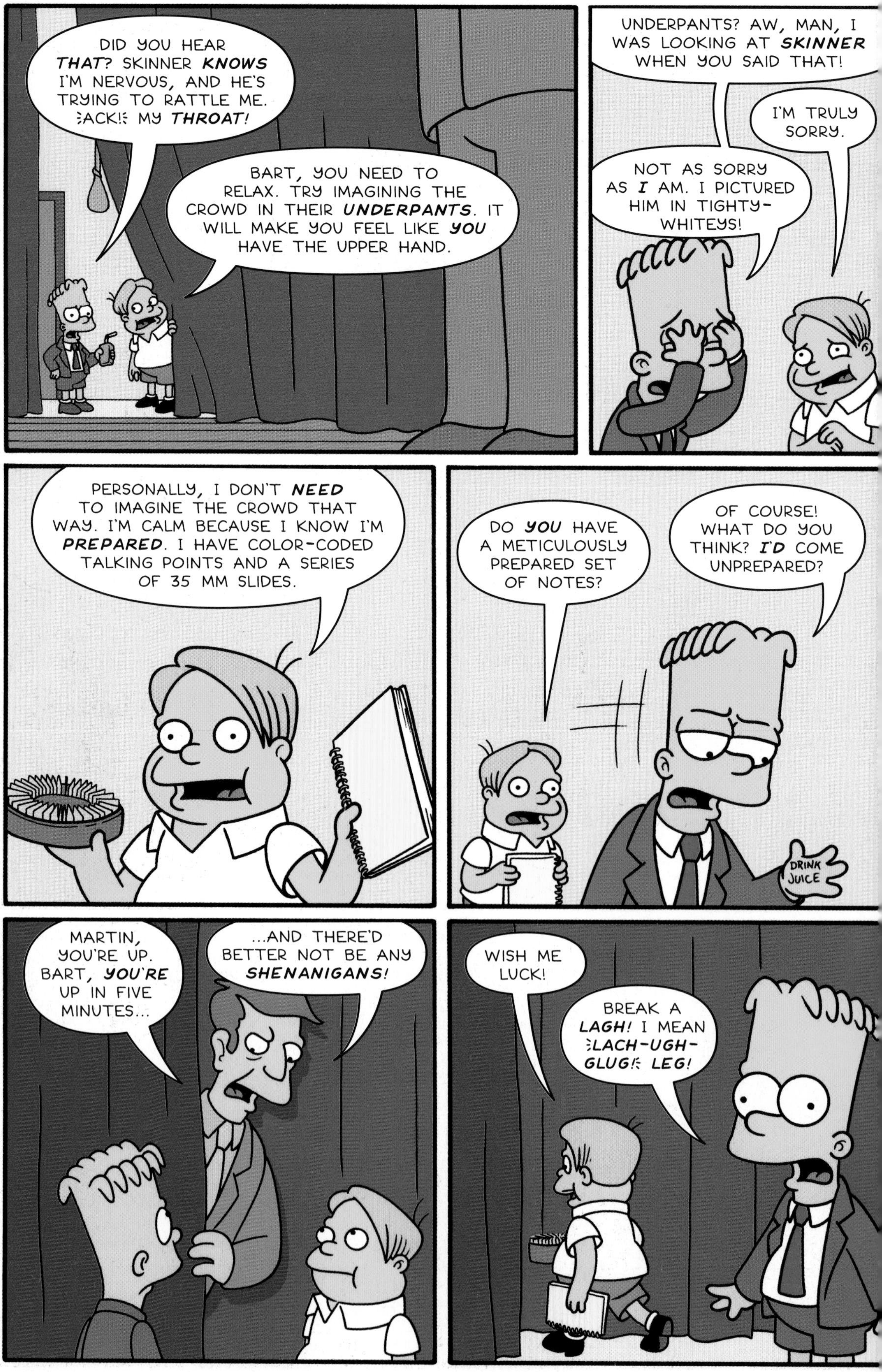
DID YOU HEAR THAT? SKINNER KNOWS I'M NERVOUS, AND HE'S TRYING TO RATTLE ME. ACK!! MY THROAT!
BART, YOU NEED TO RELAX. TRY IMAGINING THE CROWD IN THEIR UNDERPANTS. IT WILL MAKE YOU FEEL LIKE YOU HAVE THE UPPER HAND.
UNDERPANTS? AW, MAN, I WAS LOOKING AT SKINNER WHEN YOU SAID THAT!
I'M TRULY SORRY.
NOT AS SORRY AS I AM. I PICTURED HIM IN TIGHTY-WHITEYS!
PERSONALLY, I DON'T NEED TO IMAGINE THE CROWD THAT WAY. I'M CALM BECAUSE I KNOW I'M PREPARED. I HAVE COLOR-CODED TALKING POINTS AND A SERIES OF 35 MM SLIDES.
DO YOU HAVE A METICULOUSLY PREPARED SET OF NOTES?
OF COURSE! WHAT DO YOU THINK? I'D COME UNPREPARED?
DRINK JUICE
MARTIN, YOU'RE UP. BART, YOU'RE UP IN FIVE MINUTES...
...AND THERE'D BETTER NOT BE ANY SHENANIGANS!
WISH ME LUCK!
BREAK A LAGH! I MEAN LACH-UGH-GLUG!! LEG!

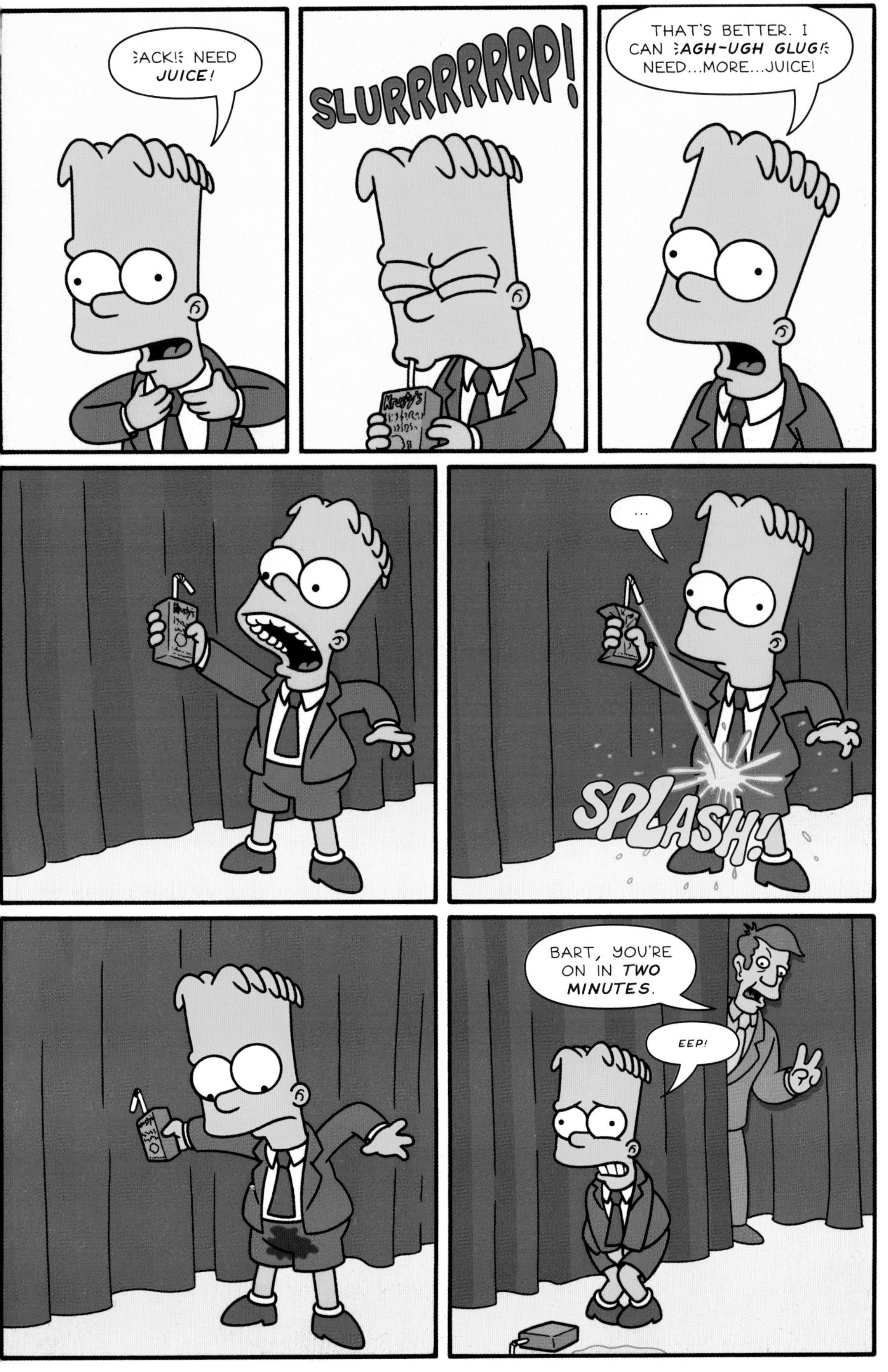
ACK! NEED JUICE!
SLURRRRRRP!
THAT'S BETTER. I CAN AGH-UGH GLUG! NEED...MORE...JUICE!
...
SPLASH!
BART, YOU'RE ON IN TWO MINUTES.
EEP!

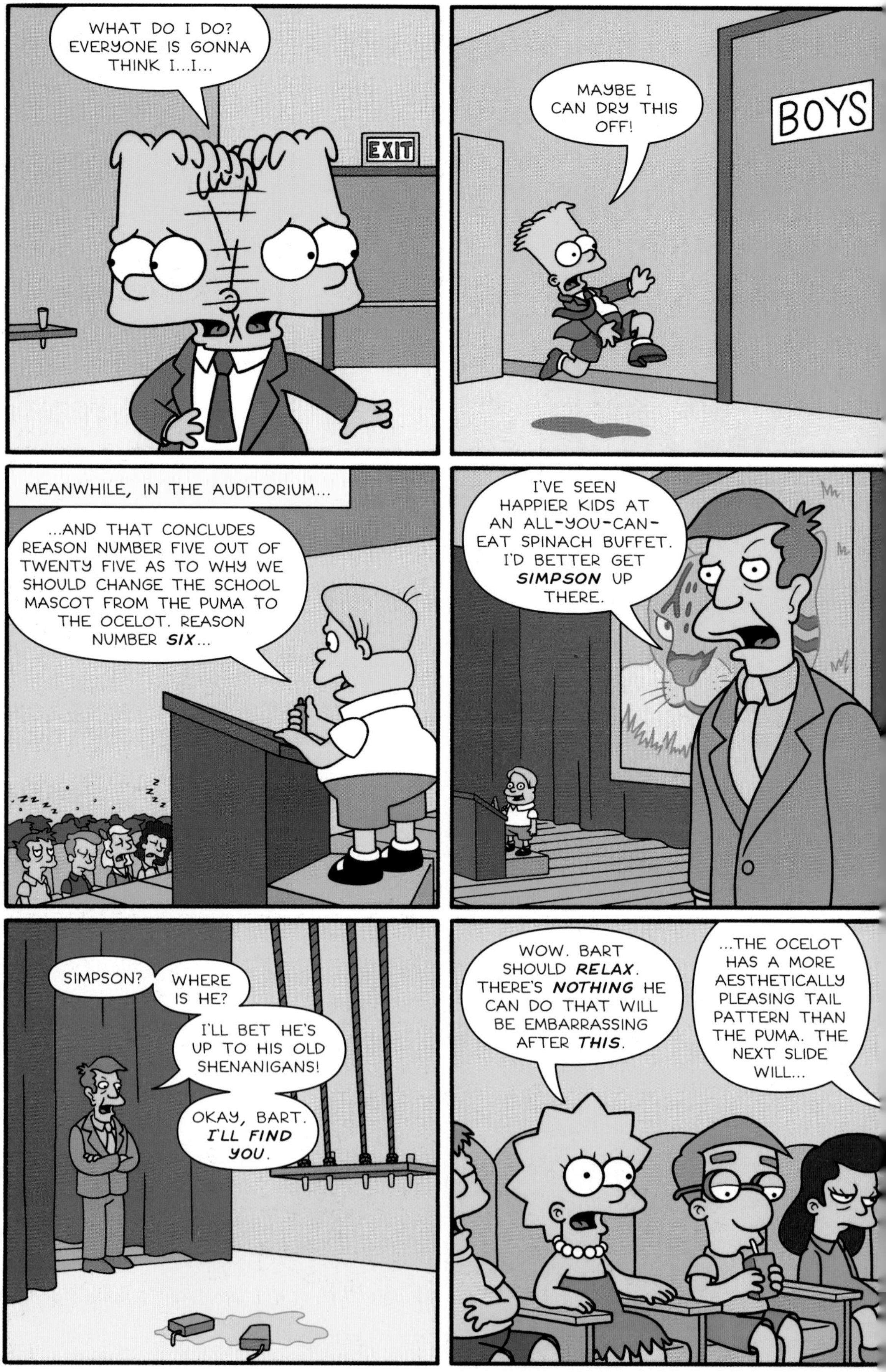
WHAT DO I DO? EVERYONE IS GONNA THINK I...I...
EXIT
MAYBE I CAN DRY THIS OFF!
BOYS
MEANWHILE, IN THE AUDITORIUM...
...AND THAT CONCLUDES REASON NUMBER FIVE OUT OF TWENTY FIVE AS TO WHY WE SHOULD CHANGE THE SCHOOL MASCOT FROM THE PUMA TO THE OCELOT. REASON NUMBER SIX...
I'VE SEEN HAPPIER KIDS AT AN ALL-YOU-CAN-EAT SPINACH BUFFET. I'D BETTER GET SIMPSON UP THERE.
SIMPSON?
WHERE IS HE?
I'LL BET HE'S UP TO HIS OLD SHENANIGANS!
OKAY, BART. I'LL FIND YOU.
WOW. BART SHOULD RELAX. THERE'S NOTHING HE CAN DO THAT WILL BE EMBARRASSING AFTER THIS.
...THE OCELOT HAS A MORE AESTHETICALLY PLEASING TAIL PATTERN THAN THE PUMA. THE NEXT SLIDE WILL...

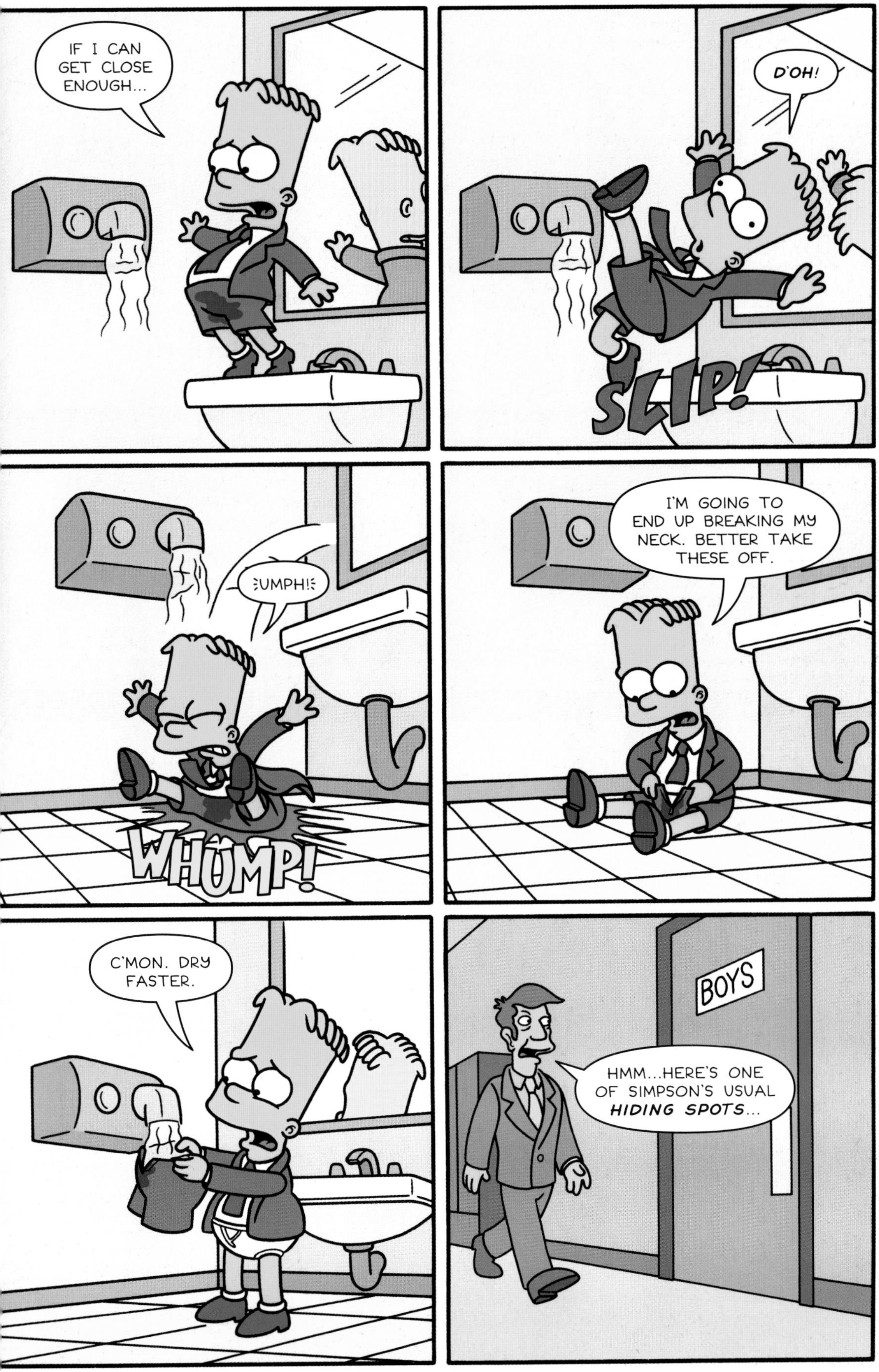
IF I CAN GET CLOSE ENOUGH...
D'OH!
SLIP!
UMPH!
WHUMP!
I'M GOING TO END UP BREAKING MY NECK. BETTER TAKE THESE OFF.
C'MON. DRY FASTER.
BOYS
HMM...HERE'S ONE OF SIMPSON'S USUAL *HIDING SPOTS*...

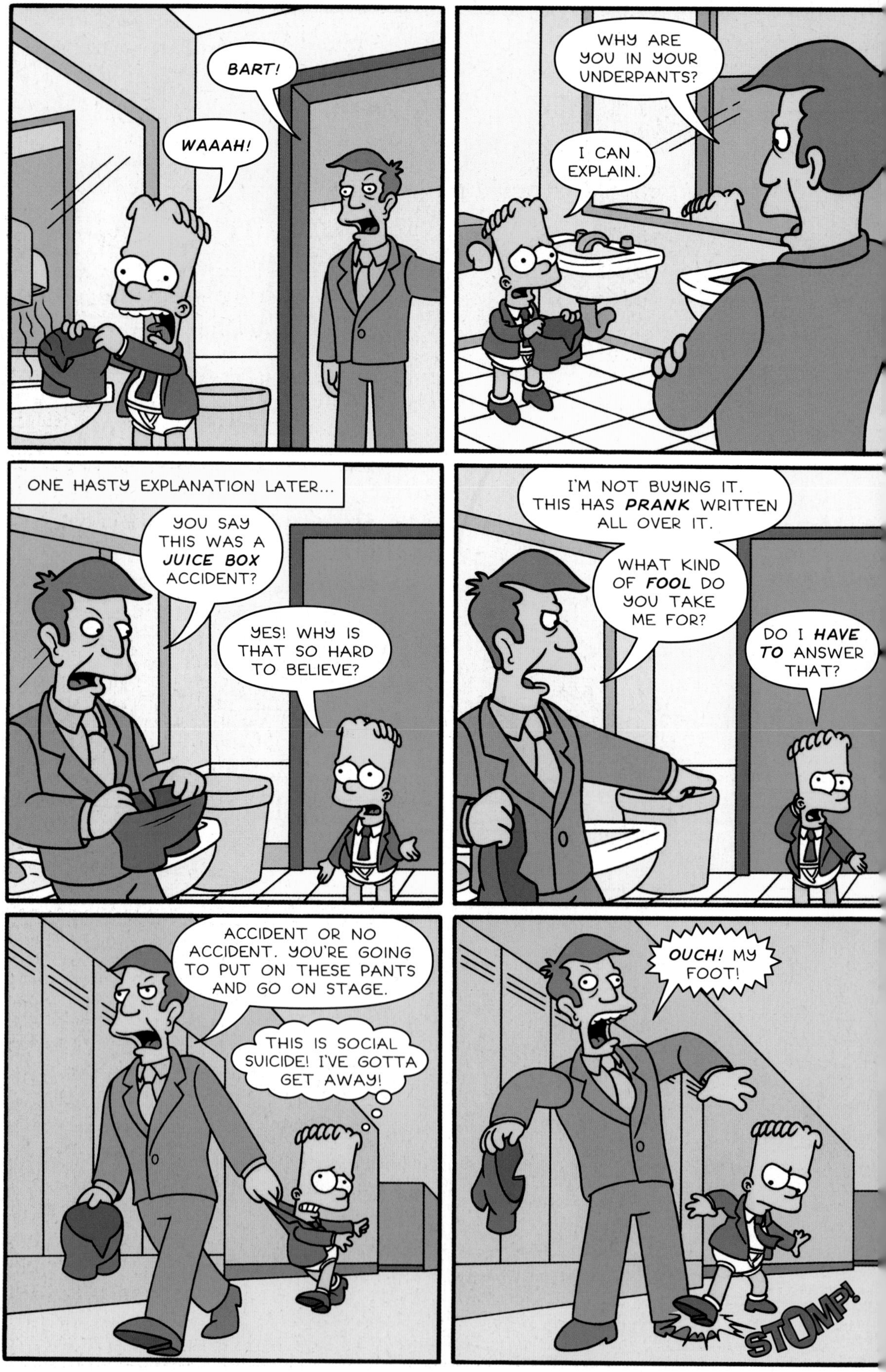
BART!
WAAAH!
WHY ARE YOU IN YOUR UNDERPANTS?
I CAN EXPLAIN.
ONE HASTY EXPLANATION LATER...
YOU SAY THIS WAS A *JUICE BOX* ACCIDENT?
YES! WHY IS THAT SO HARD TO BELIEVE?
I'M NOT BUYING IT. THIS HAS *PRANK* WRITTEN ALL OVER IT.
WHAT KIND OF *FOOL* DO YOU TAKE ME FOR?
DO I *HAVE TO* ANSWER THAT?
ACCIDENT OR NO ACCIDENT. YOU'RE GOING TO PUT ON THESE PANTS AND GO ON STAGE.
THIS IS SOCIAL SUICIDE! I'VE GOTTA GET AWAY!
OUCH! MY FOOT!
STOMP!

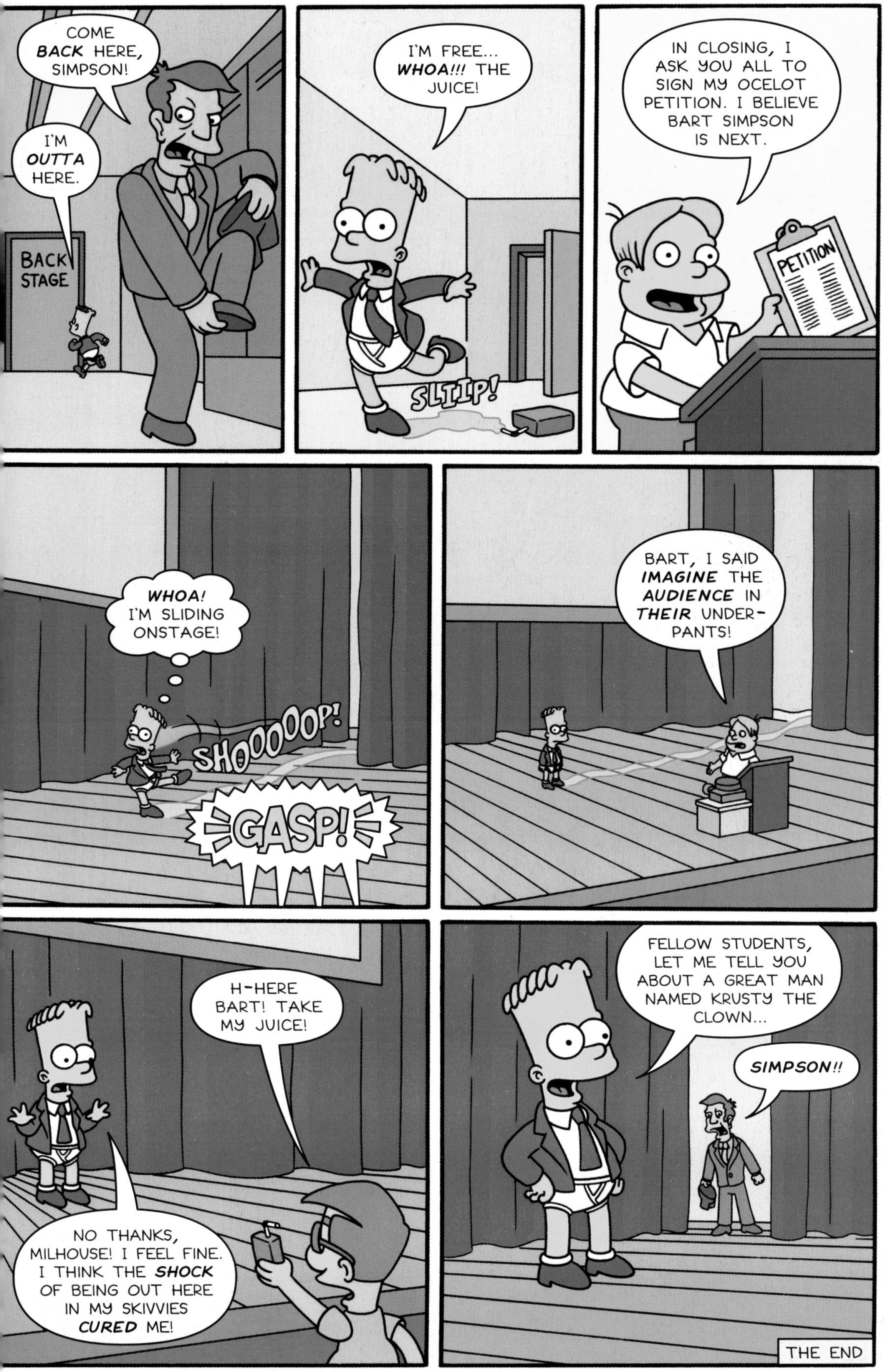
COME BACK HERE, SIMPSON!
I'M OUTTA HERE.
BACK STAGE
I'M FREE... WHOA!!! THE JUICE!
SLIIP!
IN CLOSING, I ASK YOU ALL TO SIGN MY OCELOT PETITION. I BELIEVE BART SIMPSON IS NEXT.
PETITION
WHOA! I'M SLIDING ONSTAGE!
SHOOOOOP!
GASP!
BART, I SAID IMAGINE THE AUDIENCE IN THEIR UNDER-PANTS!
H-HERE BART! TAKE MY JUICE!
NO THANKS, MILHOUSE! I FEEL FINE. I THINK THE SHOCK OF BEING OUT HERE IN MY SKIVVIES CURED ME!
FELLOW STUDENTS, LET ME TELL YOU ABOUT A GREAT MAN NAMED KRUSTY THE CLOWN...
SIMPSON!!
THE END

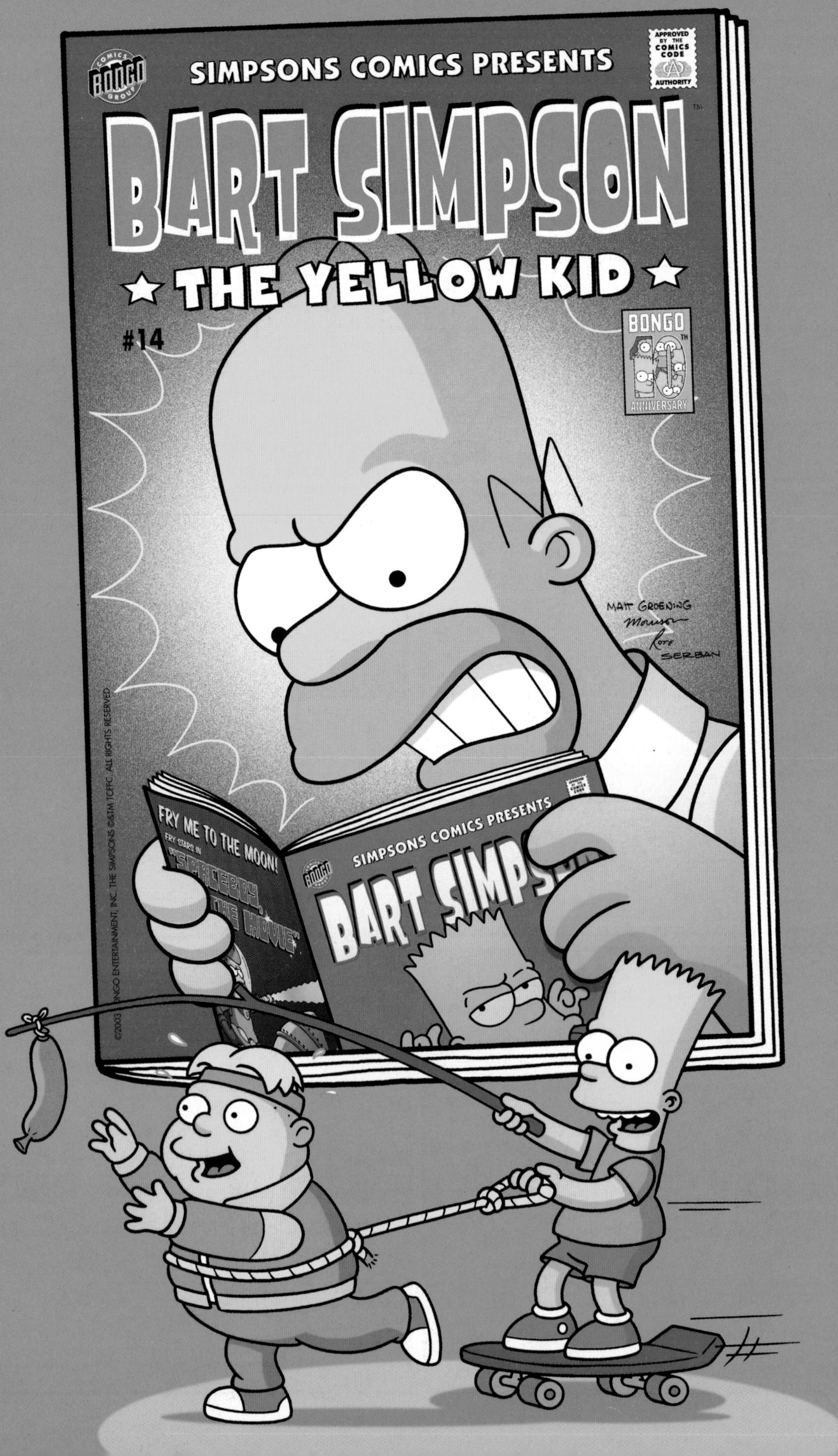
BONGO COMICS GROUP
SIMPSONS COMICS PRESENTS
APPROVED BY THE COMICS CODE AUTHORITY
BART SIMPSON™
THE YELLOW KID
#14
BONGO 10TH ANNIVERSARY
MATT GROENING
SERBAN
FRY ME TO THE MOON!
SIMPSONS COMICS PRESENTS
BART SIMPS
©2003 BONGO ENTERTAINMENT, INC. THE SIMPSONS ©&TM TCFFC. ALL RIGHTS RESERVED.

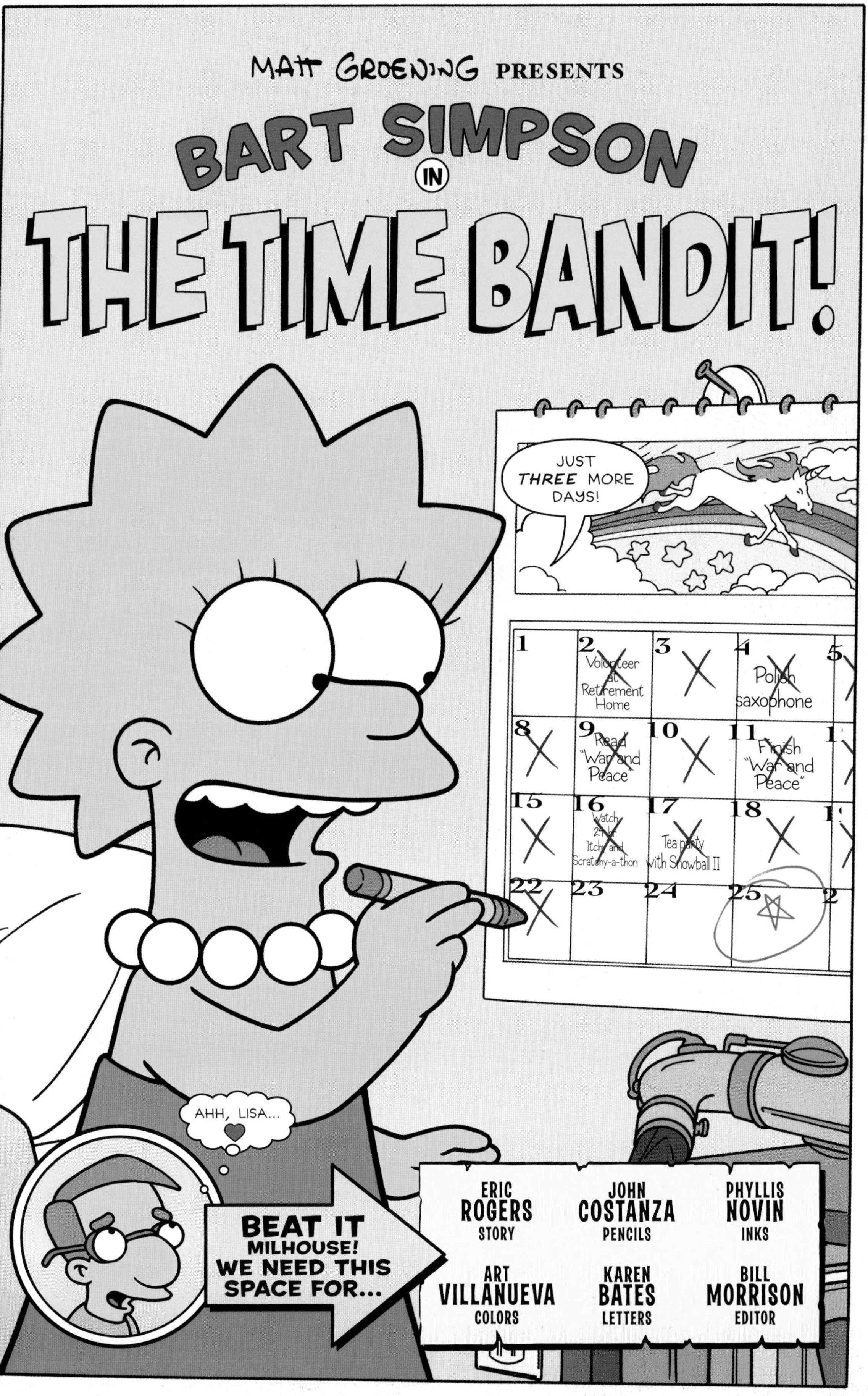
MATT GROENING PRESENTS
BART SIMPSON IN
THE TIME BANDIT!
JUST THREE MORE DAYS!
1
2 Volunteer at Retirement Home
3
4 Polish saxophone
8
9 Read "War and Peace"
10
11 Finish "War and Peace"
15
16 Watch 24 hr. Itchy and Scratchy-a-thon
17 Tea party with Snowball II
18
22
23
24
25
AHH, LISA...
BEAT IT MILHOUSE! WE NEED THIS SPACE FOR...
ERIC ROGERS STORY
JOHN COSTANZA PENCILS
PHYLLIS NOVIN INKS
ART VILLANUEVA COLORS
KAREN BATES LETTERS
BILL MORRISON EDITOR

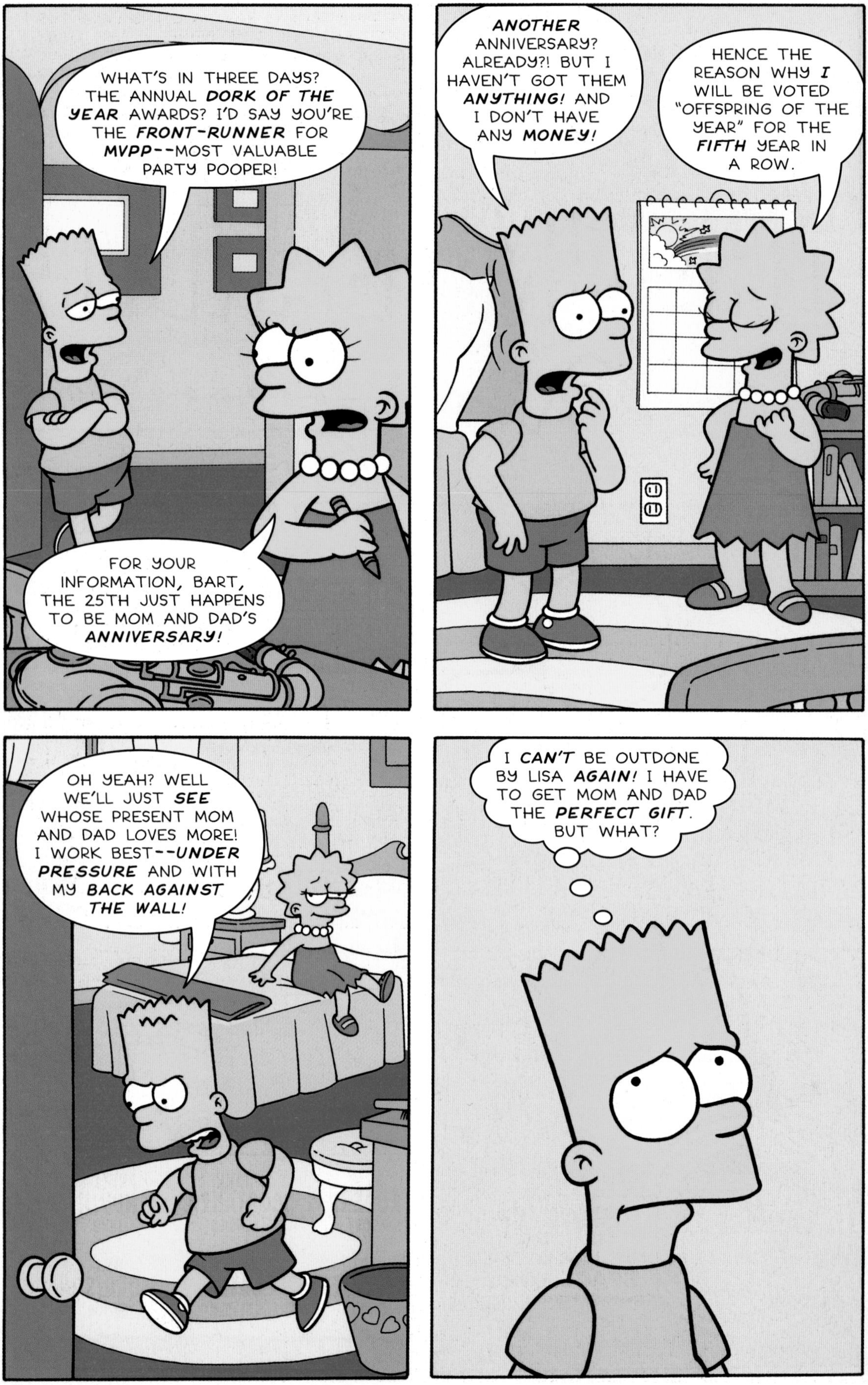
WHAT'S IN THREE DAYS? THE ANNUAL DORK OF THE YEAR AWARDS? I'D SAY YOU'RE THE FRONT-RUNNER FOR MVPP--MOST VALUABLE PARTY POOPER!
FOR YOUR INFORMATION, BART, THE 25TH JUST HAPPENS TO BE MOM AND DAD'S ANNIVERSARY!
ANOTHER ANNIVERSARY? ALREADY?! BUT I HAVEN'T GOT THEM ANYTHING! AND I DON'T HAVE ANY MONEY!
HENCE THE REASON WHY I WILL BE VOTED "OFFSPRING OF THE YEAR" FOR THE FIFTH YEAR IN A ROW.
OH YEAH? WELL WE'LL JUST SEE WHOSE PRESENT MOM AND DAD LOVES MORE! I WORK BEST--UNDER PRESSURE AND WITH MY BACK AGAINST THE WALL!
I CAN'T BE OUTDONE BY LISA AGAIN! I HAVE TO GET MOM AND DAD THE PERFECT GIFT. BUT WHAT?

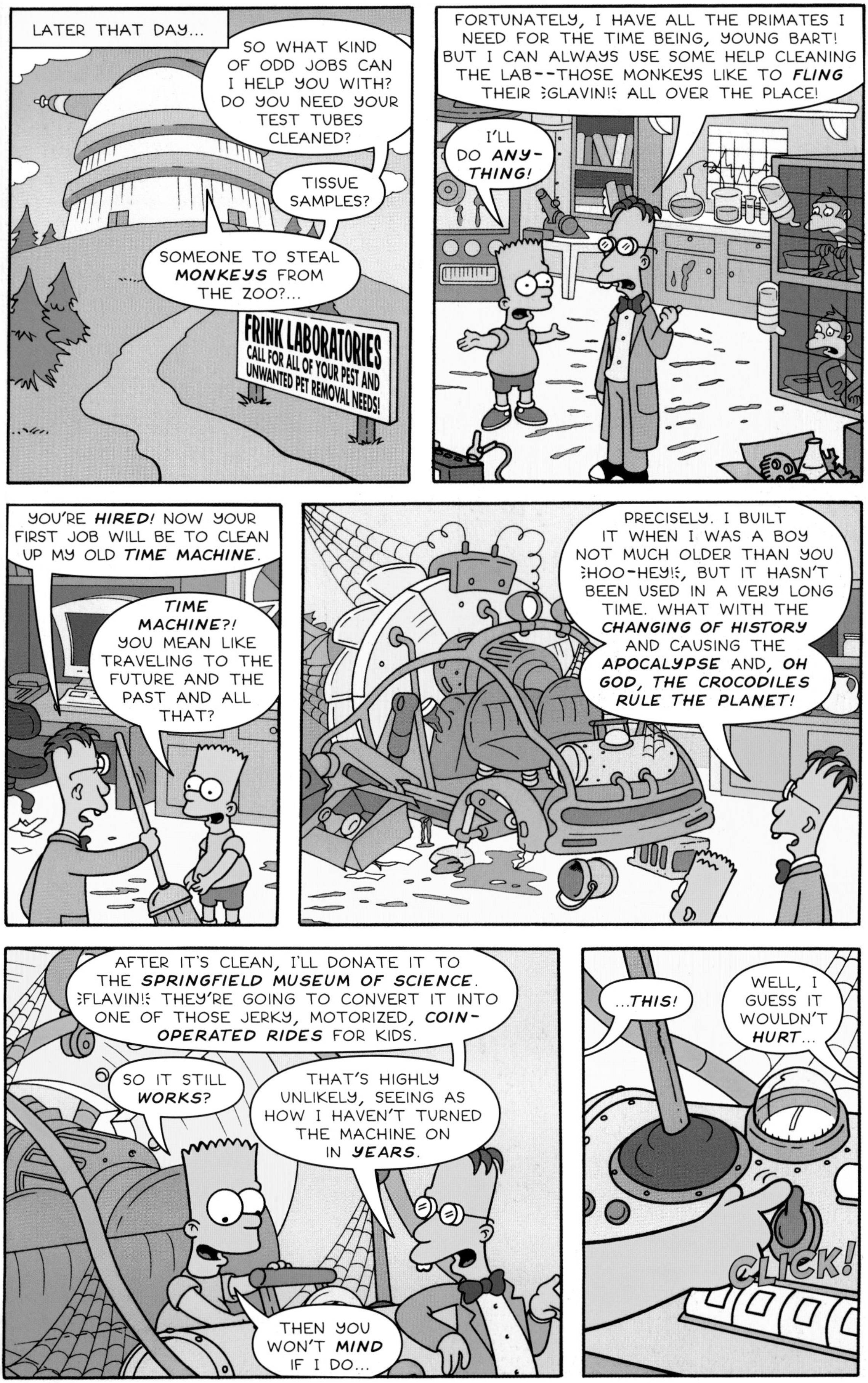
LATER THAT DAY...
SO WHAT KIND OF ODD JOBS CAN I HELP YOU WITH? DO YOU NEED YOUR TEST TUBES CLEANED?
TISSUE SAMPLES?
SOMEONE TO STEAL MONKEYS FROM THE ZOO?...
FRINK LABORATORIES CALL FOR ALL OF YOUR PEST AND UNWANTED PET REMOVAL NEEDS!
FORTUNATELY, I HAVE ALL THE PRIMATES I NEED FOR THE TIME BEING, YOUNG BART! BUT I CAN ALWAYS USE SOME HELP CLEANING THE LAB--THOSE MONKEYS LIKE TO FLING THEIR GLAVIN! ALL OVER THE PLACE!
I'LL DO ANY-THING!
YOU'RE HIRED! NOW YOUR FIRST JOB WILL BE TO CLEAN UP MY OLD TIME MACHINE.
TIME MACHINE?! YOU MEAN LIKE TRAVELING TO THE FUTURE AND THE PAST AND ALL THAT?
PRECISELY. I BUILT IT WHEN I WAS A BOY NOT MUCH OLDER THAN YOU HOO-HEY!, BUT IT HASN'T BEEN USED IN A VERY LONG TIME. WHAT WITH THE CHANGING OF HISTORY AND CAUSING THE APOCALYPSE AND, OH GOD, THE CROCODILES RULE THE PLANET!
AFTER IT'S CLEAN, I'LL DONATE IT TO THE SPRINGFIELD MUSEUM OF SCIENCE. FLAVIN! THEY'RE GOING TO CONVERT IT INTO ONE OF THOSE JERKY, MOTORIZED, COIN-OPERATED RIDES FOR KIDS.
SO IT STILL WORKS?
THAT'S HIGHLY UNLIKELY, SEEING AS HOW I HAVEN'T TURNED THE MACHINE ON IN YEARS.
THEN YOU WON'T MIND IF I DO...
...THIS!
WELL, I GUESS IT WOULDN'T HURT...
CLICK!

WHN!
PROFESSOR, NO GREAT ADVENTURE STARTS WITHOUT THOSE FAMOUS LAST WORDS!
WHN!
GADZOOKS!
WHN!
WHN!
WHN!
WHN!
POOF!
WH-WHERE ARE WE, PROFESSOR FRINK?
NOT WHERE ARE WE! NG-HEY! WHEN ARE WE?
IT LOOKS LIKE MY MACHINE STILL FUNCTIONS, AND IT HAS TRANSPORTED US BACK IN TIME!
AYE, CARUMBA!
HOLY COW PASTURE! THIS MUST BE THE SITE ON WHICH MY LABORATORY STANDS IN THE FUTURE!
WHAT DO WE DO NOW?
YOU DON'T HAPPEN TO HAVE ANY "AQUA SHELL" HAIRSPRAY ON YOU, DO YOU?
NO!
THEN I'LL HAVE TO FIND SOME BECAUSE THAT'S WHAT THE TIME MACHINE RUNS ON, AND WE'RE ALL OUT OF FUEL GLAVIN! YOU STAY HERE AND GUARD THE MACHINE WHILE I FIND A NICE HAIR SALON OR A HOUSEWIFE WITH A BOUFFANT WHO MIGHT HAVE SOME AQUA SHELL HANDY NG-HEY!

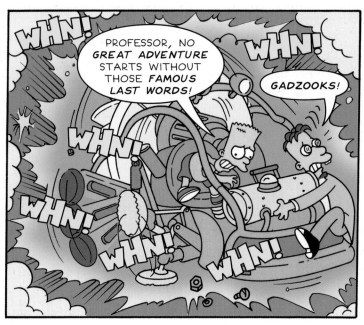

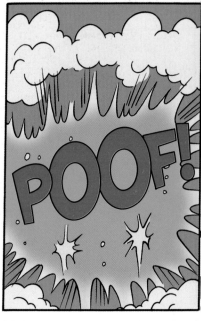

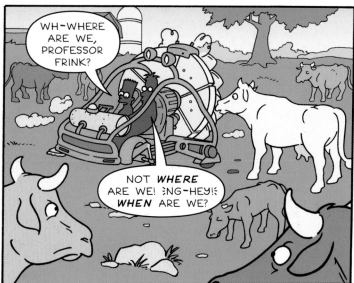

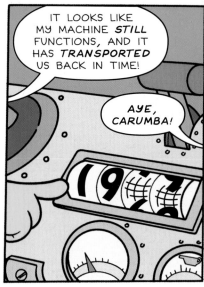

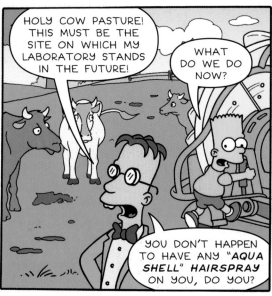

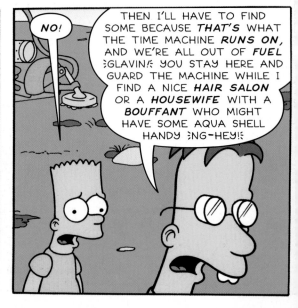

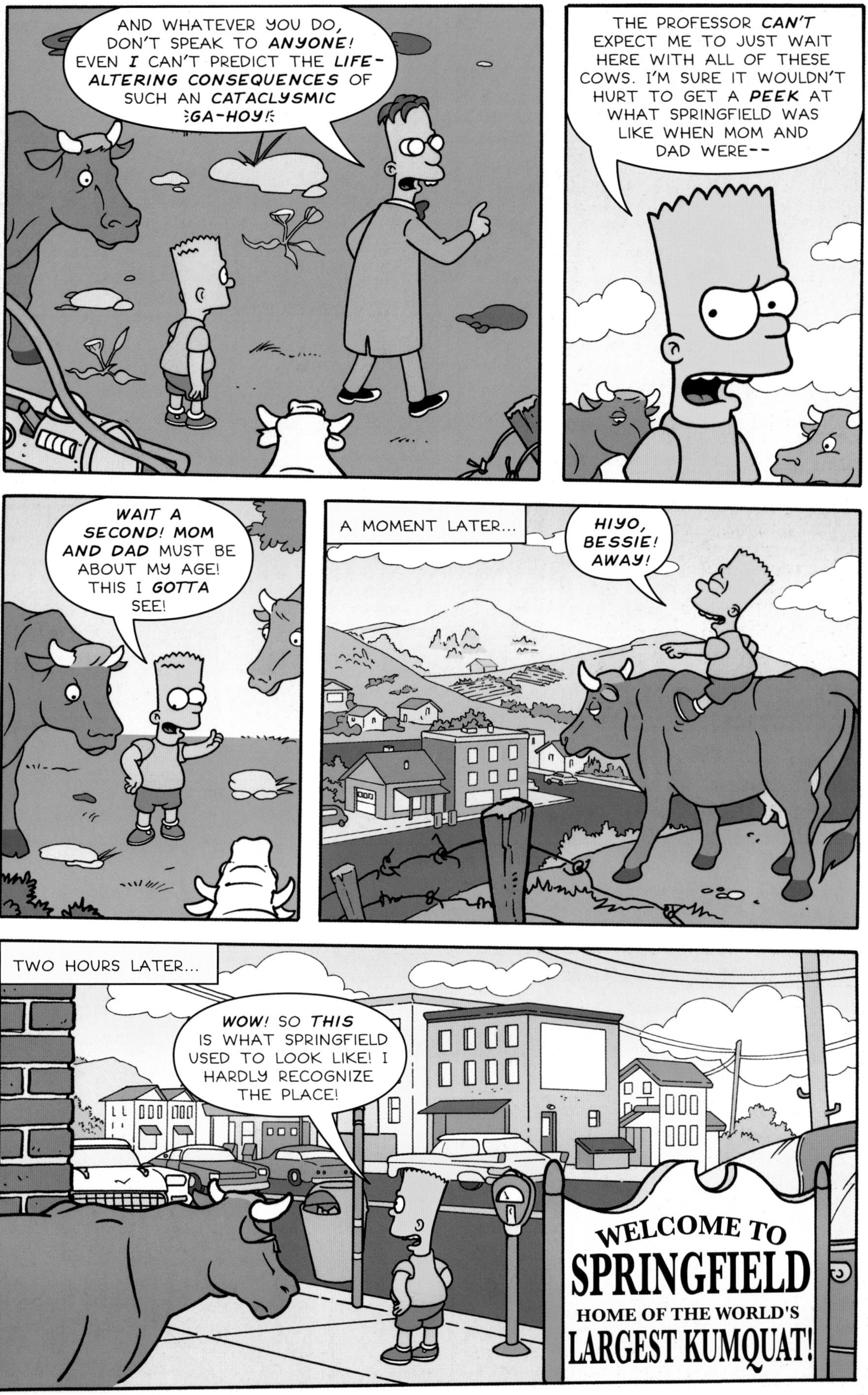
AND WHATEVER YOU DO, DON'T SPEAK TO ANYONE! EVEN I CAN'T PREDICT THE LIFE-ALTERING CONSEQUENCES OF SUCH AN CATACLYSMIC GA-HOY!
THE PROFESSOR CAN'T EXPECT ME TO JUST WAIT HERE WITH ALL OF THESE COWS. I'M SURE IT WOULDN'T HURT TO GET A PEEK AT WHAT SPRINGFIELD WAS LIKE WHEN MOM AND DAD WERE--
WAIT A SECOND! MOM AND DAD MUST BE ABOUT MY AGE! THIS I GOTTA SEE!
A MOMENT LATER...
HIYO, BESSIE! AWAY!
TWO HOURS LATER...
WOW! SO THIS IS WHAT SPRINGFIELD USED TO LOOK LIKE! I HARDLY RECOGNIZE THE PLACE!
WELCOME TO SPRINGFIELD HOME OF THE WORLD'S LARGEST KUMQUAT!

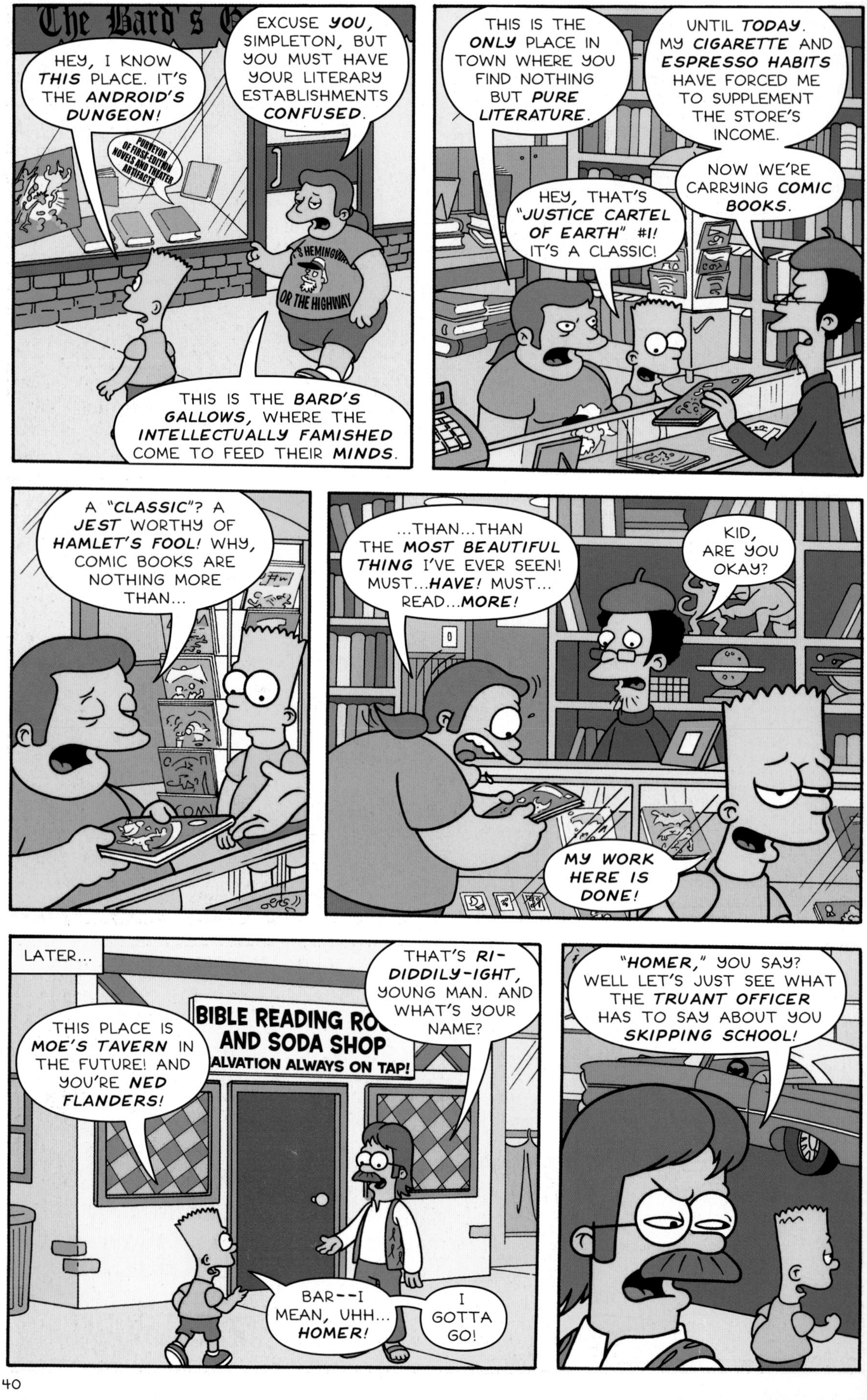
The Bard's G
HEY, I KNOW THIS PLACE. IT'S THE ANDROID'S DUNGEON!
EXCUSE YOU, SIMPLETON, BUT YOU MUST HAVE YOUR LITERARY ESTABLISHMENTS CONFUSED.
PURVEYOR OF FIRST-EDITION NOVELS AND THEATER ARTIFACTS
IT'S HEMINGWAY OR THE HIGHWAY
THIS IS THE BARD'S GALLOWS, WHERE THE INTELLECTUALLY FAMISHED COME TO FEED THEIR MINDS.
THIS IS THE ONLY PLACE IN TOWN WHERE YOU FIND NOTHING BUT PURE LITERATURE.
UNTIL TODAY. MY CIGARETTE AND ESPRESSO HABITS HAVE FORCED ME TO SUPPLEMENT THE STORE'S INCOME.
NOW WE'RE CARRYING COMIC BOOKS.
HEY, THAT'S "JUSTICE CARTEL OF EARTH" #1! IT'S A CLASSIC!
A "CLASSIC"? A JEST WORTHY OF HAMLET'S FOOL! WHY, COMIC BOOKS ARE NOTHING MORE THAN...
...THAN...THAN THE MOST BEAUTIFUL THING I'VE EVER SEEN! MUST...HAVE! MUST... READ...MORE!
KID, ARE YOU OKAY?
MY WORK HERE IS DONE!
LATER...
BIBLE READING RO AND SODA SHOP
ALVATION ALWAYS ON TAP!
THIS PLACE IS MOE'S TAVERN IN THE FUTURE! AND YOU'RE NED FLANDERS!
THAT'S RI-DIDDILY-IGHT, YOUNG MAN. AND WHAT'S YOUR NAME?
BAR--I MEAN, UHH... HOMER!
I GOTTA GO!
"HOMER," YOU SAY? WELL LET'S JUST SEE WHAT THE TRUANT OFFICER HAS TO SAY ABOUT YOU SKIPPING SCHOOL!

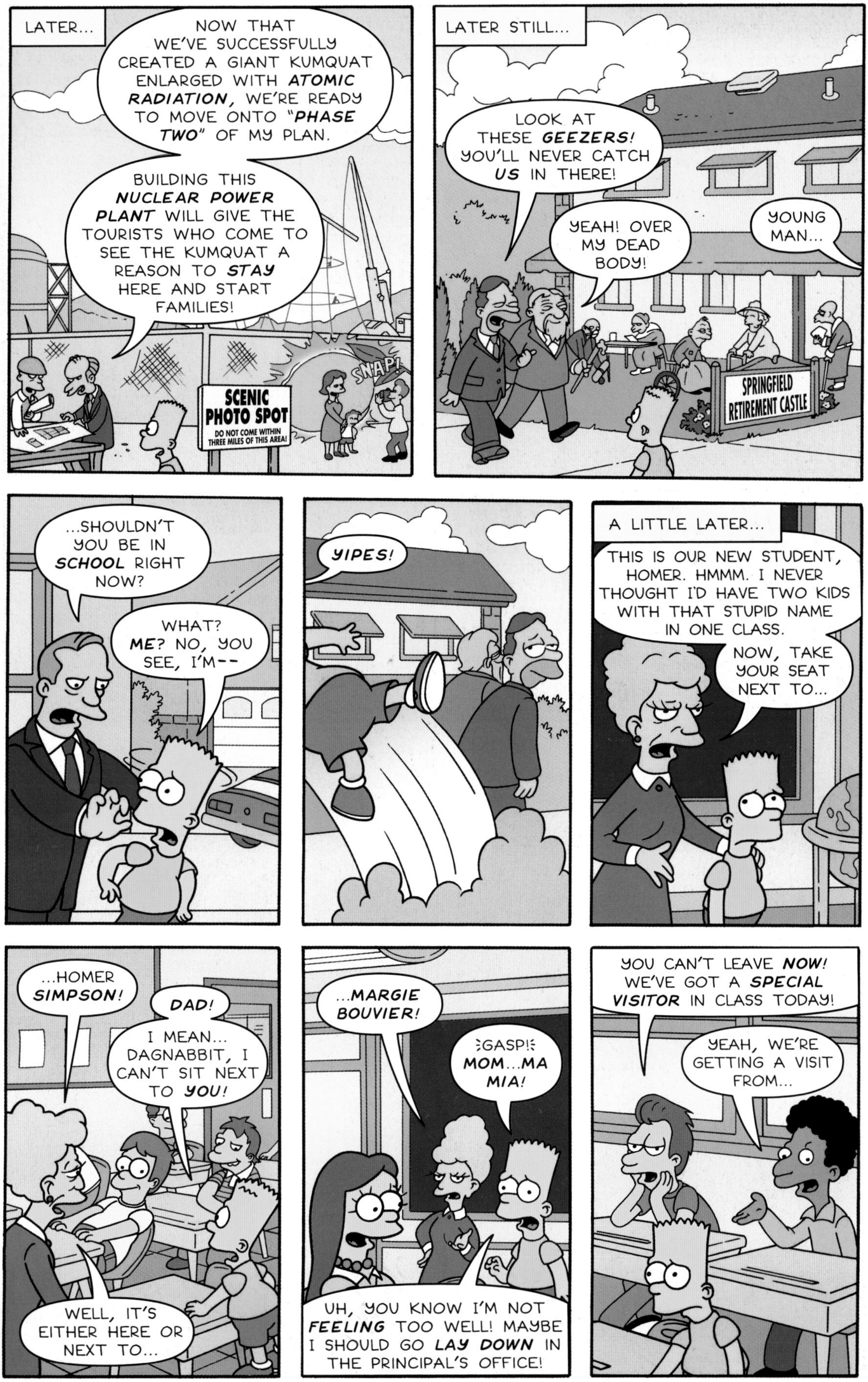
LATER...
NOW THAT WE'VE SUCCESSFULLY CREATED A GIANT KUMQUAT ENLARGED WITH ATOMIC RADIATION, WE'RE READY TO MOVE ONTO "PHASE TWO" OF MY PLAN.
BUILDING THIS NUCLEAR POWER PLANT WILL GIVE THE TOURISTS WHO COME TO SEE THE KUMQUAT A REASON TO STAY HERE AND START FAMILIES!
SCENIC PHOTO SPOT
DO NOT COME WITHIN THREE MILES OF THIS AREA!
SNAP!
LATER STILL...
LOOK AT THESE GEEZERS! YOU'LL NEVER CATCH US IN THERE!
YEAH! OVER MY DEAD BODY!
YOUNG MAN...
SPRINGFIELD RETIREMENT CASTLE
...SHOULDN'T YOU BE IN SCHOOL RIGHT NOW?
WHAT? ME? NO, YOU SEE, I'M--
YIPES!
A LITTLE LATER...
THIS IS OUR NEW STUDENT, HOMER. HMMM. I NEVER THOUGHT I'D HAVE TWO KIDS WITH THAT STUPID NAME IN ONE CLASS.
NOW, TAKE YOUR SEAT NEXT TO...
...HOMER SIMPSON!
DAD!
I MEAN... DAGNABBIT, I CAN'T SIT NEXT TO YOU!
WELL, IT'S EITHER HERE OR NEXT TO...
...MARGIE BOUVIER!
GASP! MOM...MA MIA!
UH, YOU KNOW I'M NOT FEELING TOO WELL! MAYBE I SHOULD GO LAY DOWN IN THE PRINCIPAL'S OFFICE!
YOU CAN'T LEAVE NOW! WE'VE GOT A SPECIAL VISITOR IN CLASS TODAY!
YEAH, WE'RE GETTING A VISIT FROM...

HEY, HEY, KIDS! NOW LET'S GET THIS SHOW ON THE ROAD. YOU'VE GOT A HALF HOUR, AND YOU'RE OFFICIALLY ON THE CLOCK!

CAN SOMEONE GET ME AN ASHTRAY?

UH, HI, KRUSTY. I'M HOMEY SIMPSON AND I'M YOUR BIGGEST FAN. BECAUSE OF YOU, I WANT TO BE A COMEDIAN TOO SOMEDAY, AND I WAS HOPING YOU COULD HELP ME WITH MY ACT.

WHAT'S YOUR SCHTICK, KID?

WELL IT INVOLVES A WATERMELON AND A SLEDGEHAMMER, AND I'VE GOT THIS JOKE BOOK WITH ALL OF MY ORIGINAL MATERIAL IN IT--

HEY, KRUSTY, CHECK THIS OUT!

BETTER GET SOME SPF, HOMEBOY, BECAUSE YOU'RE ABOUT TO GET BURNED BY MY MOON SHINE!

HAHAHA! SHOCK HUMOR! I LOVE IT! YOU'VE GOT A REAL FUTURE IN COMEDY, KID!

BWAAA-HAA HAA!

AT RECESS...

WELL, IT WAS COOL SEEING MOM AND DAD AS KIDS, BUT I BETTER GET BACK TO THE TIME MACHINE BEFORE PROFESSOR FRINK DOES.

HOLD THE PHONE...WHAT DO WE HAVE HERE?

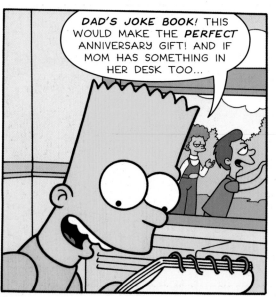

DAD'S JOKE BOOK! THIS WOULD MAKE THE PERFECT ANNIVERSARY GIFT! AND IF MOM HAS SOMETHING IN HER DESK TOO...

A MOMENT LATER...

AWESOME! IT'S MOM'S PERSONAL DIARY, TOO! I'LL DEFINITELY BEAT LISA THIS YEAR IF I TAKE THESE BACK TO THE FUTURE WITH ME...

STOP RIGHT THERE, THIEF!

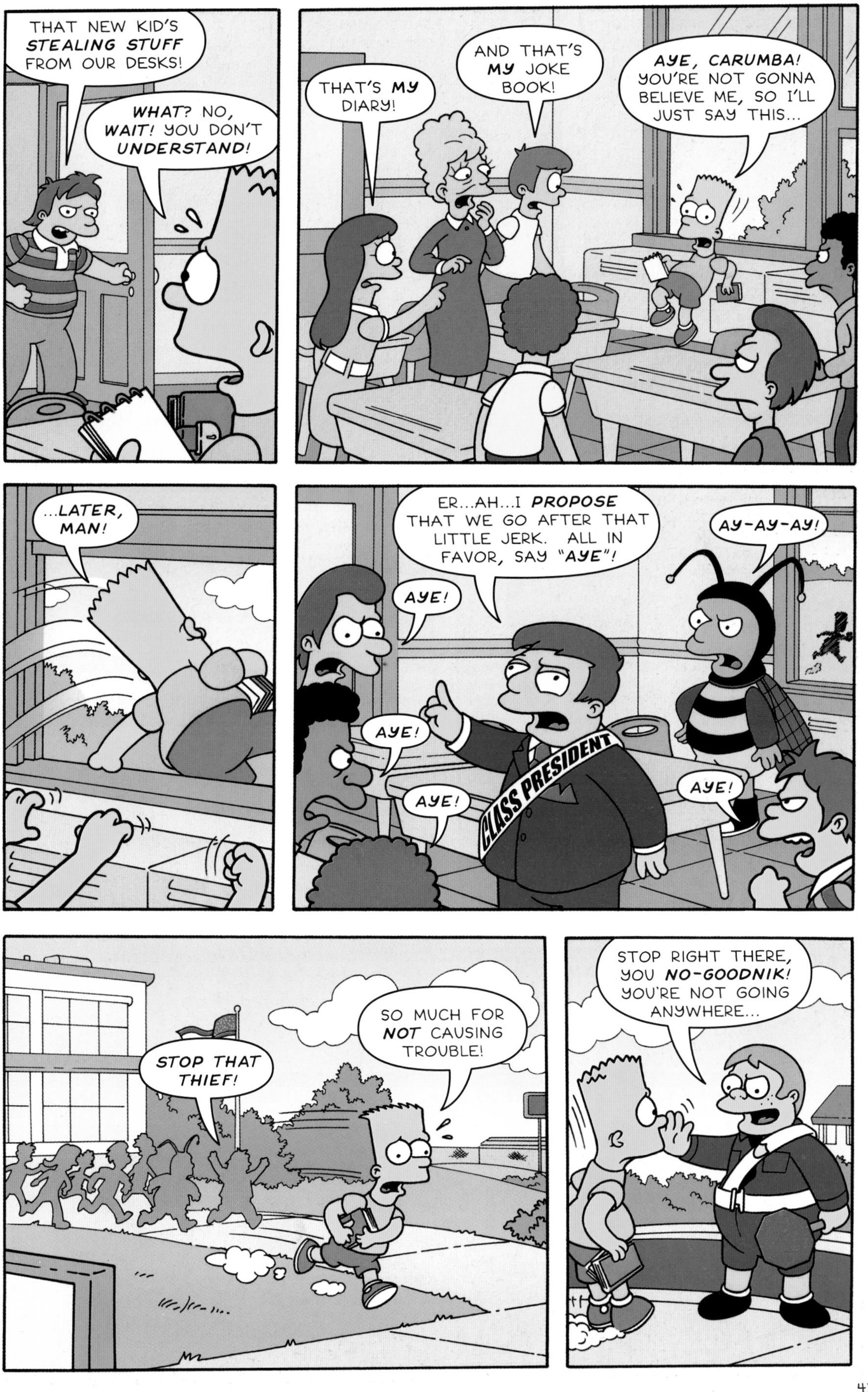
THAT NEW KID'S STEALING STUFF FROM OUR DESKS!
WHAT? NO, WAIT! YOU DON'T UNDERSTAND!
THAT'S MY DIARY!
AND THAT'S MY JOKE BOOK!
AYE, CARUMBA! YOU'RE NOT GONNA BELIEVE ME, SO I'LL JUST SAY THIS...
...LATER, MAN!
ER...AH...I PROPOSE THAT WE GO AFTER THAT LITTLE JERK. ALL IN FAVOR, SAY "AYE"!
AY-AY-AY!
AYE!
AYE!
AYE!
AYE!
CLASS PRESIDENT
STOP THAT THIEF!
SO MUCH FOR NOT CAUSING TROUBLE!
STOP RIGHT THERE, YOU NO-GOODNIK! YOU'RE NOT GOING ANYWHERE...

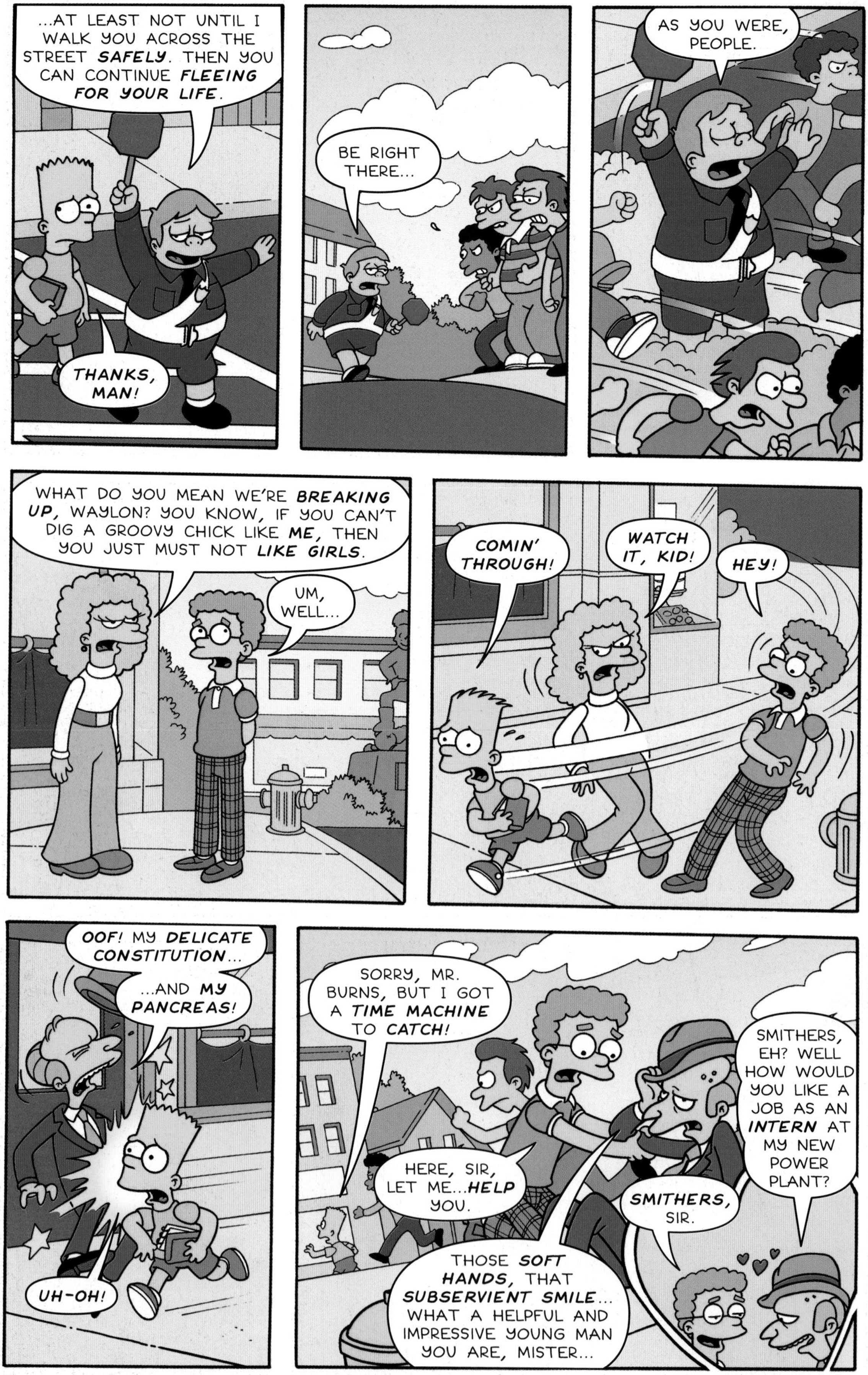
...AT LEAST NOT UNTIL I WALK YOU ACROSS THE STREET SAFELY. THEN YOU CAN CONTINUE FLEEING FOR YOUR LIFE.
THANKS, MAN!
BE RIGHT THERE...
AS YOU WERE, PEOPLE.
WHAT DO YOU MEAN WE'RE BREAKING UP, WAYLON? YOU KNOW, IF YOU CAN'T DIG A GROOVY CHICK LIKE ME, THEN YOU JUST MUST NOT LIKE GIRLS.
UM, WELL...
COMIN' THROUGH!
WATCH IT, KID!
HEY!
OOF! MY DELICATE CONSTITUTION...
...AND MY PANCREAS!
UH-OH!
SORRY, MR. BURNS, BUT I GOT A TIME MACHINE TO CATCH!
HERE, SIR, LET ME...HELP YOU.
THOSE SOFT HANDS, THAT SUBSERVIENT SMILE... WHAT A HELPFUL AND IMPRESSIVE YOUNG MAN YOU ARE, MISTER...
SMITHERS, SIR.
SMITHERS, EH? WELL HOW WOULD YOU LIKE A JOB AS AN INTERN AT MY NEW POWER PLANT?

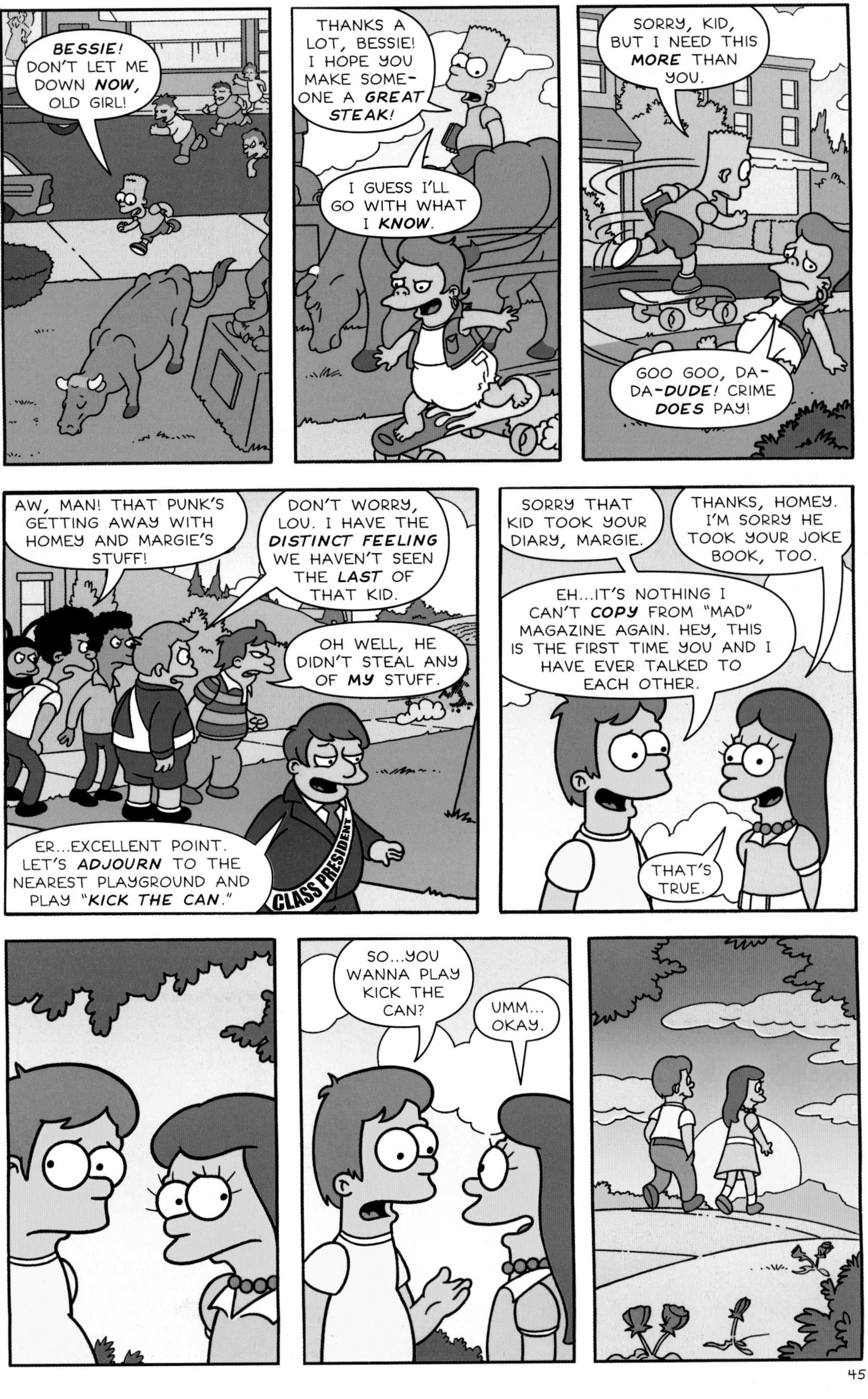
BESSIE! DON'T LET ME DOWN NOW, OLD GIRL!
THANKS A LOT, BESSIE! I HOPE YOU MAKE SOMEONE A GREAT STEAK!
I GUESS I'LL GO WITH WHAT I KNOW.
SORRY, KID, BUT I NEED THIS MORE THAN YOU.
GOO GOO, DA-DA-DUDE! CRIME DOES PAY!
AW, MAN! THAT PUNK'S GETTING AWAY WITH HOMEY AND MARGIE'S STUFF!
DON'T WORRY, LOU. I HAVE THE DISTINCT FEELING WE HAVEN'T SEEN THE LAST OF THAT KID.
OH WELL, HE DIDN'T STEAL ANY OF MY STUFF.
ER...EXCELLENT POINT. LET'S ADJOURN TO THE NEAREST PLAYGROUND AND PLAY "KICK THE CAN."
CLASS PRESIDENT
SORRY THAT KID TOOK YOUR DIARY, MARGIE.
THANKS, HOMEY. I'M SORRY HE TOOK YOUR JOKE BOOK, TOO.
EH...IT'S NOTHING I CAN'T COPY FROM "MAD" MAGAZINE AGAIN. HEY, THIS IS THE FIRST TIME YOU AND I HAVE EVER TALKED TO EACH OTHER.
THAT'S TRUE.
SO...YOU WANNA PLAY KICK THE CAN?
UMM... OKAY.

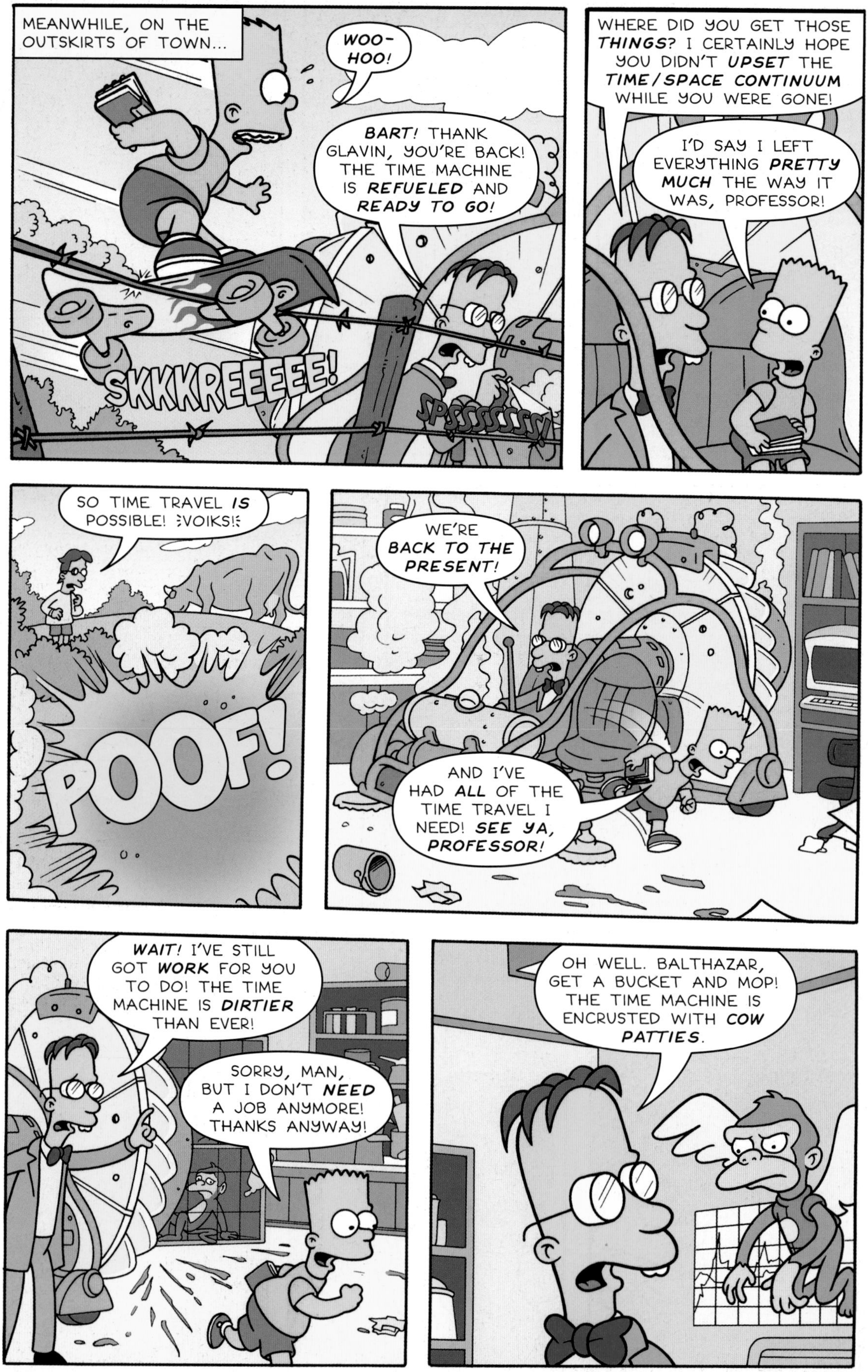
MEANWHILE, ON THE OUTSKIRTS OF TOWN...
WOO-HOO!
BART! THANK GLAVIN, YOU'RE BACK! THE TIME MACHINE IS REFUELED AND READY TO GO!
SKKKREEEEEE!
SPSSSSSSSS!
WHERE DID YOU GET THOSE THINGS? I CERTAINLY HOPE YOU DIDN'T UPSET THE TIME/SPACE CONTINUUM WHILE YOU WERE GONE!
I'D SAY I LEFT EVERYTHING PRETTY MUCH THE WAY IT WAS, PROFESSOR!
SO TIME TRAVEL IS POSSIBLE! VOIKS!
POOF!
WE'RE BACK TO THE PRESENT!
AND I'VE HAD ALL OF THE TIME TRAVEL I NEED! SEE YA, PROFESSOR!
WAIT! I'VE STILL GOT WORK FOR YOU TO DO! THE TIME MACHINE IS DIRTIER THAN EVER!
SORRY, MAN, BUT I DON'T NEED A JOB ANYMORE! THANKS ANYWAY!
OH WELL. BALTHAZAR, GET A BUCKET AND MOP! THE TIME MACHINE IS ENCRUSTED WITH COW PATTIES.

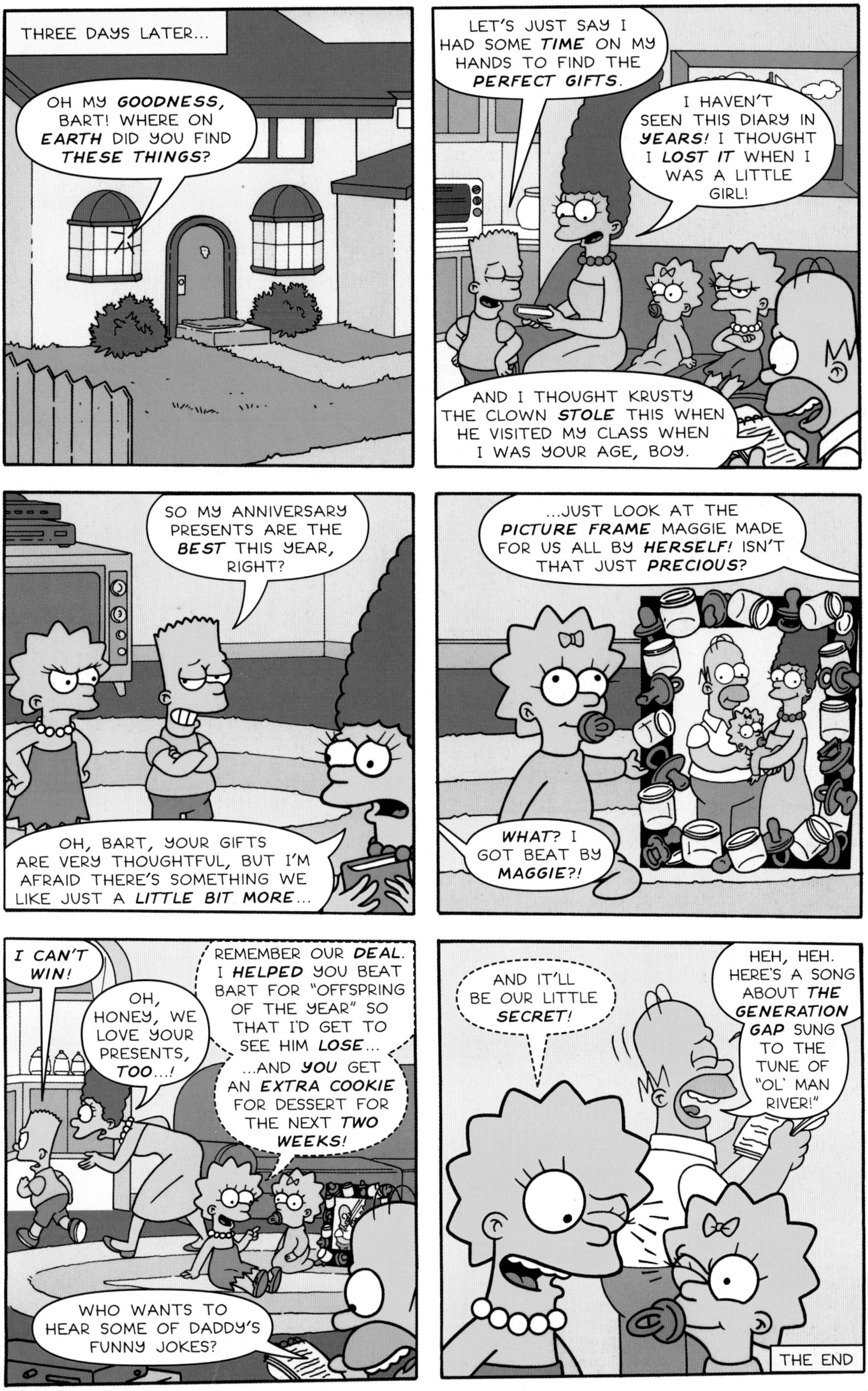
THREE DAYS LATER...
OH MY GOODNESS, BART! WHERE ON EARTH DID YOU FIND THESE THINGS?
LET'S JUST SAY I HAD SOME TIME ON MY HANDS TO FIND THE PERFECT GIFTS.
I HAVEN'T SEEN THIS DIARY IN YEARS! I THOUGHT I LOST IT WHEN I WAS A LITTLE GIRL!
AND I THOUGHT KRUSTY THE CLOWN STOLE THIS WHEN HE VISITED MY CLASS WHEN I WAS YOUR AGE, BOY.
SO MY ANNIVERSARY PRESENTS ARE THE BEST THIS YEAR, RIGHT?
OH, BART, YOUR GIFTS ARE VERY THOUGHTFUL, BUT I'M AFRAID THERE'S SOMETHING WE LIKE JUST A LITTLE BIT MORE...
...JUST LOOK AT THE PICTURE FRAME MAGGIE MADE FOR US ALL BY HERSELF! ISN'T THAT JUST PRECIOUS?
WHAT? I GOT BEAT BY MAGGIE?!
I CAN'T WIN!
OH, HONEY, WE LOVE YOUR PRESENTS, TOO...!
REMEMBER OUR DEAL. I HELPED YOU BEAT BART FOR "OFFSPRING OF THE YEAR" SO THAT I'D GET TO SEE HIM LOSE...
...AND YOU GET AN EXTRA COOKIE FOR DESSERT FOR THE NEXT TWO WEEKS!
WHO WANTS TO HEAR SOME OF DADDY'S FUNNY JOKES?
AND IT'LL BE OUR LITTLE SECRET!
HEH, HEH. HERE'S A SONG ABOUT THE GENERATION GAP SUNG TO THE TUNE OF "OL' MAN RIVER!"
THE END

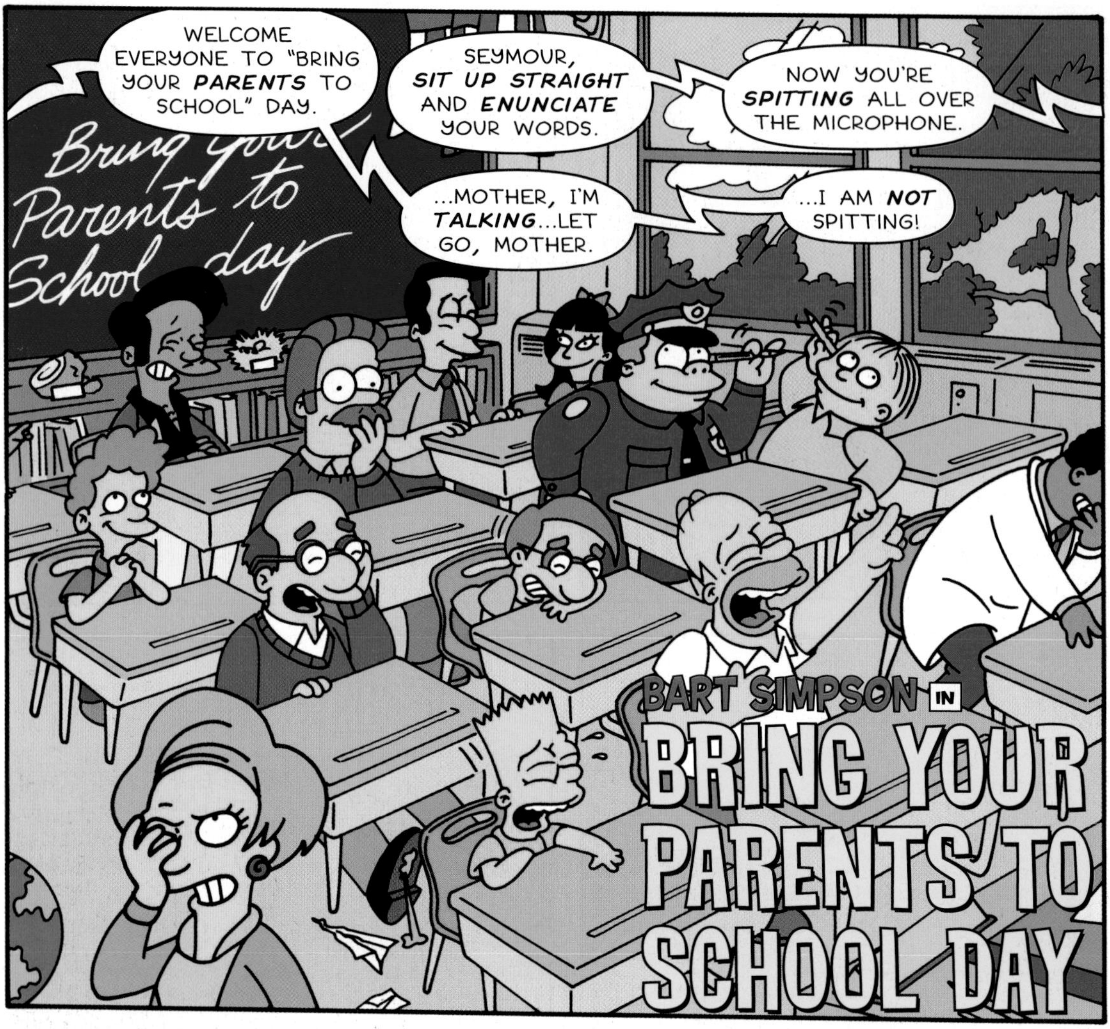
WELCOME EVERYONE TO "BRING YOUR **PARENTS** TO SCHOOL" DAY.
SEYMOUR, **SIT UP STRAIGHT** AND **ENUNCIATE** YOUR WORDS.
NOW YOU'RE **SPITTING** ALL OVER THE MICROPHONE.
...MOTHER, I'M **TALKING**...LET GO, MOTHER.
...I AM **NOT** SPITTING!
Bring your Parents to School day
BART SIMPSON IN
BRING YOUR PARENTS TO SCHOOL DAY

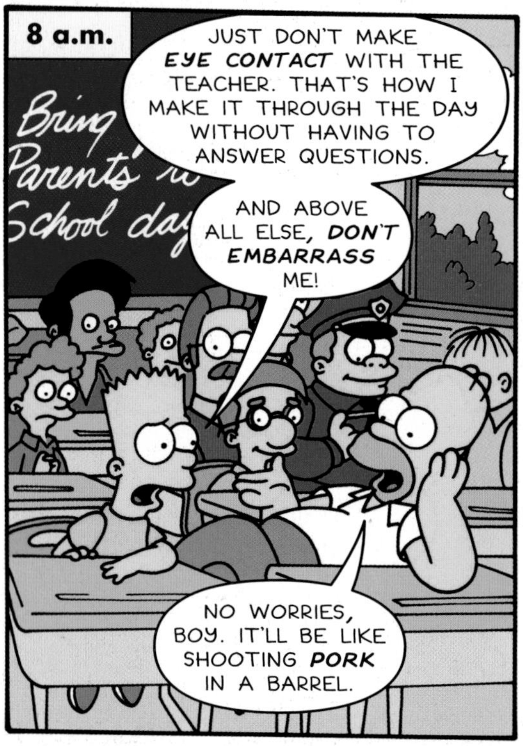
8 a.m.
JUST DON'T MAKE **EYE CONTACT** WITH THE TEACHER. THAT'S HOW I MAKE IT THROUGH THE DAY WITHOUT HAVING TO ANSWER QUESTIONS.
AND ABOVE ALL ELSE, **DON'T EMBARRASS** ME!
NO WORRIES, BOY. IT'LL BE LIKE SHOOTING **PORK** IN A BARREL.

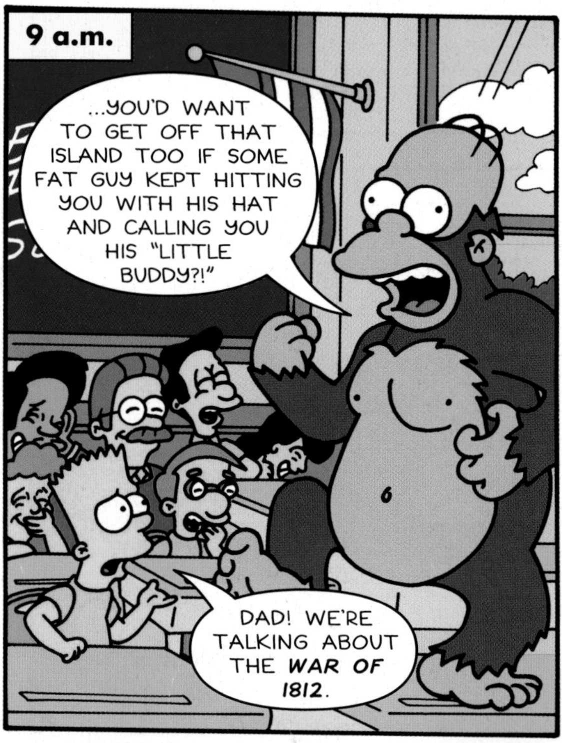
9 a.m.
...YOU'D WANT TO GET OFF THAT ISLAND TOO IF SOME FAT GUY KEPT HITTING YOU WITH HIS HAT AND CALLING YOU HIS "LITTLE BUDDY?!"
DAD! WE'RE TALKING ABOUT THE **WAR OF 1812**.

JESSE LEON MCCANN
ABBY DENSON
STORY

JOHN COSTANZA
PENCILS

PATRICK OWSLEY
INKS

ART VILLANUEVA
COLORS

KAREN BATES
LETTERS

BILL MORRISON
EDITOR

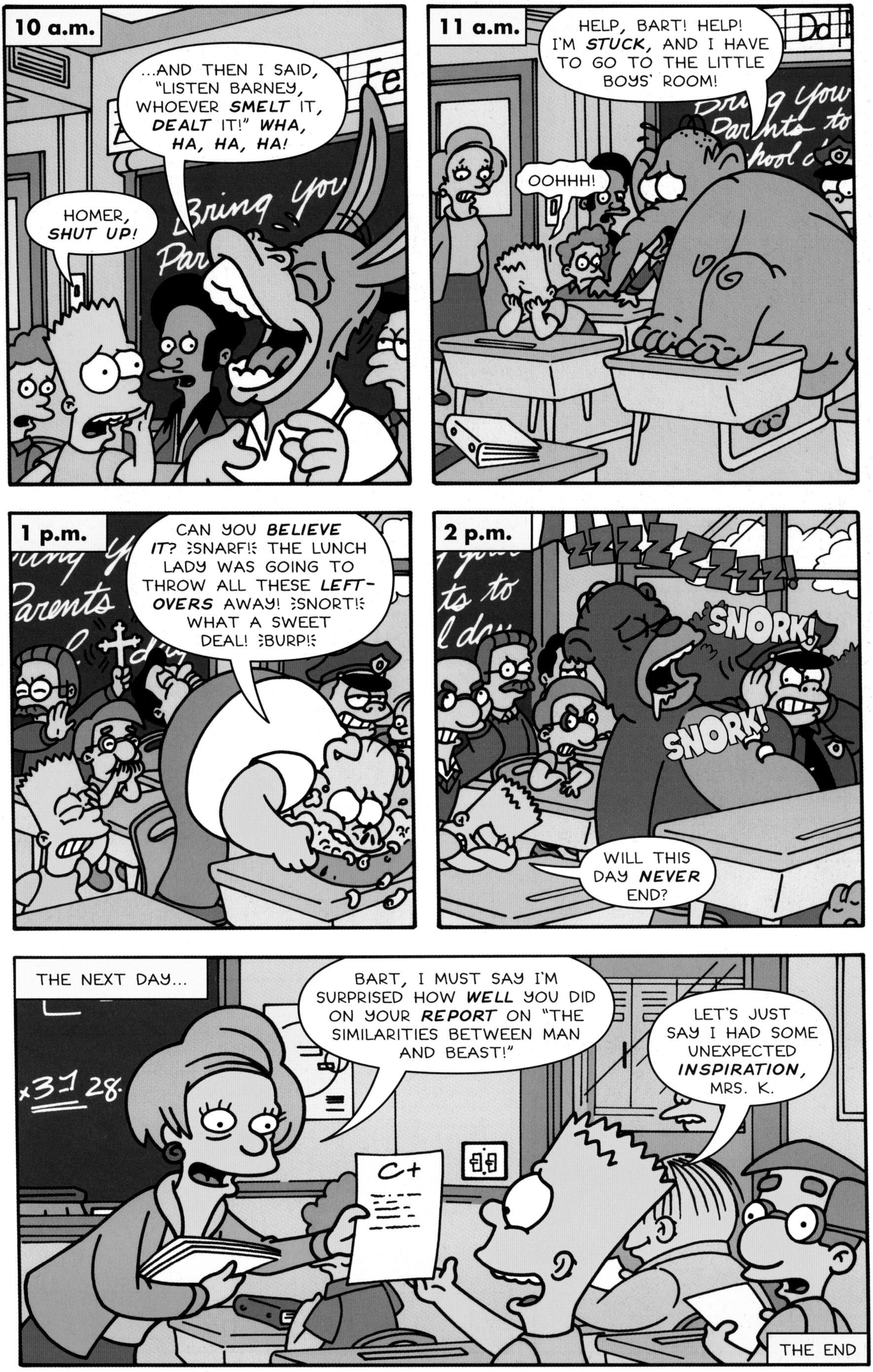

10 a.m.
...AND THEN I SAID, "LISTEN BARNEY, WHOEVER SMELT IT, DEALT IT!" WHA, HA, HA, HA!
HOMER, SHUT UP!
Bring you Par
11 a.m.
HELP, BART! HELP! I'M STUCK, AND I HAVE TO GO TO THE LITTLE BOYS' ROOM!
OOHHH!
1 p.m.
CAN YOU BELIEVE IT? ⁝SNARF!⁝ THE LUNCH LADY WAS GOING TO THROW ALL THESE LEFT-OVERS AWAY! ⁝SNORT!⁝ WHAT A SWEET DEAL! ⁝BURP!⁝
2 p.m.
ZZZZZZZZZ!
SNORK!
SNORK!
WILL THIS DAY NEVER END?
THE NEXT DAY...
BART, I MUST SAY I'M SURPRISED HOW WELL YOU DID ON YOUR REPORT ON "THE SIMILARITIES BETWEEN MAN AND BEAST!"
LET'S JUST SAY I HAD SOME UNEXPECTED INSPIRATION, MRS. K.
C+
THE END

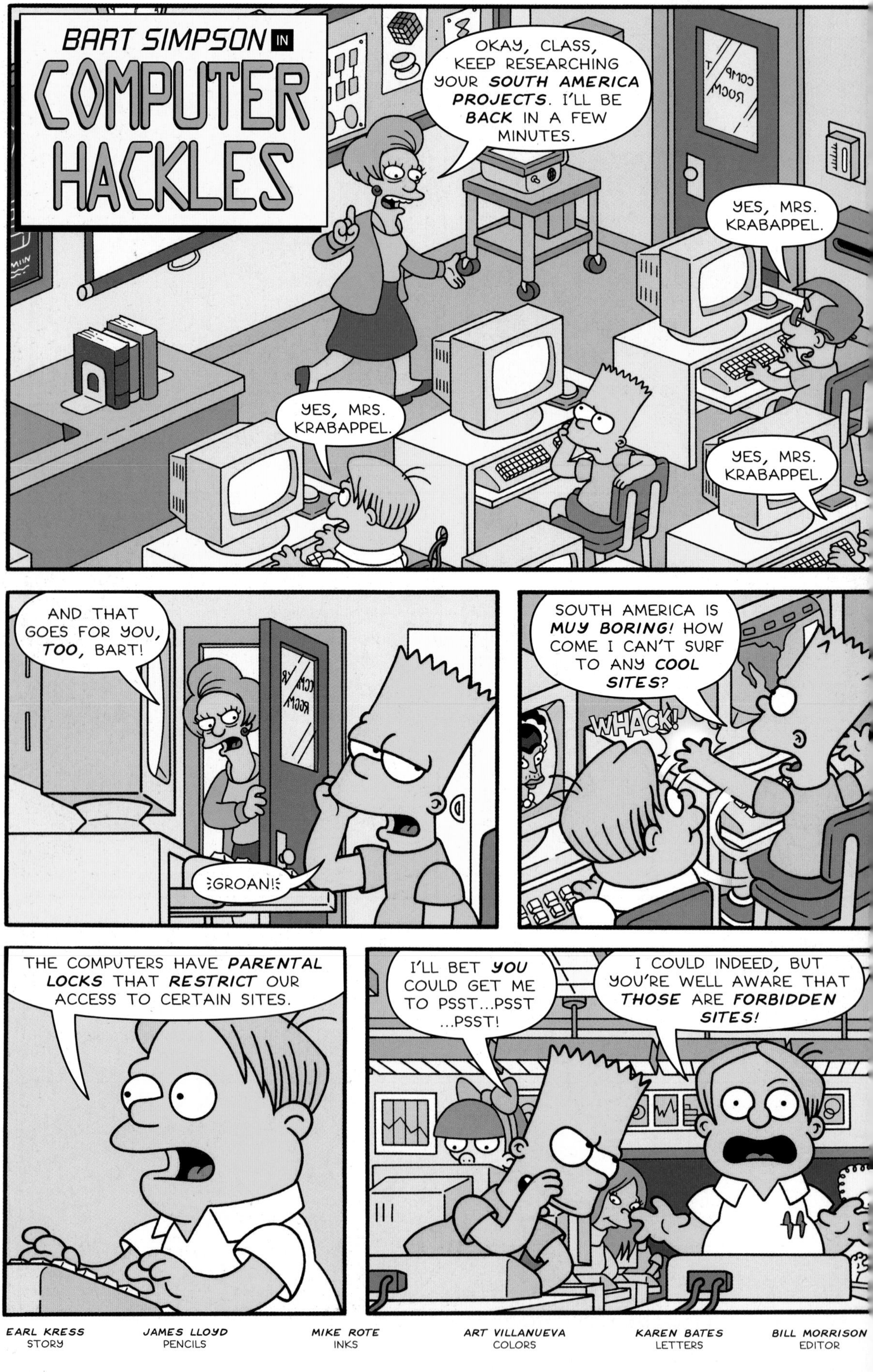

BART SIMPSON IN
COMPUTER HACKLES
OKAY, CLASS, KEEP RESEARCHING YOUR SOUTH AMERICA PROJECTS. I'LL BE BACK IN A FEW MINUTES.
YES, MRS. KRABAPPEL.
YES, MRS. KRABAPPEL.
YES, MRS. KRABAPPEL.
COMP ROOM
AND THAT GOES FOR YOU, TOO, BART!
GROAN!
SOUTH AMERICA IS MUY BORING! HOW COME I CAN'T SURF TO ANY COOL SITES?
WHACK!
THE COMPUTERS HAVE PARENTAL LOCKS THAT RESTRICT OUR ACCESS TO CERTAIN SITES.
I'LL BET YOU COULD GET ME TO PSST...PSST ...PSST!
I COULD INDEED, BUT YOU'RE WELL AWARE THAT THOSE ARE FORBIDDEN SITES!

EARL KRESS STORY | **JAMES LLOYD** PENCILS | **MIKE ROTE** INKS | **ART VILLANUEVA** COLORS | **KAREN BATES** LETTERS | **BILL MORRISON** EDITOR

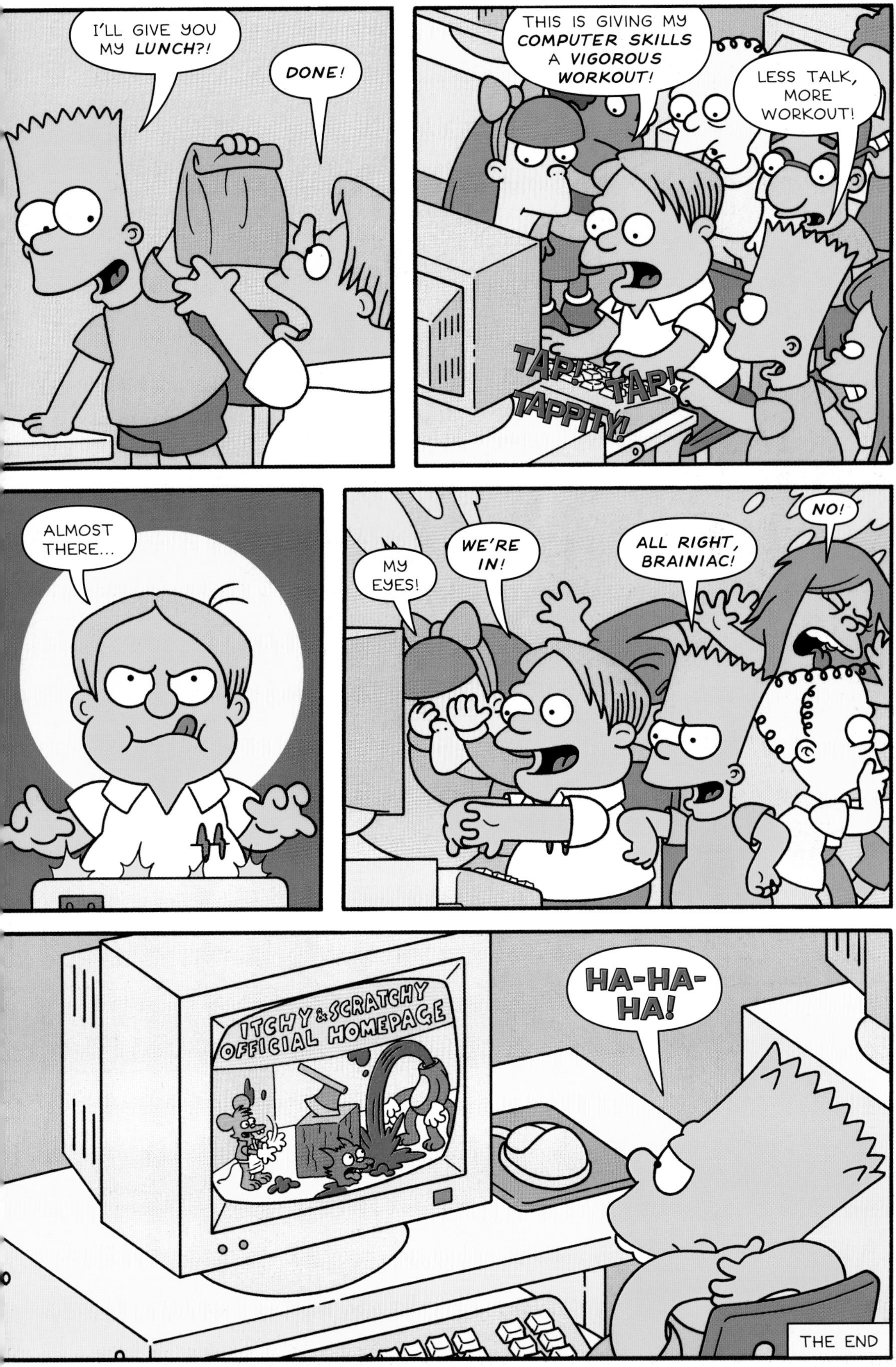
I'LL GIVE YOU MY LUNCH?!
DONE!
THIS IS GIVING MY COMPUTER SKILLS A VIGOROUS WORKOUT!
LESS TALK, MORE WORKOUT!
TAP! TAP! TAPPITY!
ALMOST THERE...
MY EYES!
WE'RE IN!
ALL RIGHT, BRAINIAC!
NO!
ITCHY & SCRATCHY OFFICIAL HOMEPAGE
HA-HA-HA!
THE END

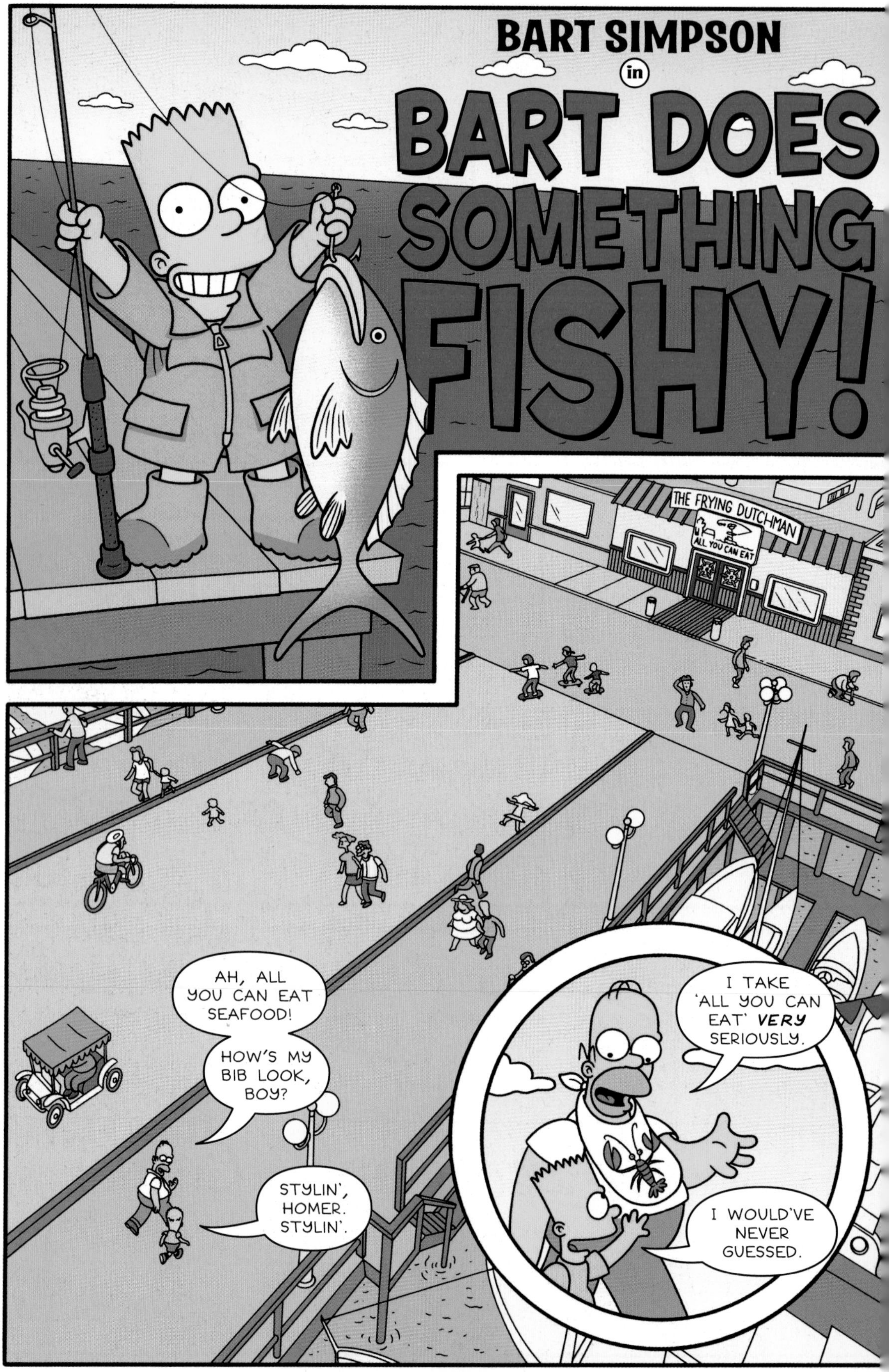
BART SIMPSON
in
BART DOES SOMETHING FISHY!
THE FRYING DUTCHMAN
ALL YOU CAN EAT
AH, ALL YOU CAN EAT SEAFOOD!
HOW'S MY BIB LOOK, BOY?
STYLIN', HOMER. STYLIN'.
I TAKE 'ALL YOU CAN EAT' VERY SERIOUSLY.
I WOULD'VE NEVER GUESSED.

JAMES BATES
STORY

ISTVAN MAJOROS
PENCILS

MIKE ROTE
INKS

ART VILLANUEVA
COLORS

KAREN BATES
LETTERS

BILL MORRISON
EDITOR

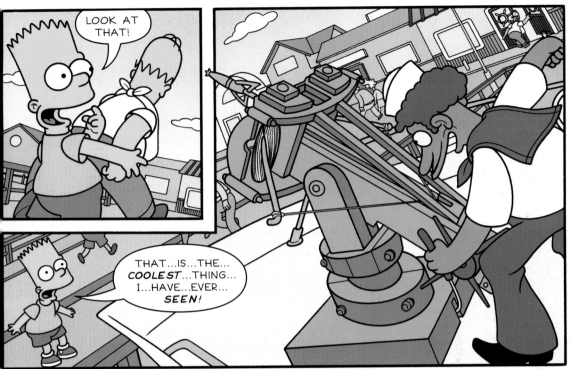

LOOK AT THAT!

THAT...IS...THE... *COOLEST*...THING... I...HAVE...EVER... *SEEN!*

HALLO, YOUNG LAD. ARE YOU A WOULD-BE FISHERMAN?

UH-HUH. CAN I SHOOT THE HARPOON?

DO NOT BE SILLY. THAT HARPOON IS FOR *FEIOS PEIXES GRANDE!*

ME AND MY CREW HAVE SAILED THE SEVEN SEAS HUNTING FEIOS PEIXES GRANDE!

WHAT'S *THAT?*

A BIG UGLY FISH.

NO. *THE* BIG UGLY FISH!

WE HAVE HUNTED OUR FOE ALL THE WAY HERE, TO THE PORT OF SPRINGFIELD.

WHOOPS!

PHEWF!

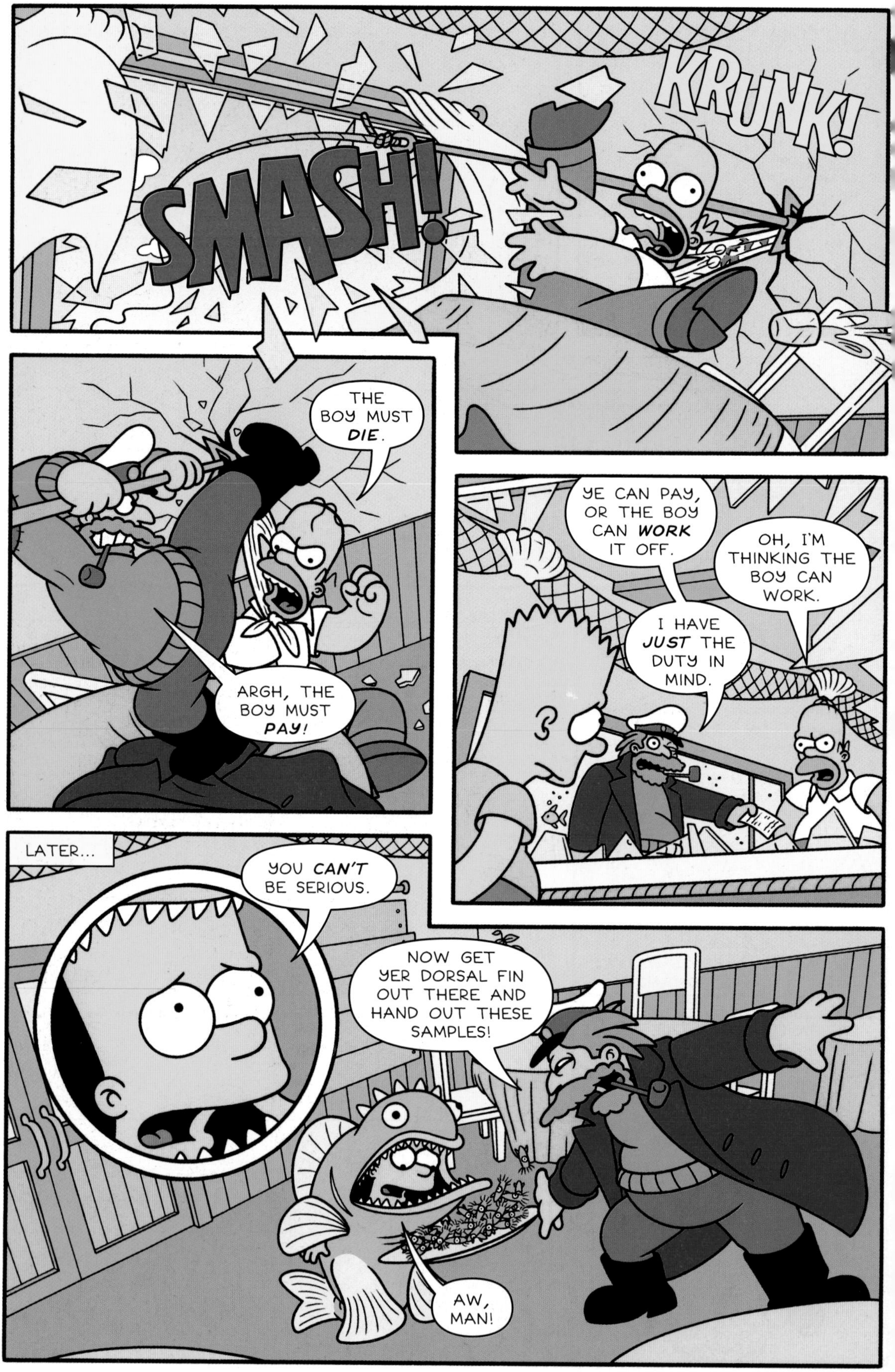
SMASH!
KRUNK!
THE BOY MUST DIE.
ARGH, THE BOY MUST PAY!
YE CAN PAY, OR THE BOY CAN WORK IT OFF.
OH, I'M THINKING THE BOY CAN WORK.
I HAVE JUST THE DUTY IN MIND.
LATER...
YOU CAN'T BE SERIOUS.
NOW GET YER DORSAL FIN OUT THERE AND HAND OUT THESE SAMPLES!
AW, MAN!

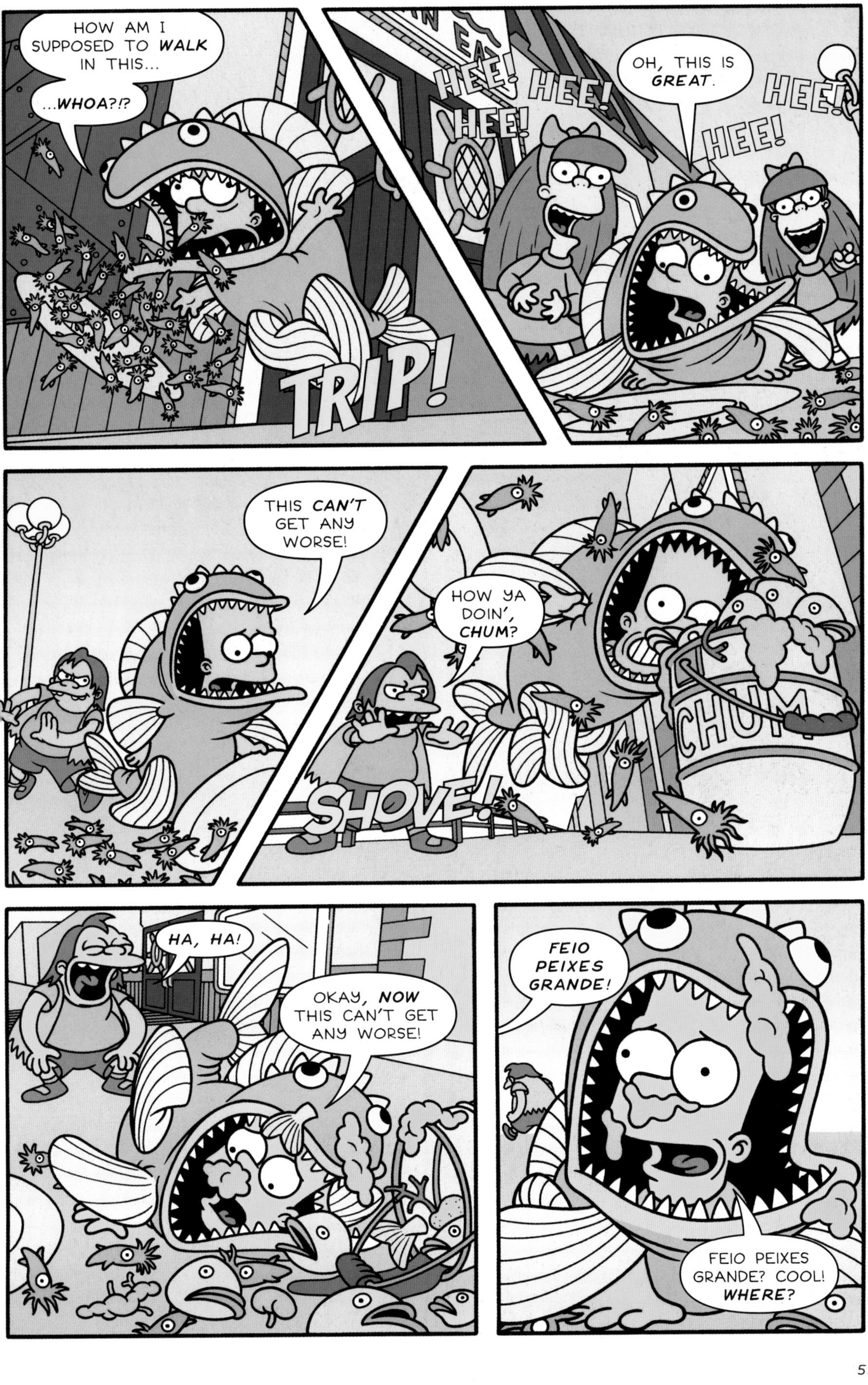
HOW AM I SUPPOSED TO WALK IN THIS...
...WHOA?!?
TRIP!
HEE! HEE! HEE!
OH, THIS IS GREAT.
HEE! HEE!
THIS CAN'T GET ANY WORSE!
HOW YA DOIN', CHUM?
CHUM
SHOVE!
HA, HA!
OKAY, NOW THIS CAN'T GET ANY WORSE!
FEIO PEIXES GRANDE!
FEIO PEIXES GRANDE? COOL! WHERE?

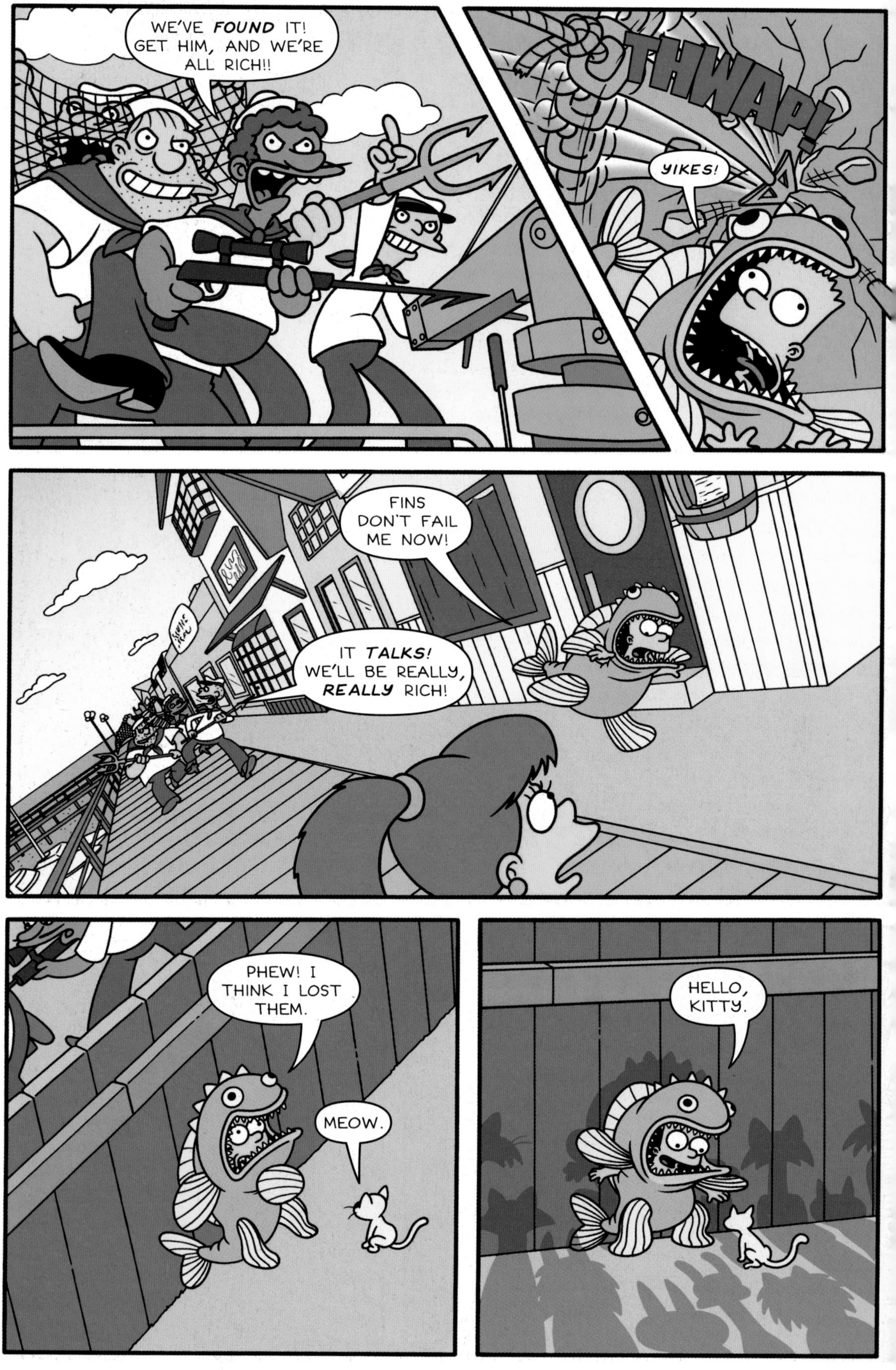
WE'VE FOUND IT! GET HIM, AND WE'RE ALL RICH!!
THWAP!
YIKES!
FINS DON'T FAIL ME NOW!
IT TALKS! WE'LL BE REALLY, REALLY RICH!
PHEW! I THINK I LOST THEM.
MEOW.
HELLO, KITTY.

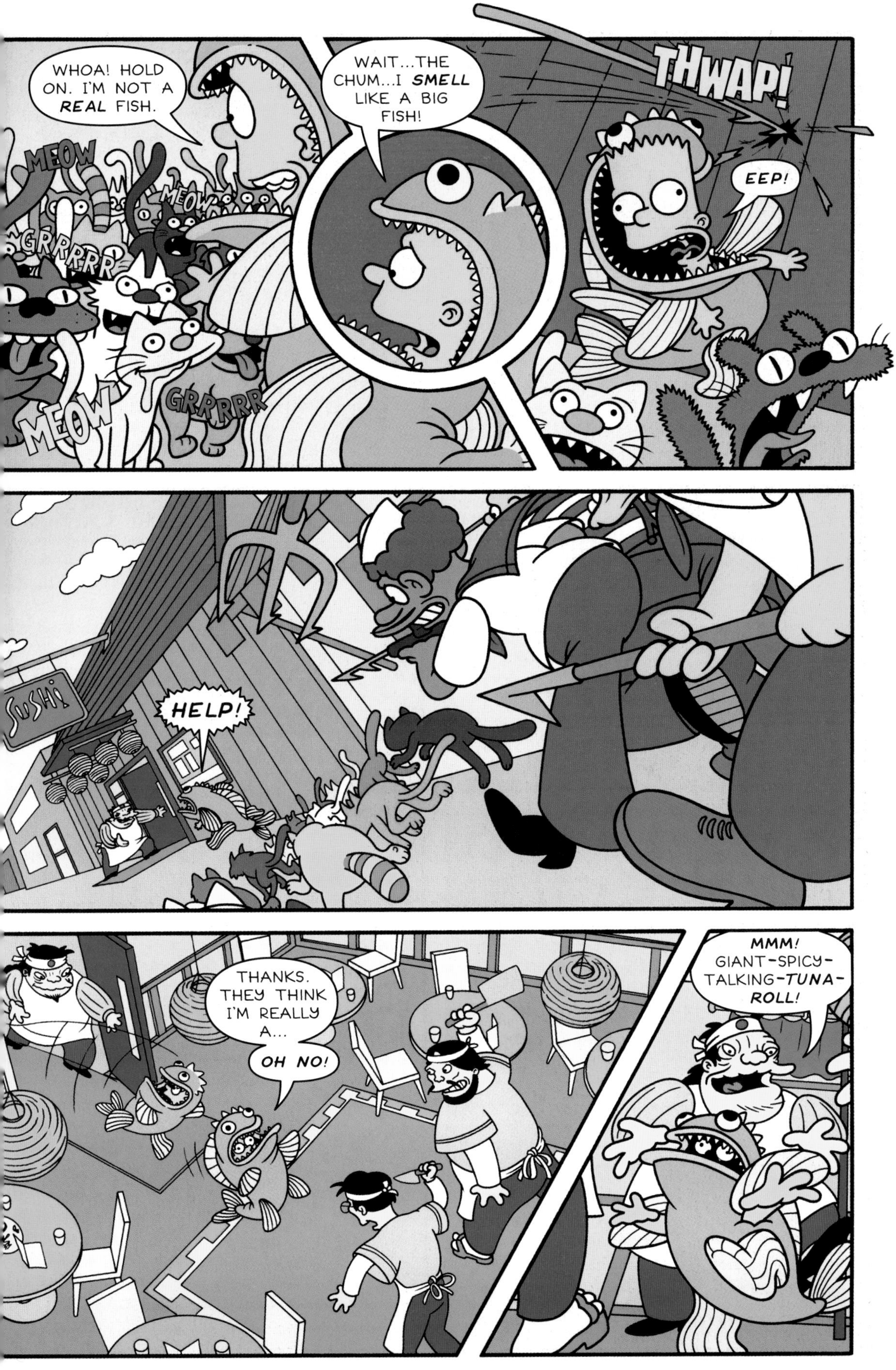
WHOA! HOLD ON. I'M NOT A *REAL* FISH.
MEOW
MEOW
GRRRRRR
MEOW
GRRRRRR
WAIT...THE CHUM...I *SMELL* LIKE A BIG FISH!
THWAP!
EEP!
SUSHI
HELP!
THANKS. THEY THINK I'M REALLY A...
OH NO!
MMM! GIANT-SPICY-TALKING-*TUNA*-*ROLL*!

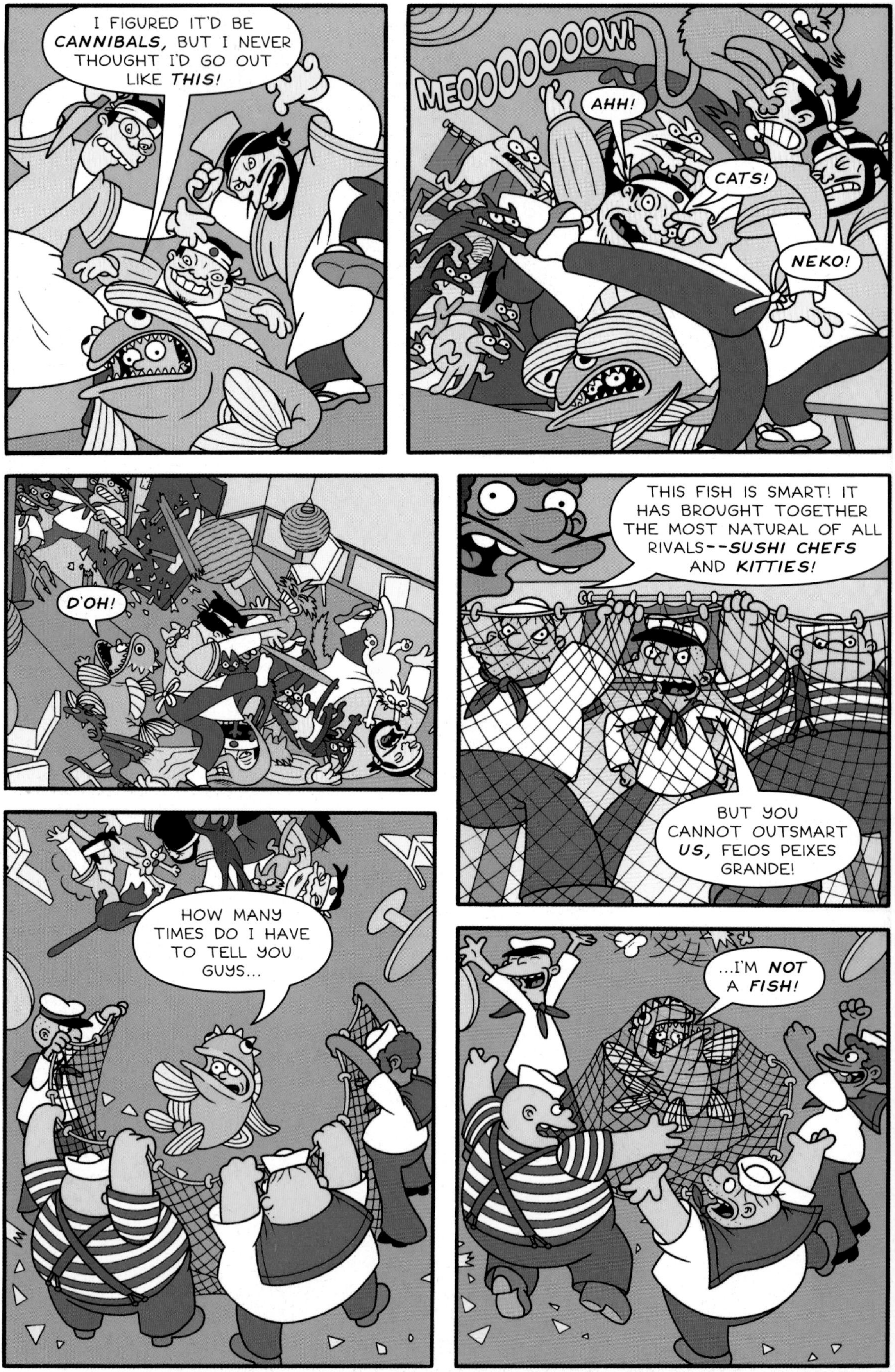
I FIGURED IT'D BE CANNIBALS, BUT I NEVER THOUGHT I'D GO OUT LIKE THIS!
MEOOOOOOOW!
AHH!
CATS!
NEKO!
D'OH!
THIS FISH IS SMART! IT HAS BROUGHT TOGETHER THE MOST NATURAL OF ALL RIVALS--SUSHI CHEFS AND KITTIES!
BUT YOU CANNOT OUTSMART US, FEIOS PEIXES GRANDE!
HOW MANY TIMES DO I HAVE TO TELL YOU GUYS...
...I'M NOT A FISH!

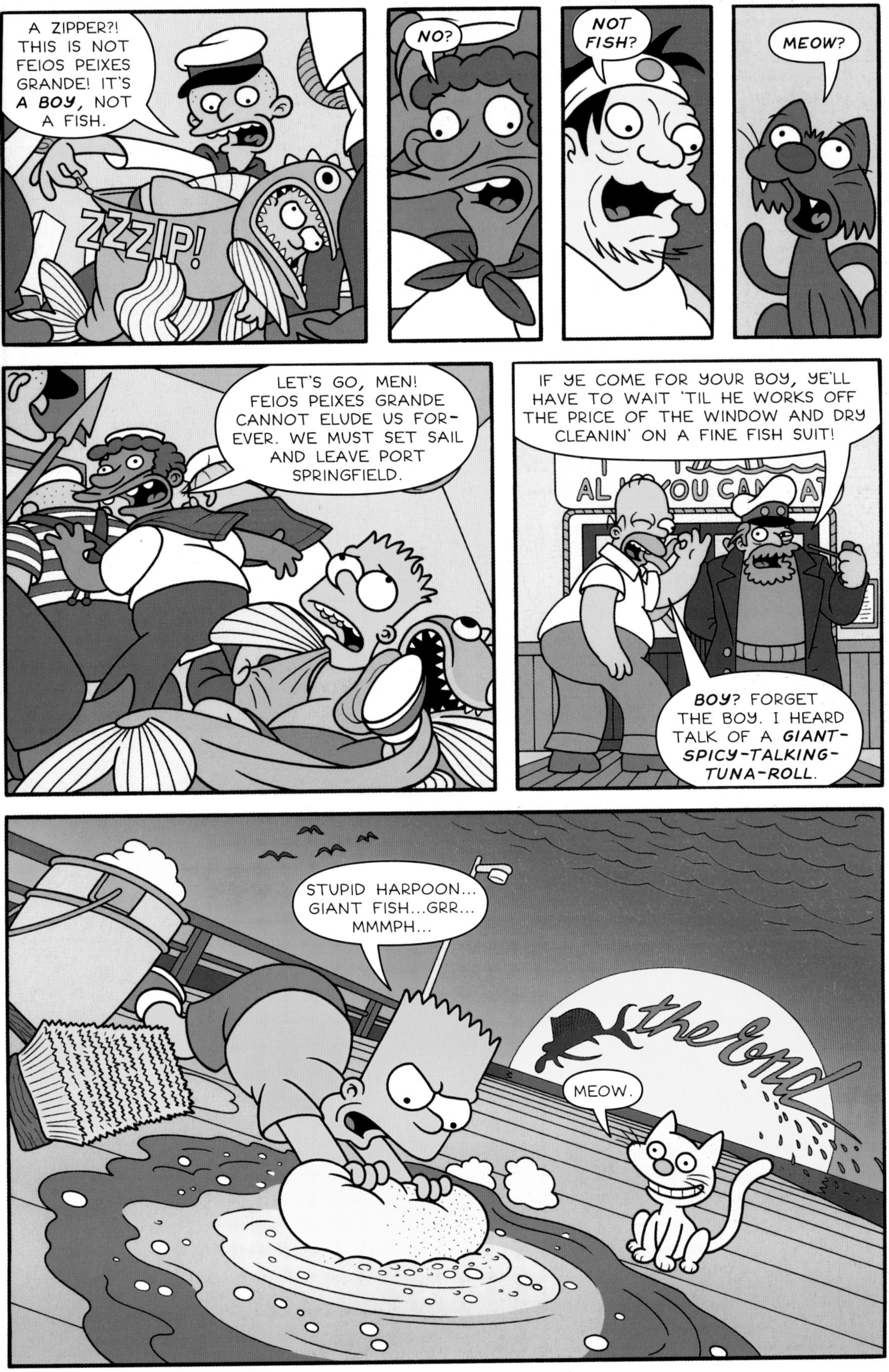
A ZIPPER?! THIS IS NOT FEIOS PEIXES GRANDE! IT'S A BOY, NOT A FISH.
ZZZIP!
NO?
NOT FISH?
MEOW?
LET'S GO, MEN! FEIOS PEIXES GRANDE CANNOT ELUDE US FOR-EVER. WE MUST SET SAIL AND LEAVE PORT SPRINGFIELD.
IF YE COME FOR YOUR BOY, YE'LL HAVE TO WAIT 'TIL HE WORKS OFF THE PRICE OF THE WINDOW AND DRY CLEANIN' ON A FINE FISH SUIT!
BOY? FORGET THE BOY. I HEARD TALK OF A GIANT-SPICY-TALKING-TUNA-ROLL.
STUPID HARPOON... GIANT FISH...GRR... MMMPH...
the end
MEOW.

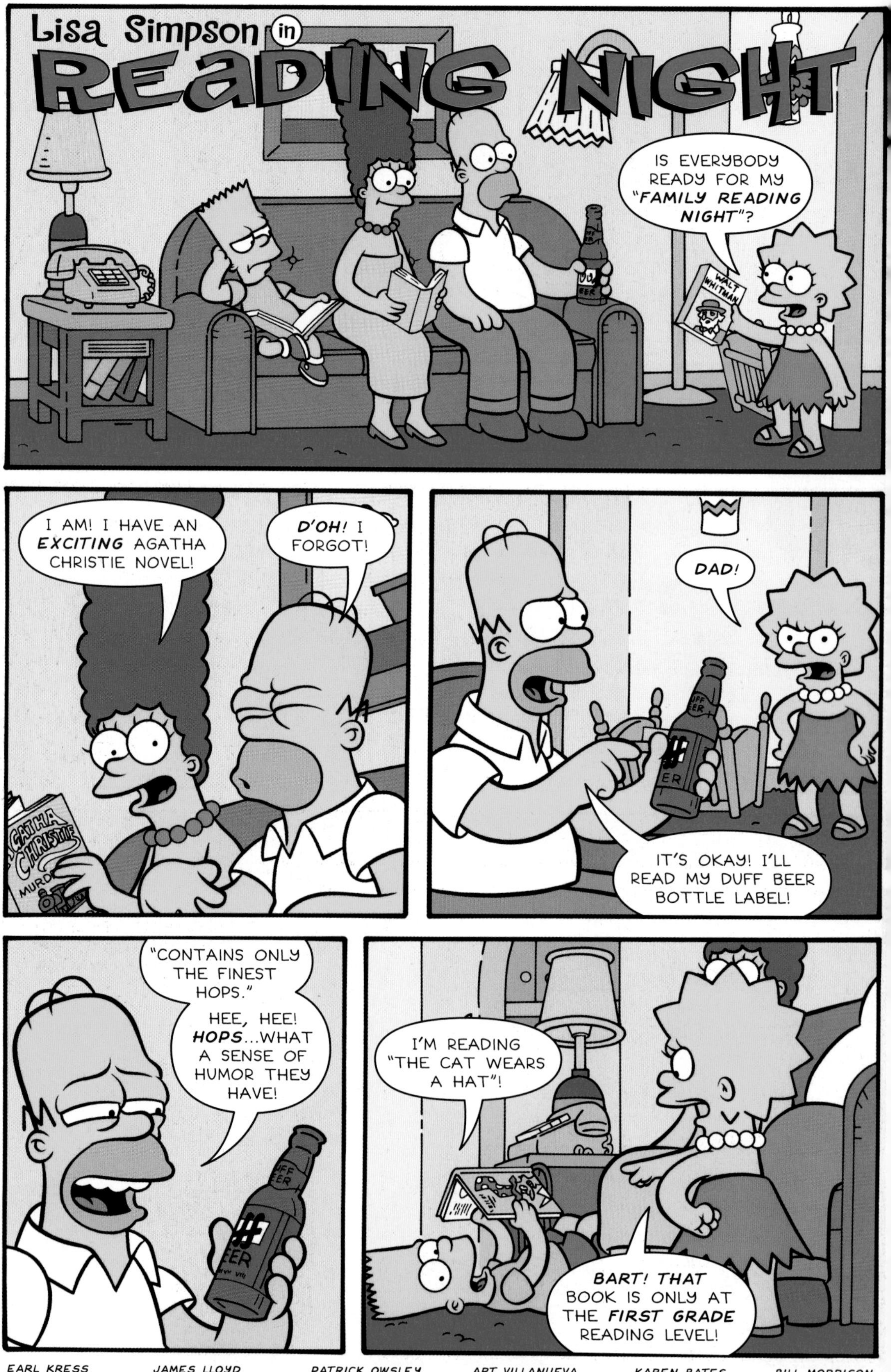
Lisa Simpson in
READING NIGHT
IS EVERYBODY READY FOR MY "FAMILY READING NIGHT"?
WALT WHITMAN
I AM! I HAVE AN EXCITING AGATHA CHRISTIE NOVEL!
D'OH! I FORGOT!
AGATHA CHRISTIE
DAD!
IT'S OKAY! I'LL READ MY DUFF BEER BOTTLE LABEL!
"CONTAINS ONLY THE FINEST HOPS."
HEE, HEE! HOPS...WHAT A SENSE OF HUMOR THEY HAVE!
I'M READING "THE CAT WEARS A HAT"!
BART! THAT BOOK IS ONLY AT THE FIRST GRADE READING LEVEL!

EARL KRESS STORY | *JAMES LLOYD* PENCILS | *PATRICK OWSLEY* INKS | *ART VILLANUEVA* COLORS | *KAREN BATES* LETTERS | *BILL MORRISON* EDITOR

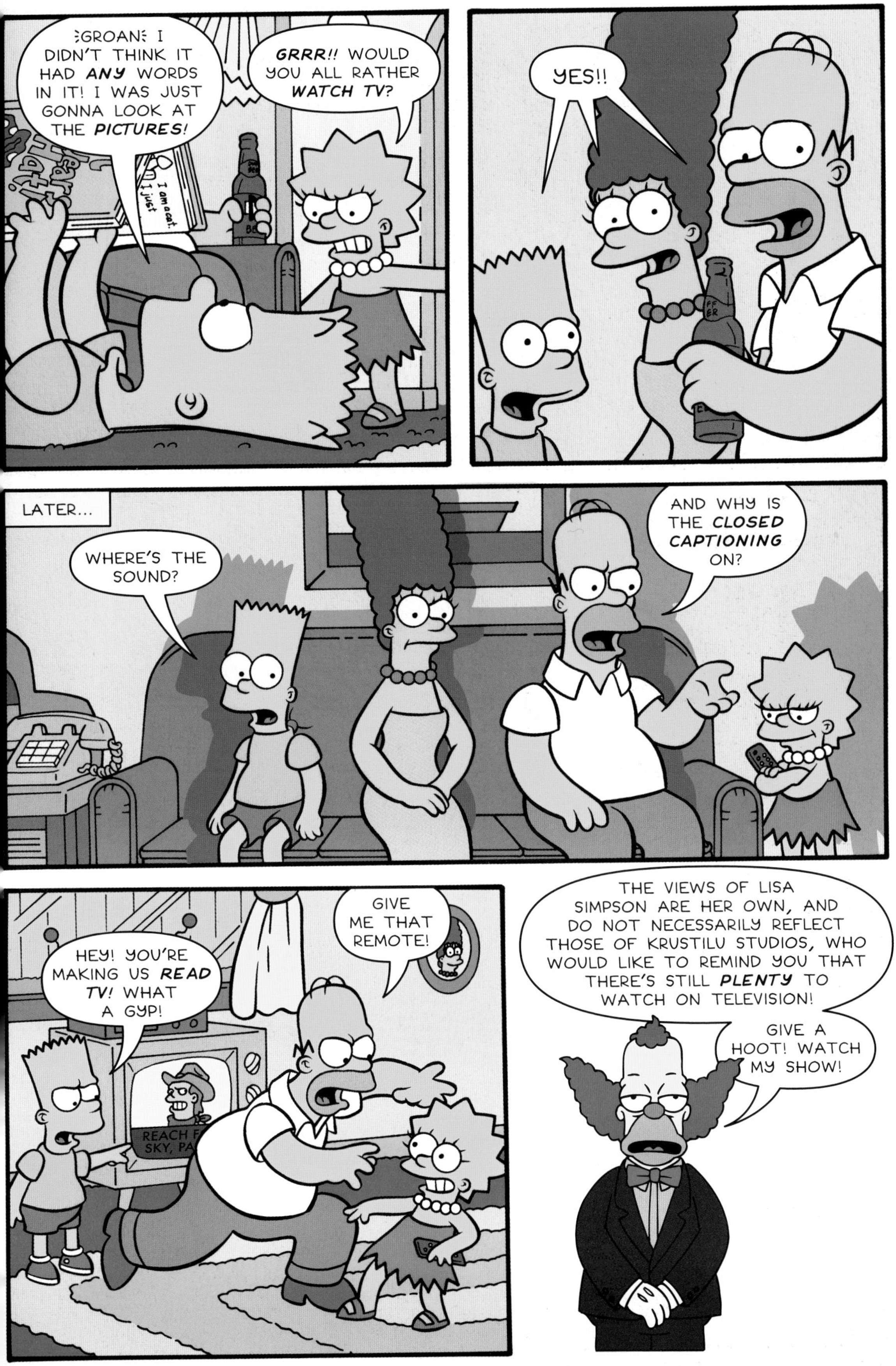
⁝GROAN⁝ I DIDN'T THINK IT HAD **ANY** WORDS IN IT! I WAS JUST GONNA LOOK AT THE **PICTURES**!
GRRR!! WOULD YOU ALL RATHER **WATCH TV**?
YES!!
LATER...
WHERE'S THE SOUND?
AND WHY IS THE **CLOSED CAPTIONING** ON?
HEY! YOU'RE MAKING US **READ TV!** WHAT A GYP!
GIVE ME THAT REMOTE!
THE VIEWS OF LISA SIMPSON ARE HER OWN, AND DO NOT NECESSARILY REFLECT THOSE OF KRUSTILU STUDIOS, WHO WOULD LIKE TO REMIND YOU THAT THERE'S STILL **PLENTY** TO WATCH ON TELEVISION!
GIVE A HOOT! WATCH MY SHOW!

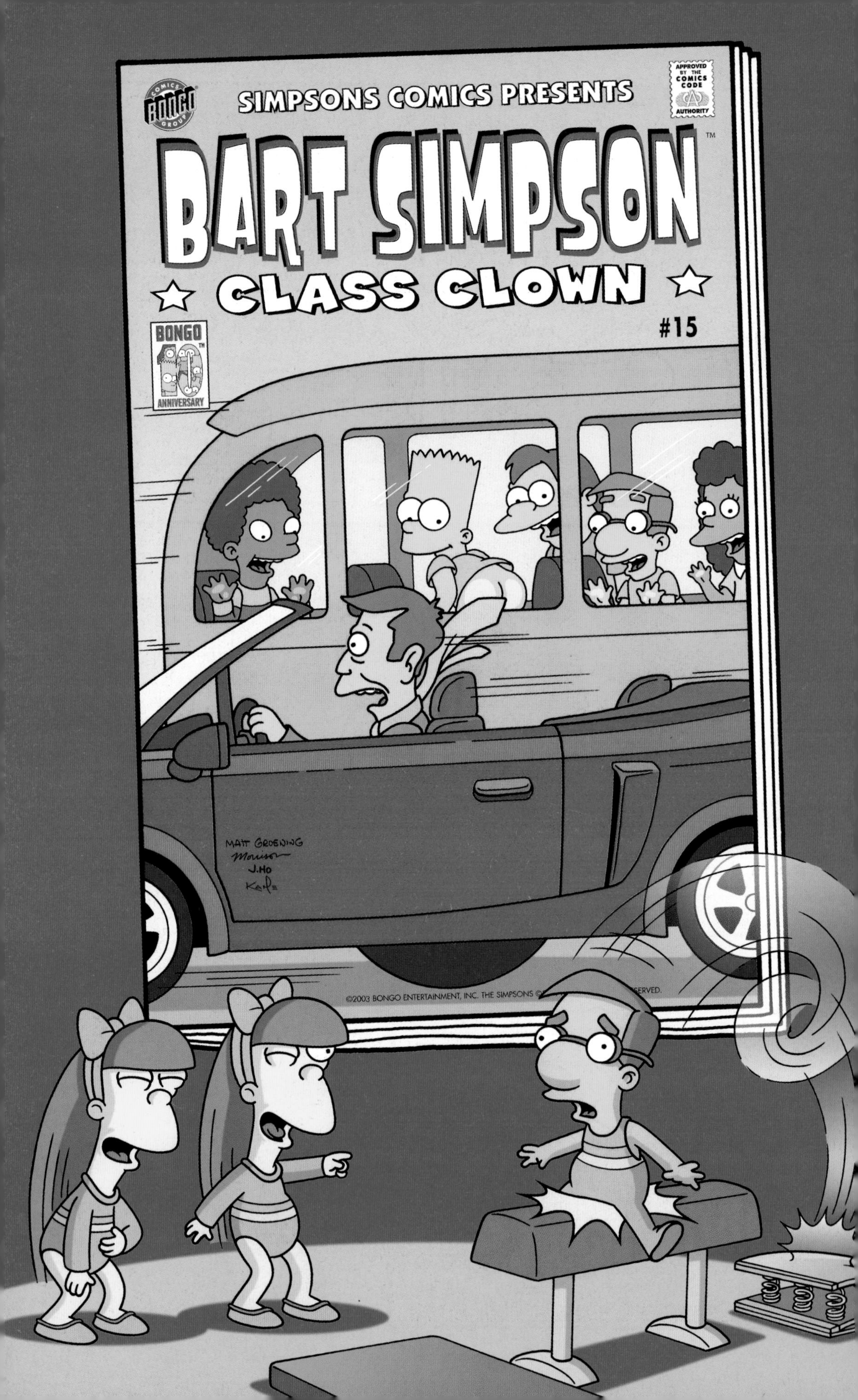
SIMPSONS COMICS PRESENTS
APPROVED BY THE COMICS CODE AUTHORITY
BART SIMPSON
CLASS CLOWN
#15
BONGO 10TH ANNIVERSARY
MATT GROENING
J.HO

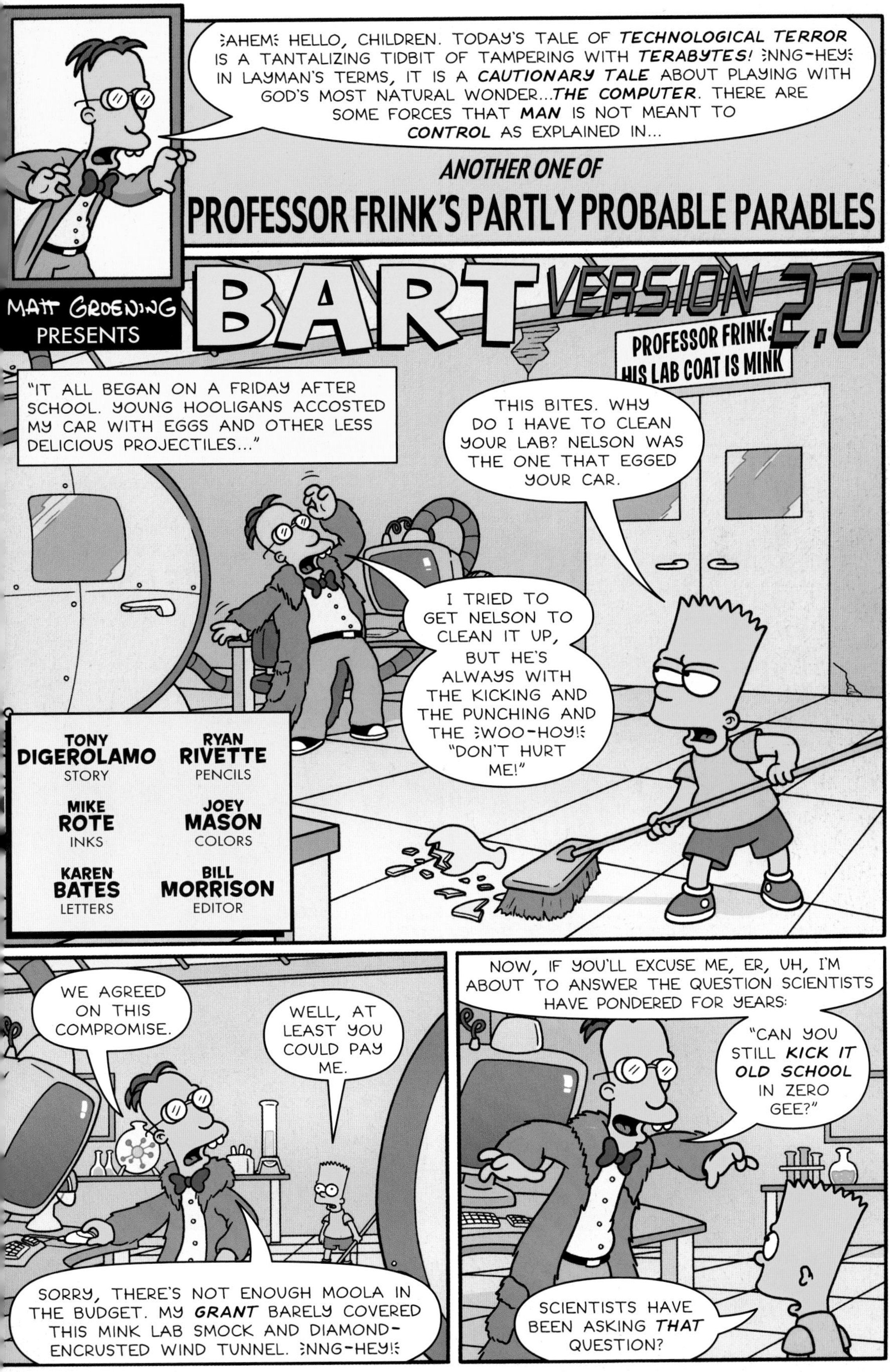

⦂AHEM⦂ HELLO, CHILDREN. TODAY'S TALE OF *TECHNOLOGICAL TERROR* IS A TANTALIZING TIDBIT OF TAMPERING WITH *TERABYTES!* ⦂NNG-HEY⦂ IN LAYMAN'S TERMS, IT IS A *CAUTIONARY TALE* ABOUT PLAYING WITH GOD'S MOST NATURAL WONDER...*THE COMPUTER*. THERE ARE SOME FORCES THAT *MAN* IS NOT MEANT TO *CONTROL* AS EXPLAINED IN...
ANOTHER ONE OF
PROFESSOR FRINK'S PARTLY PROBABLE PARABLES
MATT GROENING PRESENTS
BART VERSION 2.0
PROFESSOR FRINK: HIS LAB COAT IS MINK
"IT ALL BEGAN ON A FRIDAY AFTER SCHOOL. YOUNG HOOLIGANS ACCOSTED MY CAR WITH EGGS AND OTHER LESS DELICIOUS PROJECTILES..."
THIS BITES. WHY DO I HAVE TO CLEAN YOUR LAB? NELSON WAS THE ONE THAT EGGED YOUR CAR.
I TRIED TO GET NELSON TO CLEAN IT UP,
BUT HE'S ALWAYS WITH THE KICKING AND THE PUNCHING AND THE ⦂WOO-HOY!⦂ "DON'T HURT ME!"
TONY DIGEROLAMO STORY
RYAN RIVETTE PENCILS
MIKE ROTE INKS
JOEY MASON COLORS
KAREN BATES LETTERS
BILL MORRISON EDITOR
WE AGREED ON THIS COMPROMISE.
WELL, AT LEAST YOU COULD PAY ME.
SORRY, THERE'S NOT ENOUGH MOOLA IN THE BUDGET. MY *GRANT* BARELY COVERED THIS MINK LAB SMOCK AND DIAMOND-ENCRUSTED WIND TUNNEL. ⦂NNG-HEY!⦂
NOW, IF YOU'LL EXCUSE ME, ER, UH, I'M ABOUT TO ANSWER THE QUESTION SCIENTISTS HAVE PONDERED FOR YEARS:
"CAN YOU STILL *KICK IT OLD SCHOOL* IN ZERO GEE?"
SCIENTISTS HAVE BEEN ASKING *THAT* QUESTION?

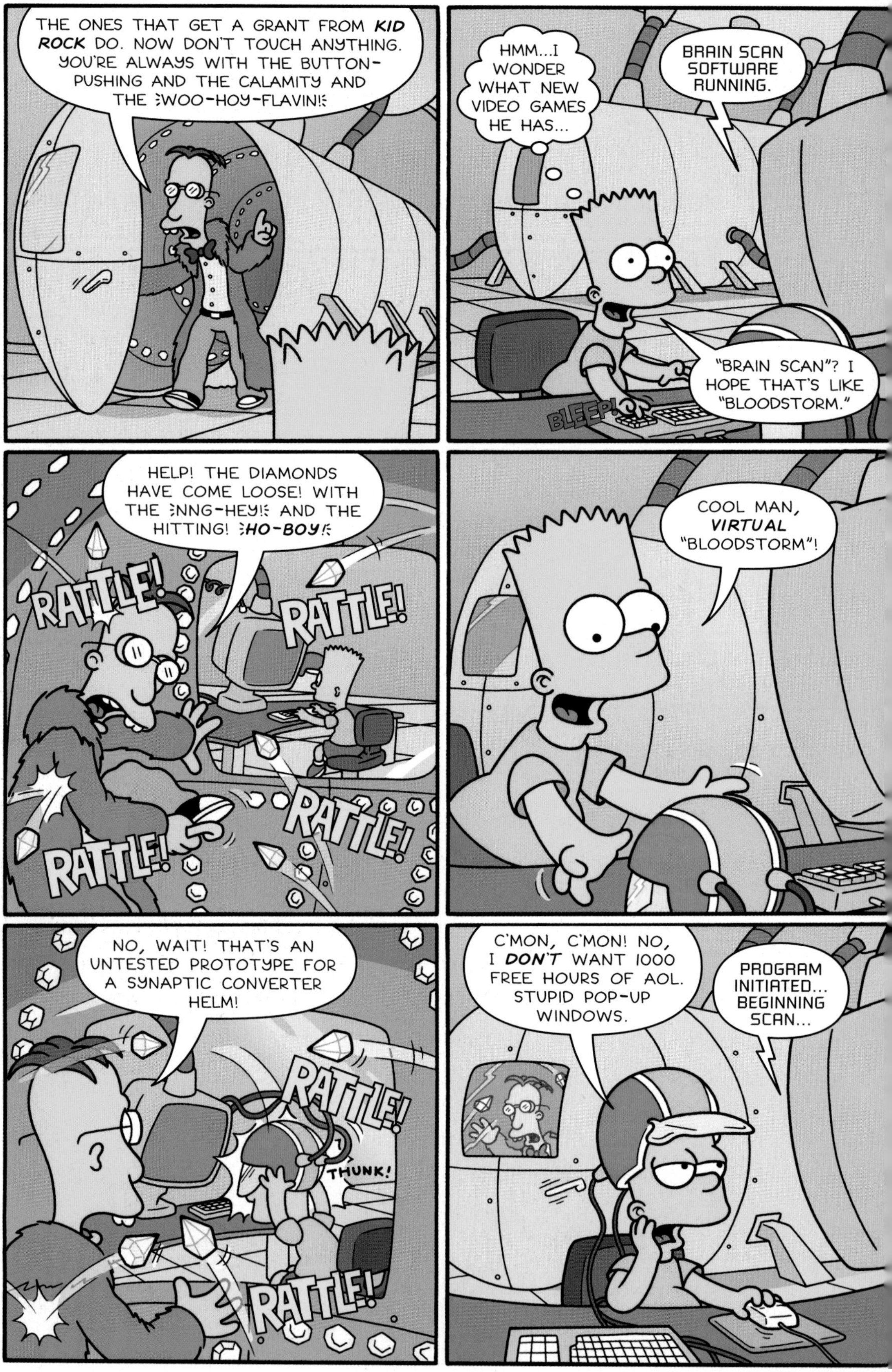
THE ONES THAT GET A GRANT FROM KID ROCK DO. NOW DON'T TOUCH ANYTHING. YOU'RE ALWAYS WITH THE BUTTON-PUSHING AND THE CALAMITY AND THE WOO-HOY-FLAVIN!
HMM...I WONDER WHAT NEW VIDEO GAMES HE HAS...
BRAIN SCAN SOFTWARE RUNNING.
"BRAIN SCAN"? I HOPE THAT'S LIKE "BLOODSTORM."
BLEEP!
HELP! THE DIAMONDS HAVE COME LOOSE! WITH THE NNG-HEY! AND THE HITTING! HO-BOY!
RATTLE!
RATTLE!
RATTLE!
RATTLE!
COOL MAN, VIRTUAL "BLOODSTORM"!
NO, WAIT! THAT'S AN UNTESTED PROTOTYPE FOR A SYNAPTIC CONVERTER HELM!
RATTLE!
THUNK!
RATTLE!
C'MON, C'MON! NO, I DON'T WANT 1000 FREE HOURS OF AOL. STUPID POP-UP WINDOWS.
PROGRAM INITIATED... BEGINNING SCAN...

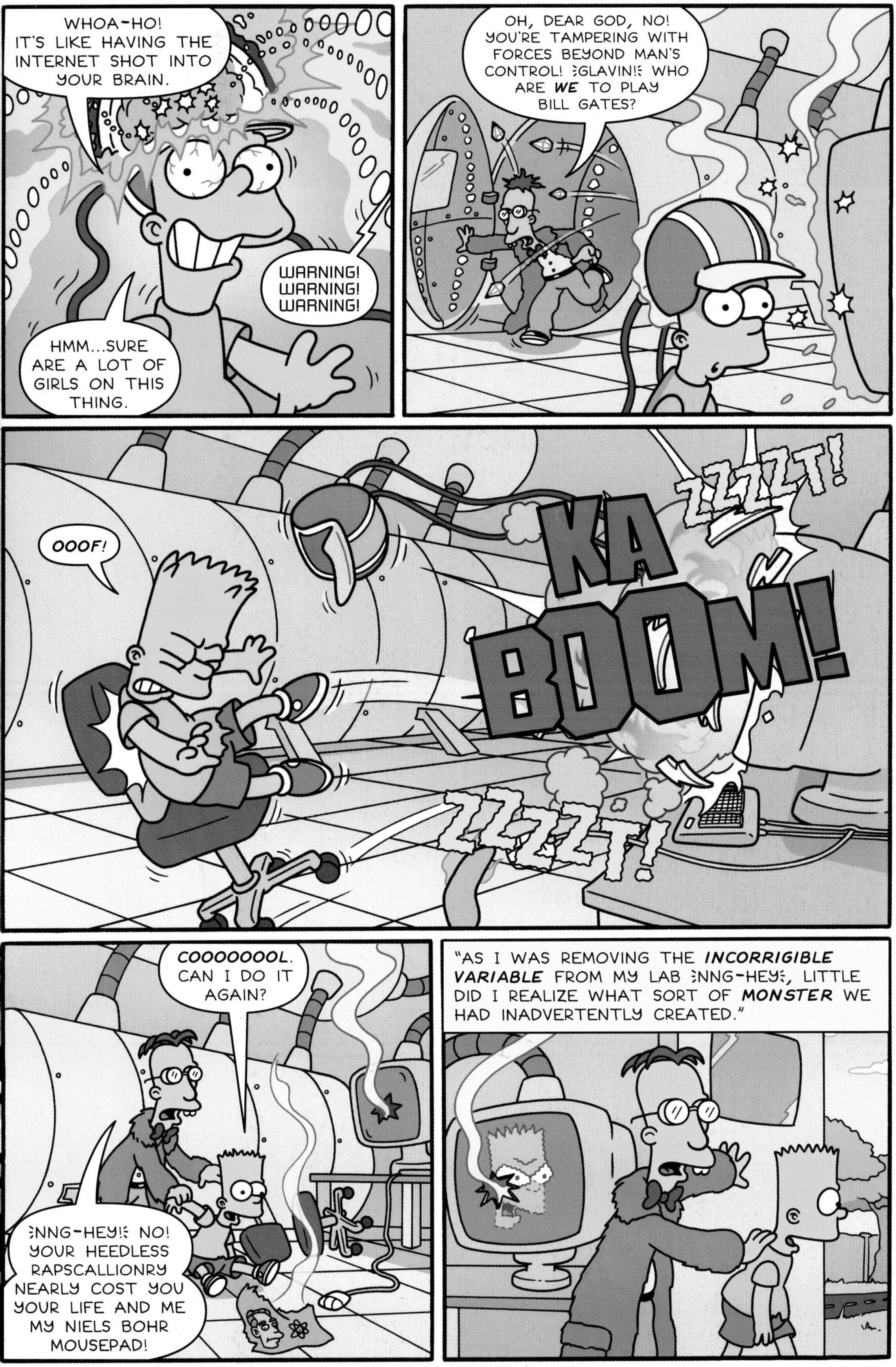
WHOA-HO! IT'S LIKE HAVING THE INTERNET SHOT INTO YOUR BRAIN.
WARNING! WARNING! WARNING!
HMM...SURE ARE A LOT OF GIRLS ON THIS THING.
OH, DEAR GOD, NO! YOU'RE TAMPERING WITH FORCES BEYOND MAN'S CONTROL! GLAVIN! WHO ARE WE TO PLAY BILL GATES?
OOOF!
KA BOOM!
ZZZZT!
ZZZZT!
COOOOOOOL. CAN I DO IT AGAIN?
NNG-HEY! NO! YOUR HEEDLESS RAPSCALLIONRY NEARLY COST YOU YOUR LIFE AND ME MY NIELS BOHR MOUSEPAD!
"AS I WAS REMOVING THE INCORRIGIBLE VARIABLE FROM MY LAB NNG-HEY, LITTLE DID I REALIZE WHAT SORT OF MONSTER WE HAD INADVERTENTLY CREATED."

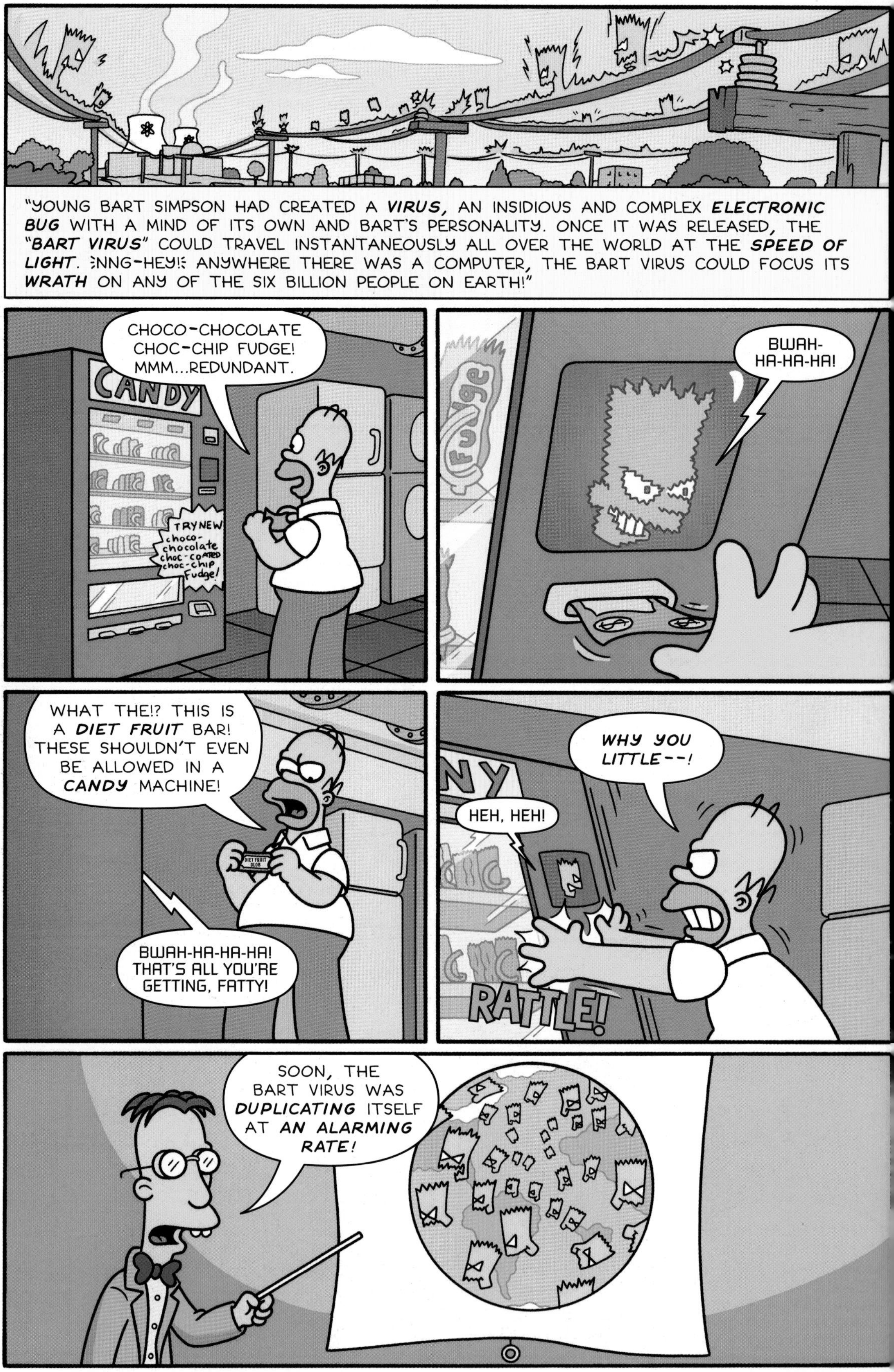
"YOUNG BART SIMPSON HAD CREATED A ***VIRUS,*** AN INSIDIOUS AND COMPLEX ***ELECTRONIC BUG*** WITH A MIND OF ITS OWN AND BART'S PERSONALITY. ONCE IT WAS RELEASED, THE "***BART VIRUS***" COULD TRAVEL INSTANTANEOUSLY ALL OVER THE WORLD AT THE ***SPEED OF LIGHT***. ƐNNG-HEY!Ǝ ANYWHERE THERE WAS A COMPUTER, THE BART VIRUS COULD FOCUS ITS ***WRATH*** ON ANY OF THE SIX BILLION PEOPLE ON EARTH!"
CANDY
CHOCO-CHOCOLATE CHOC-CHIP FUDGE! MMM...REDUNDANT.
TRY NEW choco-chocolate choc-coATED choc-chip Fudge!
Fudge
BWAH-HA-HA-HA!
WHAT THE!? THIS IS A ***DIET FRUIT*** BAR! THESE SHOULDN'T EVEN BE ALLOWED IN A ***CANDY*** MACHINE!
BWAH-HA-HA-HA! THAT'S ALL YOU'RE GETTING, FATTY!
WHY YOU LITTLE--!
HEH, HEH!
RATTLE!
SOON, THE BART VIRUS WAS ***DUPLICATING*** ITSELF AT ***AN ALARMING RATE!***

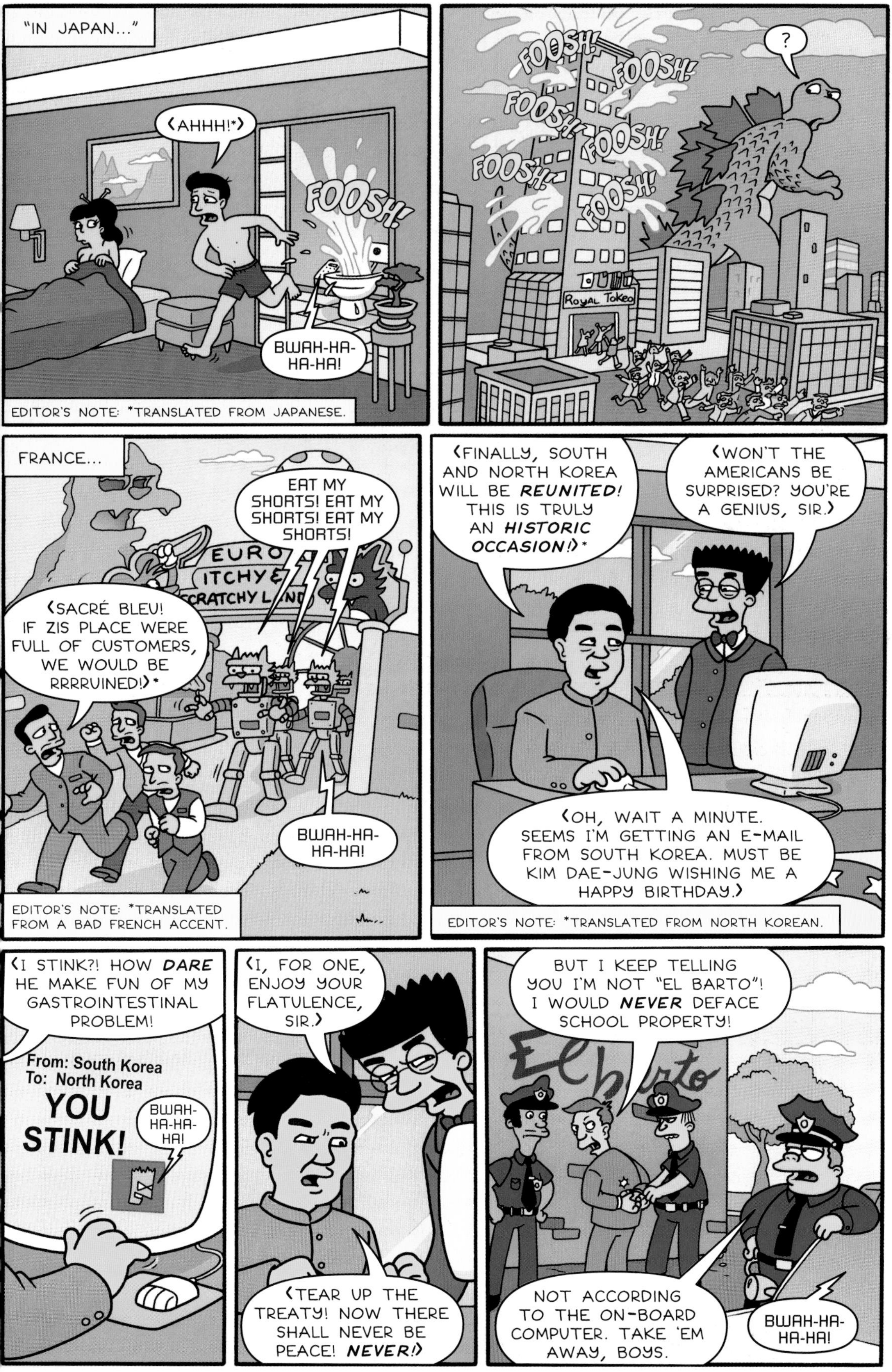
"IN JAPAN..."
‹AHHH!*›
FOOSH!
BWAH-HA-HA-HA!
EDITOR'S NOTE: *TRANSLATED FROM JAPANESE.
FOOSH! FOOSH! FOOSH! FOOSH! FOOSH! FOOSH!
?
ROYAL TOKEO
FRANCE...
EURO ITCHY & SCRATCHY LAND
EAT MY SHORTS! EAT MY SHORTS! EAT MY SHORTS!
‹SACRÉ BLEU! IF ZIS PLACE WERE FULL OF CUSTOMERS, WE WOULD BE RRRRUINED!›*
BWAH-HA-HA-HA!
EDITOR'S NOTE: *TRANSLATED FROM A BAD FRENCH ACCENT.
‹FINALLY, SOUTH AND NORTH KOREA WILL BE REUNITED! THIS IS TRULY AN HISTORIC OCCASION!›*
‹WON'T THE AMERICANS BE SURPRISED? YOU'RE A GENIUS, SIR.›
‹OH, WAIT A MINUTE. SEEMS I'M GETTING AN E-MAIL FROM SOUTH KOREA. MUST BE KIM DAE-JUNG WISHING ME A HAPPY BIRTHDAY.›
EDITOR'S NOTE: *TRANSLATED FROM NORTH KOREAN.
‹I STINK?! HOW DARE HE MAKE FUN OF MY GASTROINTESTINAL PROBLEM!
From: South Korea
To: North Korea
YOU STINK!
BWAH-HA-HA-HA!
‹I, FOR ONE, ENJOY YOUR FLATULENCE, SIR.›
‹TEAR UP THE TREATY! NOW THERE SHALL NEVER BE PEACE! NEVER!›
BUT I KEEP TELLING YOU I'M NOT "EL BARTO"! I WOULD NEVER DEFACE SCHOOL PROPERTY!
El Barto
NOT ACCORDING TO THE ON-BOARD COMPUTER. TAKE 'EM AWAY, BOYS.
BWAH-HA-HA-HA!

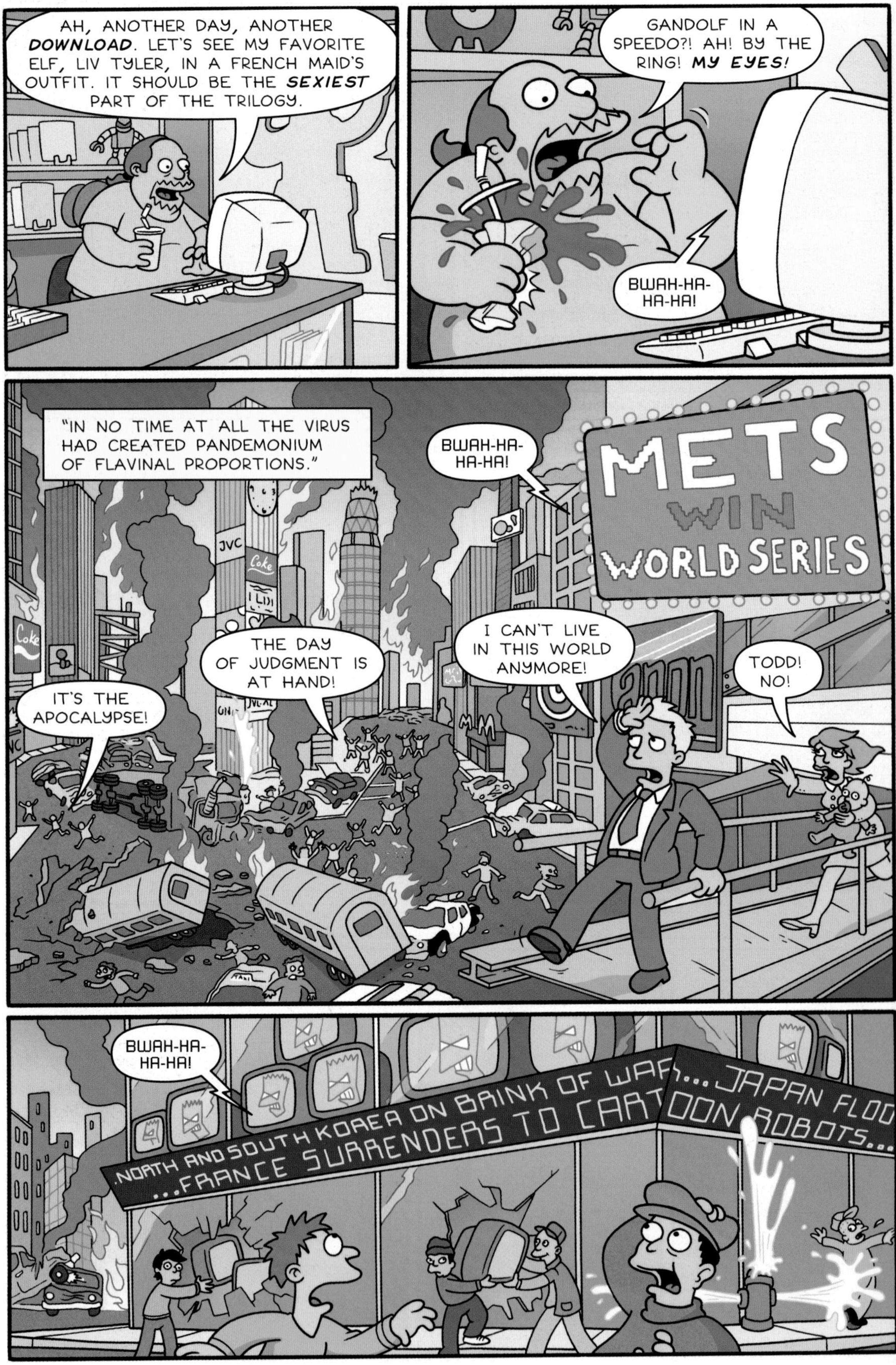
AH, ANOTHER DAY, ANOTHER **DOWNLOAD**. LET'S SEE MY FAVORITE ELF, LIV TYLER, IN A FRENCH MAID'S OUTFIT. IT SHOULD BE THE ***SEXIEST*** PART OF THE TRILOGY.
GANDOLF IN A SPEEDO?! AH! BY THE RING! ***MY EYES!***
BWAH-HA-HA-HA!
"IN NO TIME AT ALL THE VIRUS HAD CREATED PANDEMONIUM OF FLAVINAL PROPORTIONS."
BWAH-HA-HA-HA!
METS WIN WORLD SERIES
JVC
Coke
IT'S THE APOCALYPSE!
THE DAY OF JUDGMENT IS AT HAND!
I CAN'T LIVE IN THIS WORLD ANYMORE!
TODD! NO!
BWAH-HA-HA-HA!
NORTH AND SOUTH KOREA ON BRINK OF WAR... JAPAN FLOO
...FRANCE SURRENDERS TO CARTOON ROBOTS...

"BACK AT MY LAB, THE FULL SCOPE OF THE PROBLEM WAS ABOUT TO ∋NNG-HEY∋ DAWN ON ME!"

BUT, MR. ROCK, THE TEST WAS *INCONCLUSIVE!* IF YOU'LL LET ME BUILD THE *SOLID GOLD* WIND TUNNEL, I'M SURE--

GOOD GLAVIN! IT'S THE END OF THE WORLD WITH THE FIRE AND THE DYING AND SUCH! I'LL HAVE TO CALL YOU BACK, MR. ROCK.

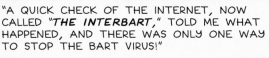

"A QUICK CHECK OF THE INTERNET, NOW CALLED *"THE INTERBART,"* TOLD ME WHAT HAPPENED, AND THERE WAS ONLY ONE WAY TO STOP THE BART VIRUS!"

MR. SIMPSON! MR. SIMPSON!

HEY, *YOU'RE* AN EGGHEAD. MAYBE YOU KNOW WHAT A COAXIAL CABLE IS.

YOU DON'T UNDERSTAND! THE WORLD IS IN *GRAVE DANGER!*

PFFF! YOU THINK *YOU* GOT IT BAD. TODAY THE *SNACK* MACHINE CALLED ME FAT AND THEN THE *SODA* MACHINE SENT ME HOME TO INSTALL CABLE TV IN BART'S TREEHOUSE. TALK ABOUT YOUR HUMP DAYS! WHEW! BART'S INSIDE...

ONE EXPLANATION, LATER...

SO, YOU SEE, THE BART VIRUS HAS BROUGHT ALL OF MANKIND TO THE *BRINK OF TOTAL DESTRUCTION!*

BOY, WHAT DID I TELL YOU ABOUT DOOMING ALL OF MANKIND?! *GO TO YOUR ROOM!*

PROFESSOR FRINK, SURELY IF THE BART VIRUS IS *SENTIENT*, IT CAN BE *REASONED* WITH, JUST LIKE BART.

NO-NO, I TRIED THAT, AND IT DESTROYED MY CREDIT RATING AND LEGALLY CHANGED MY NAME TO "ROSIE BUTTCHEEKS" ∋NNG-HEY∋

WELL, WHAT IF YOU RECREATED THE ACCIDENT AND CREATED A *NEW* BART VIRUS?

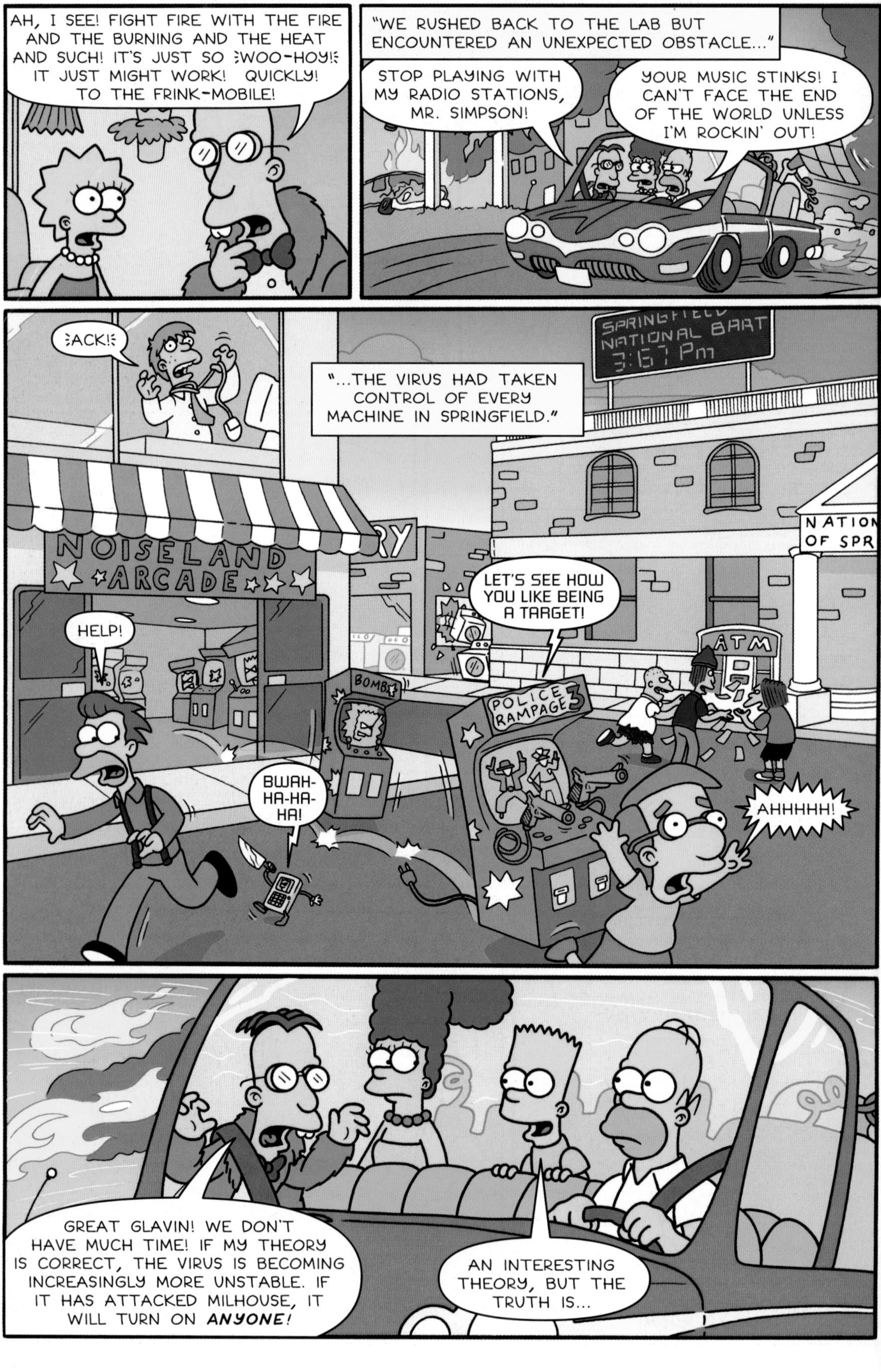
AH, I SEE! FIGHT FIRE WITH THE FIRE AND THE BURNING AND THE HEAT AND SUCH! IT'S JUST SO WOO-HOY! IT JUST MIGHT WORK! QUICKLY! TO THE FRINK-MOBILE!
"WE RUSHED BACK TO THE LAB BUT ENCOUNTERED AN UNEXPECTED OBSTACLE..."
STOP PLAYING WITH MY RADIO STATIONS, MR. SIMPSON!
YOUR MUSIC STINKS! I CAN'T FACE THE END OF THE WORLD UNLESS I'M ROCKIN' OUT!
ACK!
"...THE VIRUS HAD TAKEN CONTROL OF EVERY MACHINE IN SPRINGFIELD."
NOISELAND ARCADE
HELP!
LET'S SEE HOW YOU LIKE BEING A TARGET!
ATM
POLICE RAMPAGE 3
BOMB
BWAH-HA-HA-HA!
AHHHHH!
GREAT GLAVIN! WE DON'T HAVE MUCH TIME! IF MY THEORY IS CORRECT, THE VIRUS IS BECOMING INCREASINGLY MORE UNSTABLE. IF IT HAS ATTACKED MILHOUSE, IT WILL TURN ON ANYONE!
AN INTERESTING THEORY, BUT THE TRUTH IS...

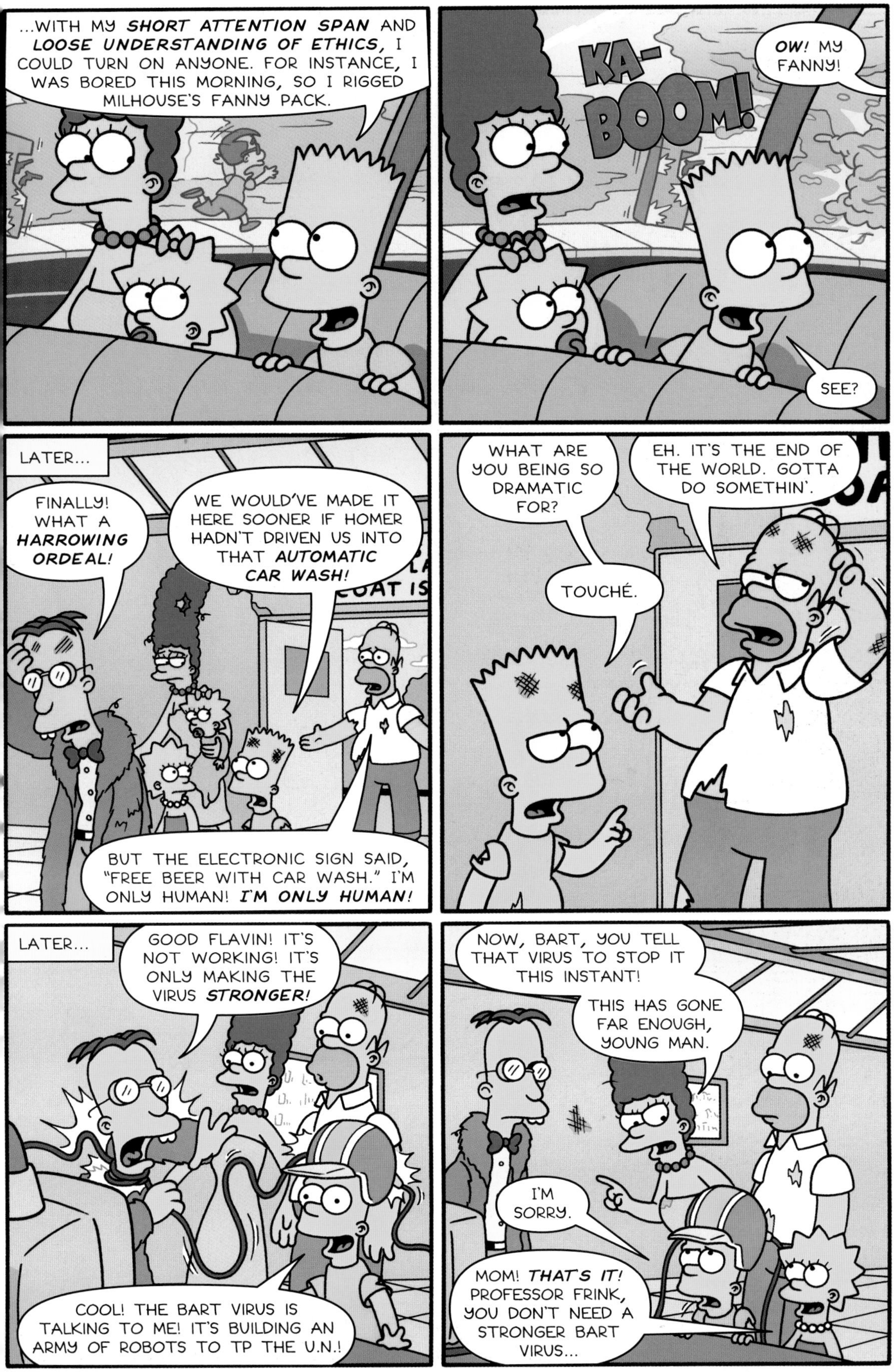
...WITH MY SHORT ATTENTION SPAN AND LOOSE UNDERSTANDING OF ETHICS, I COULD TURN ON ANYONE. FOR INSTANCE, I WAS BORED THIS MORNING, SO I RIGGED MILHOUSE'S FANNY PACK.
KA-BOOM!
OW! MY FANNY!
SEE?
LATER...
FINALLY! WHAT A HARROWING ORDEAL!
WE WOULD'VE MADE IT HERE SOONER IF HOMER HADN'T DRIVEN US INTO THAT AUTOMATIC CAR WASH!
BUT THE ELECTRONIC SIGN SAID, "FREE BEER WITH CAR WASH." I'M ONLY HUMAN! I'M ONLY HUMAN!
WHAT ARE YOU BEING SO DRAMATIC FOR?
EH. IT'S THE END OF THE WORLD. GOTTA DO SOMETHIN'.
TOUCHÉ.
LATER...
GOOD FLAVIN! IT'S NOT WORKING! IT'S ONLY MAKING THE VIRUS STRONGER!
COOL! THE BART VIRUS IS TALKING TO ME! IT'S BUILDING AN ARMY OF ROBOTS TO TP THE U.N.!
NOW, BART, YOU TELL THAT VIRUS TO STOP IT THIS INSTANT!
THIS HAS GONE FAR ENOUGH, YOUNG MAN.
I'M SORRY.
MOM! THAT'S IT! PROFESSOR FRINK, YOU DON'T NEED A STRONGER BART VIRUS...

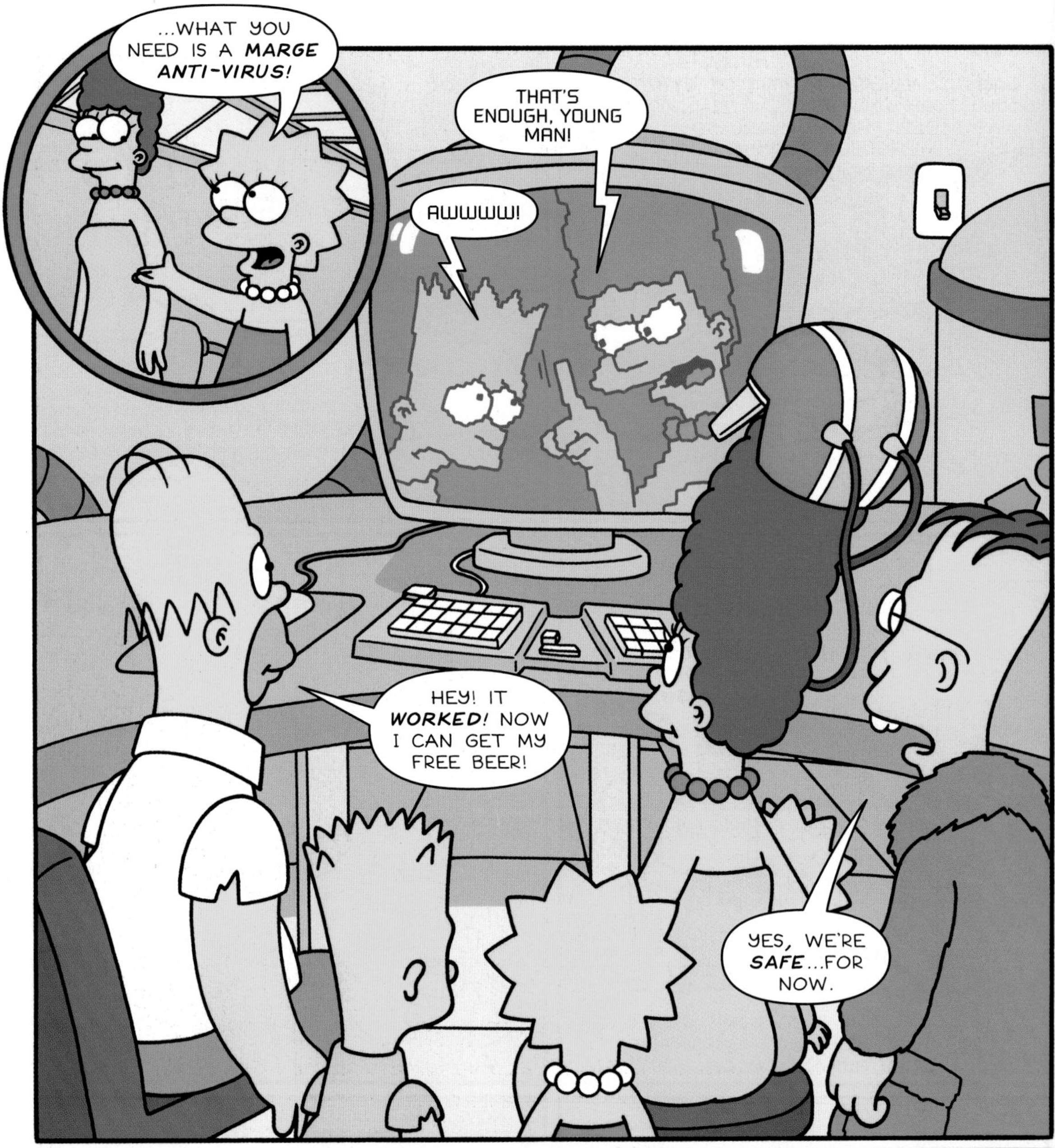
...WHAT YOU NEED IS A **MARGE ANTI-VIRUS**!
THAT'S ENOUGH, YOUNG MAN!
AWWWW!
HEY! IT **WORKED**! NOW I CAN GET MY FREE BEER!
YES, WE'RE **SAFE**...FOR NOW.

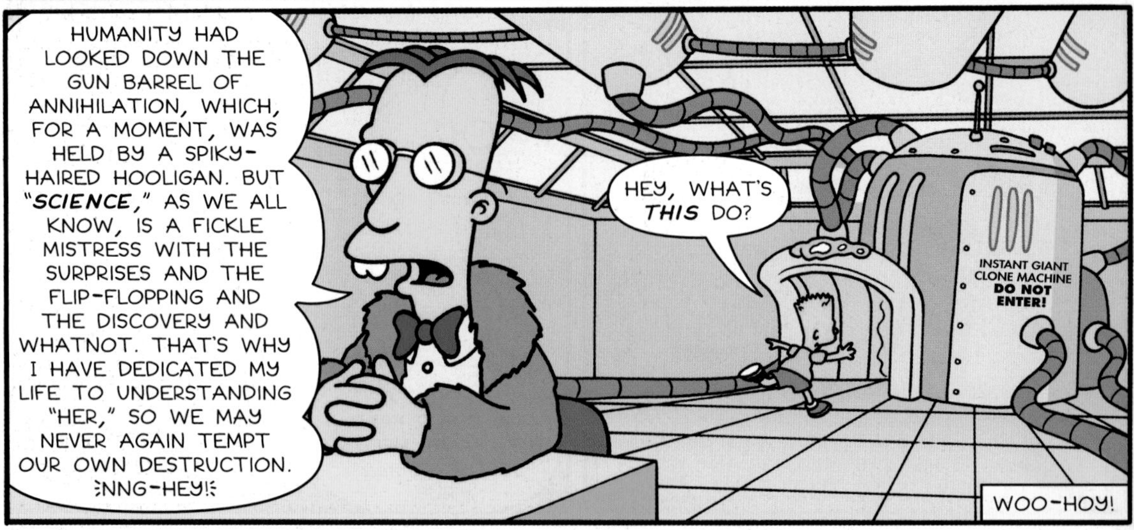
HUMANITY HAD LOOKED DOWN THE GUN BARREL OF ANNIHILATION, WHICH, FOR A MOMENT, WAS HELD BY A SPIKY-HAIRED HOOLIGAN. BUT "**SCIENCE**," AS WE ALL KNOW, IS A FICKLE MISTRESS WITH THE SURPRISES AND THE FLIP-FLOPPING AND THE DISCOVERY AND WHATNOT. THAT'S WHY I HAVE DEDICATED MY LIFE TO UNDERSTANDING "HER," SO WE MAY NEVER AGAIN TEMPT OUR OWN DESTRUCTION. ⁝NNG-HEY!⁝
HEY, WHAT'S **THIS** DO?
INSTANT GIANT CLONE MACHINE DO NOT ENTER!
WOO-HOY!

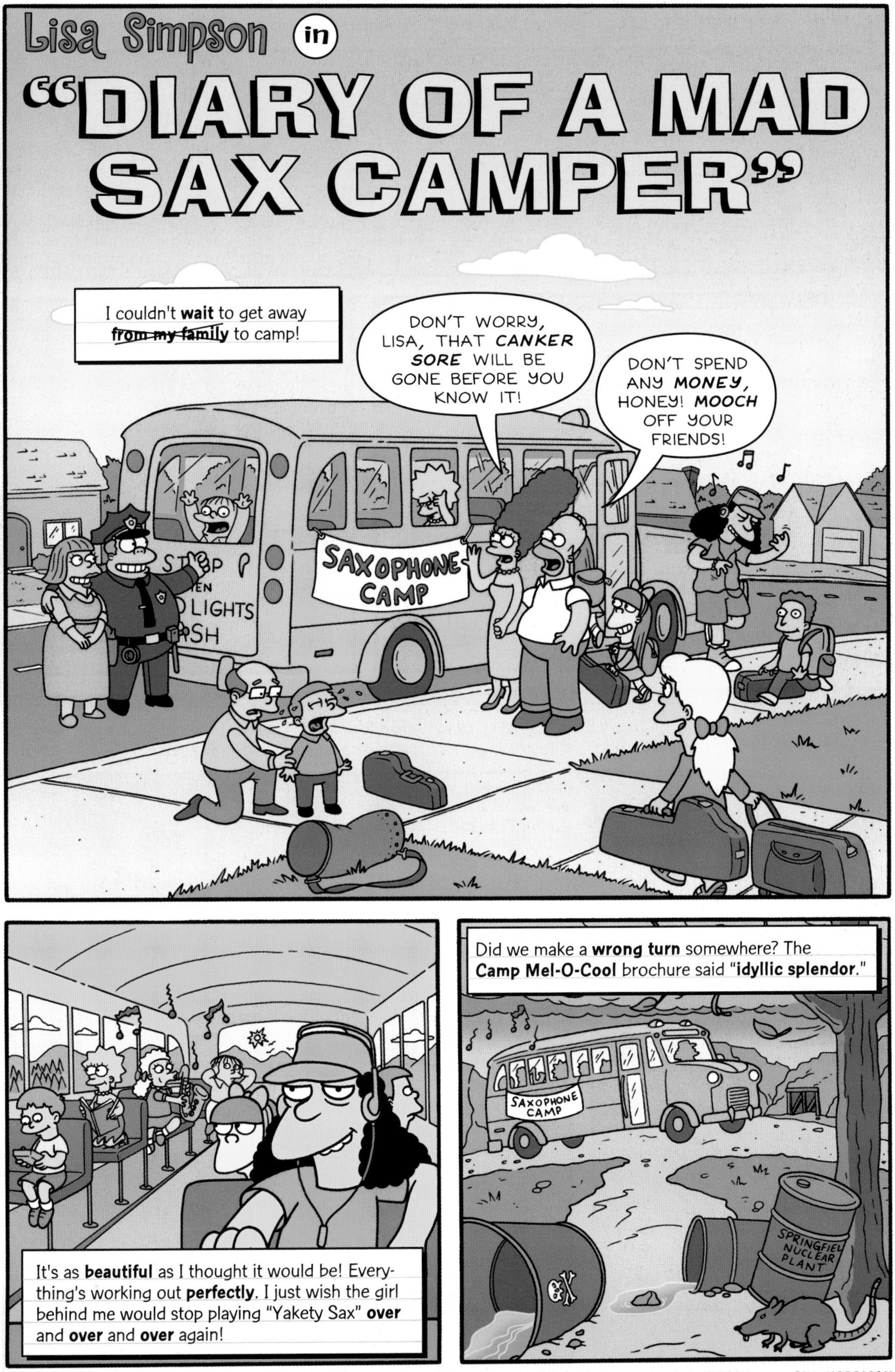

Lisa Simpson in
"DIARY OF A MAD SAX CAMPER"
I couldn't **wait** to get away ~~from my family~~ to camp!
DON'T WORRY, LISA, THAT **CANKER SORE** WILL BE GONE BEFORE YOU KNOW IT!
DON'T SPEND ANY **MONEY**, HONEY! **MOOCH** OFF YOUR FRIENDS!
SAXOPHONE CAMP
It's as **beautiful** as I thought it would be! Everything's working out **perfectly**. I just wish the girl behind me would stop playing "Yakety Sax" **over** and **over** and **over** again!
Did we make a **wrong turn** somewhere? The **Camp Mel-O-Cool** brochure said "**idyllic splendor**."
SAXOPHONE CAMP
SPRINGFIEL NUCLEAR PLANT

JESSE MCCANN & SERAN WILLIAMS STORY — BRIAN ILES PENCILS — MIKE ROTE INKS — CHRIS UNGAR COLORS — KAREN BATES LETTERS — BILL MORRISON EDITOR

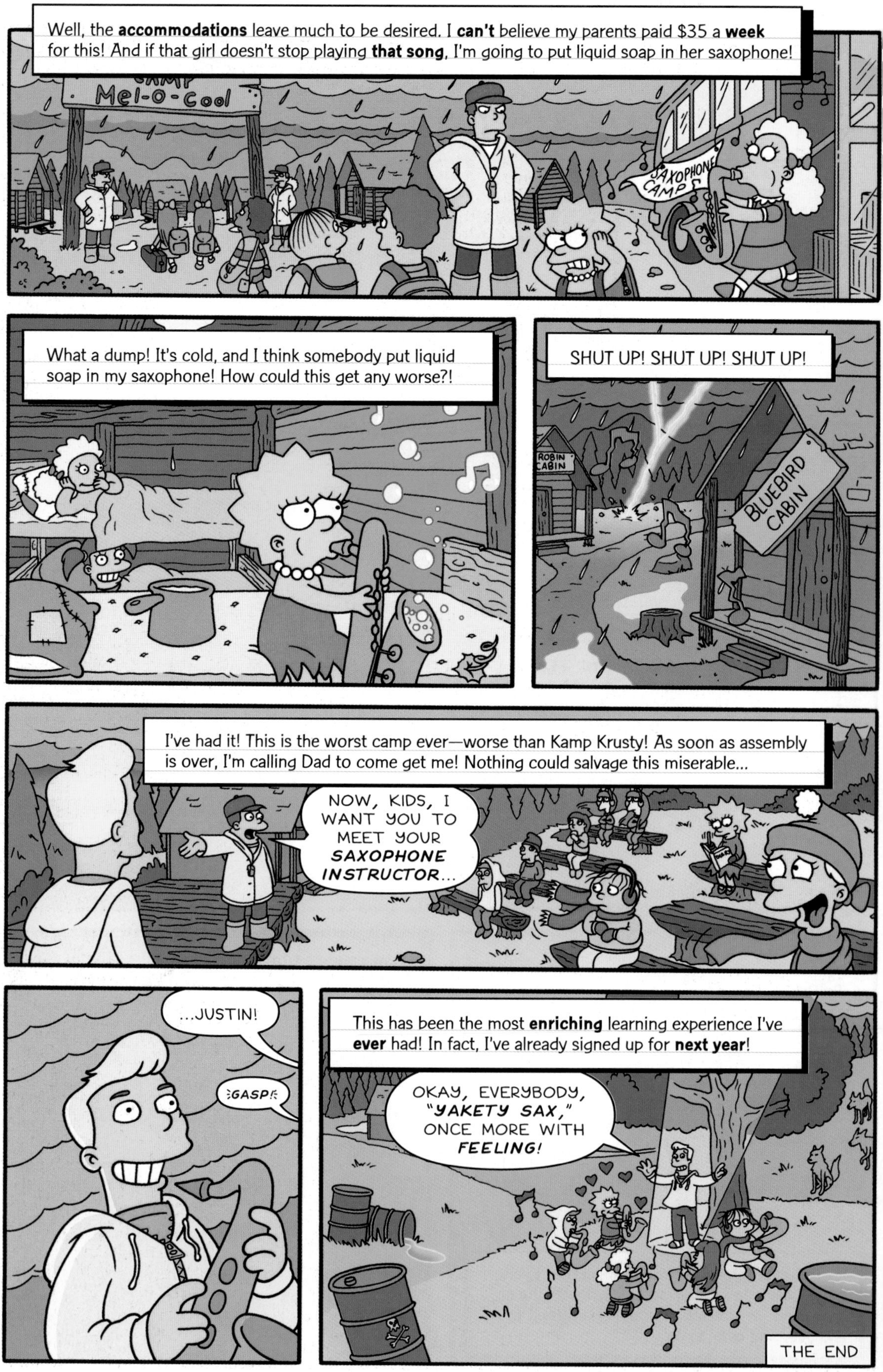
Well, the **accommodations** leave much to be desired. I **can't** believe my parents paid $35 a **week** for this! And if that girl doesn't stop playing **that song**, I'm going to put liquid soap in her saxophone!
Mel-O-Cool
SAXOPHONE CAMP
What a dump! It's cold, and I think somebody put liquid soap in my saxophone! How could this get any worse?!
SHUT UP! SHUT UP! SHUT UP!
ROBIN CABIN
BLUEBIRD CABIN
I've had it! This is the worst camp ever—worse than Kamp Krusty! As soon as assembly is over, I'm calling Dad to come get me! Nothing could salvage this miserable...
NOW, KIDS, I WANT YOU TO MEET YOUR ***SAXOPHONE INSTRUCTOR***...
...JUSTIN!
GASP!
This has been the most **enriching** learning experience I've **ever** had! In fact, I've already signed up for **next year**!
OKAY, EVERYBODY, ***"YAKETY SAX,"*** ONCE MORE WITH ***FEELING!***
THE END

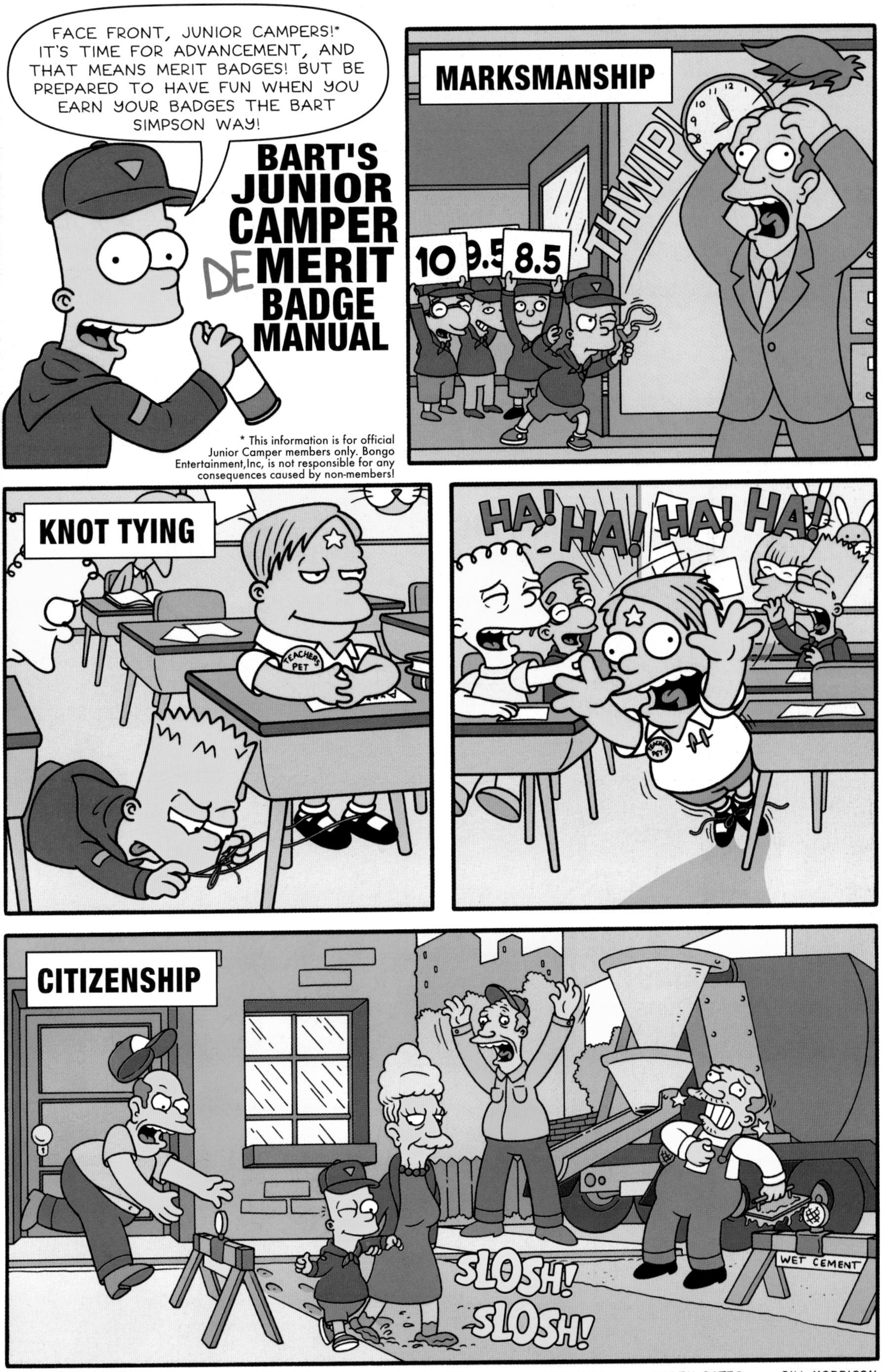

FACE FRONT, JUNIOR CAMPERS!* IT'S TIME FOR ADVANCEMENT, AND THAT MEANS MERIT BADGES! BUT BE PREPARED TO HAVE FUN WHEN YOU EARN YOUR BADGES THE BART SIMPSON WAY!
BART'S JUNIOR CAMPER DEMERIT BADGE MANUAL
* This information is for official Junior Camper members only. Bongo Entertainment,Inc, is not responsible for any consequences caused by non-members!
MARKSMANSHIP
THWIP!
10
8.5
KNOT TYING
TEACHER'S PET
HA! HA! HA! HA!
CITIZENSHIP
SLOSH! SLOSH!
WET CEMENT

GEORGE GLADIR & ERIC ROGERS STORY | MIKE WORLEY PENCILS | MIKE ROTE INKS | CHRIS UNGAR COLORS | KAREN BATES LETTERS | BILL MORRISON EDITOR

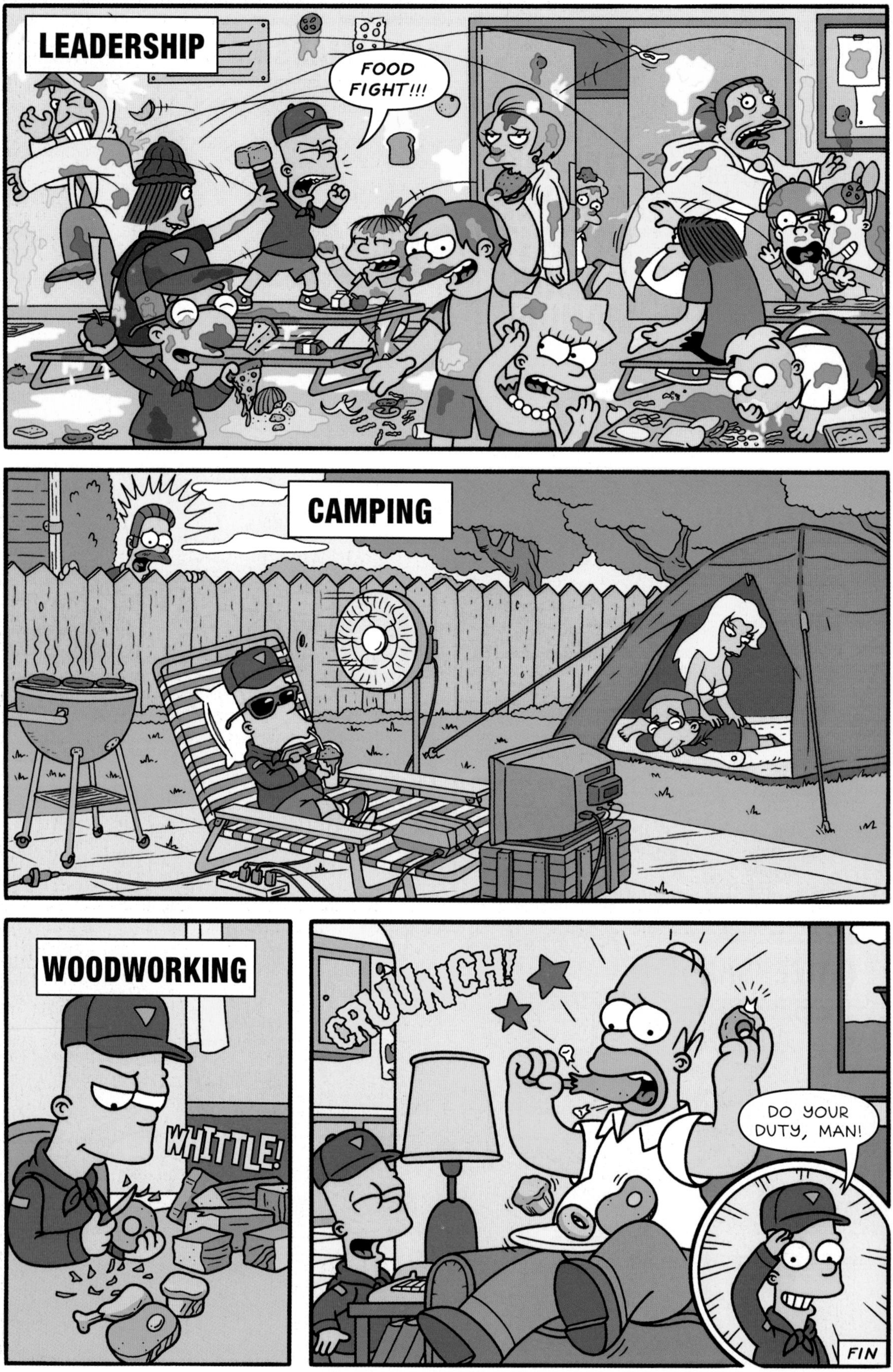
LEADERSHIP
FOOD FIGHT!!!
CAMPING
WOODWORKING
WHITTLE!
CRUUNCH!
DO YOUR DUTY, MAN!
FIN

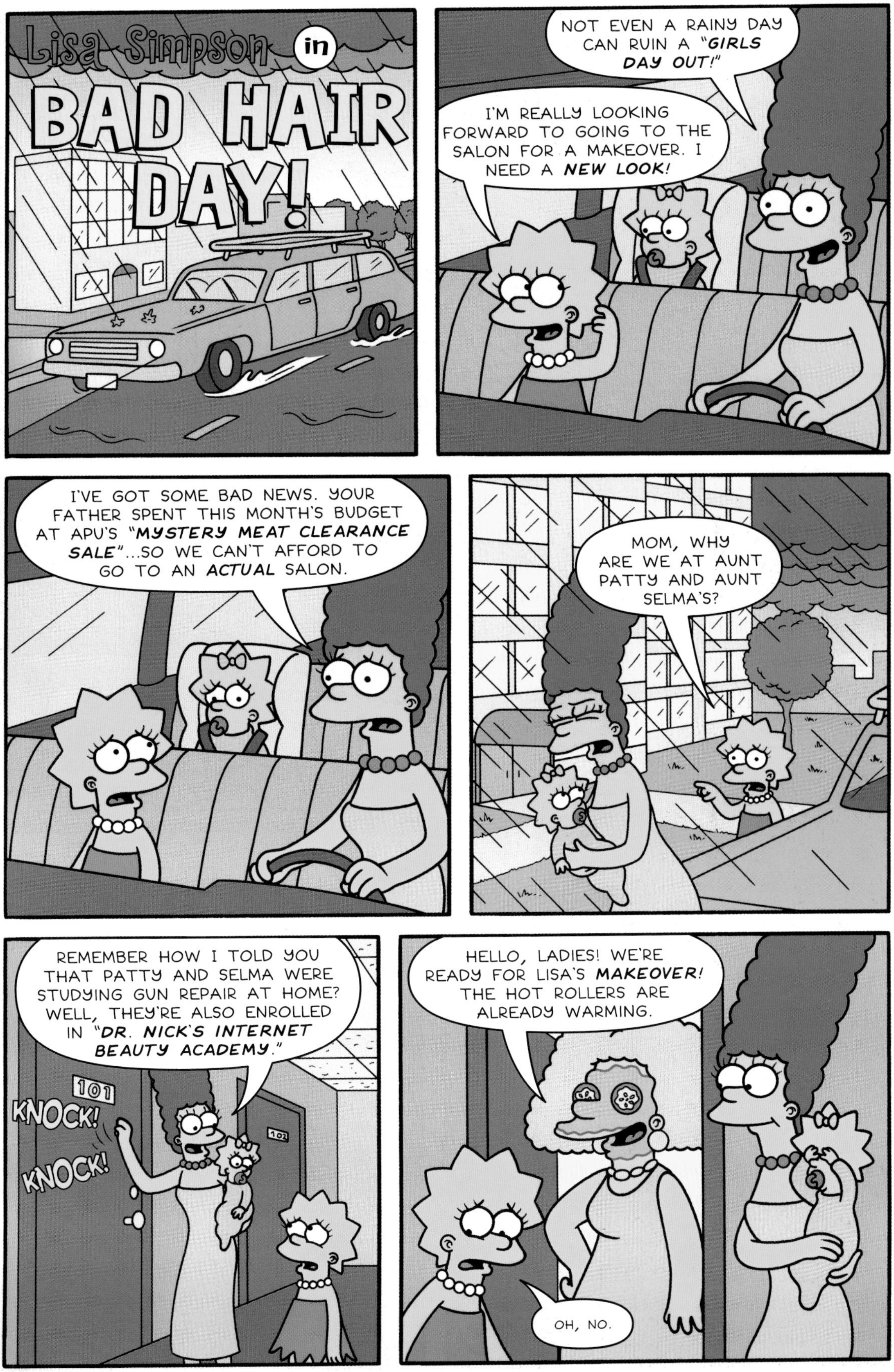

Lisa Simpson in
BAD HAIR DAY!
NOT EVEN A RAINY DAY CAN RUIN A "GIRLS DAY OUT!"
I'M REALLY LOOKING FORWARD TO GOING TO THE SALON FOR A MAKEOVER. I NEED A NEW LOOK!
I'VE GOT SOME BAD NEWS. YOUR FATHER SPENT THIS MONTH'S BUDGET AT APU'S "MYSTERY MEAT CLEARANCE SALE"...SO WE CAN'T AFFORD TO GO TO AN ACTUAL SALON.
MOM, WHY ARE WE AT AUNT PATTY AND AUNT SELMA'S?
REMEMBER HOW I TOLD YOU THAT PATTY AND SELMA WERE STUDYING GUN REPAIR AT HOME? WELL, THEY'RE ALSO ENROLLED IN "DR. NICK'S INTERNET BEAUTY ACADEMY."
101
KNOCK!
KNOCK!
102
HELLO, LADIES! WE'RE READY FOR LISA'S MAKEOVER! THE HOT ROLLERS ARE ALREADY WARMING.
OH, NO.

JAMES W. BATES
STORY

JOEY NILGES
PENCILS

MIKE ROTE
INKS

ART VILLANUEVA
COLORS

KAREN BATES
LETTERS

BILL MORRISON
EDITOR

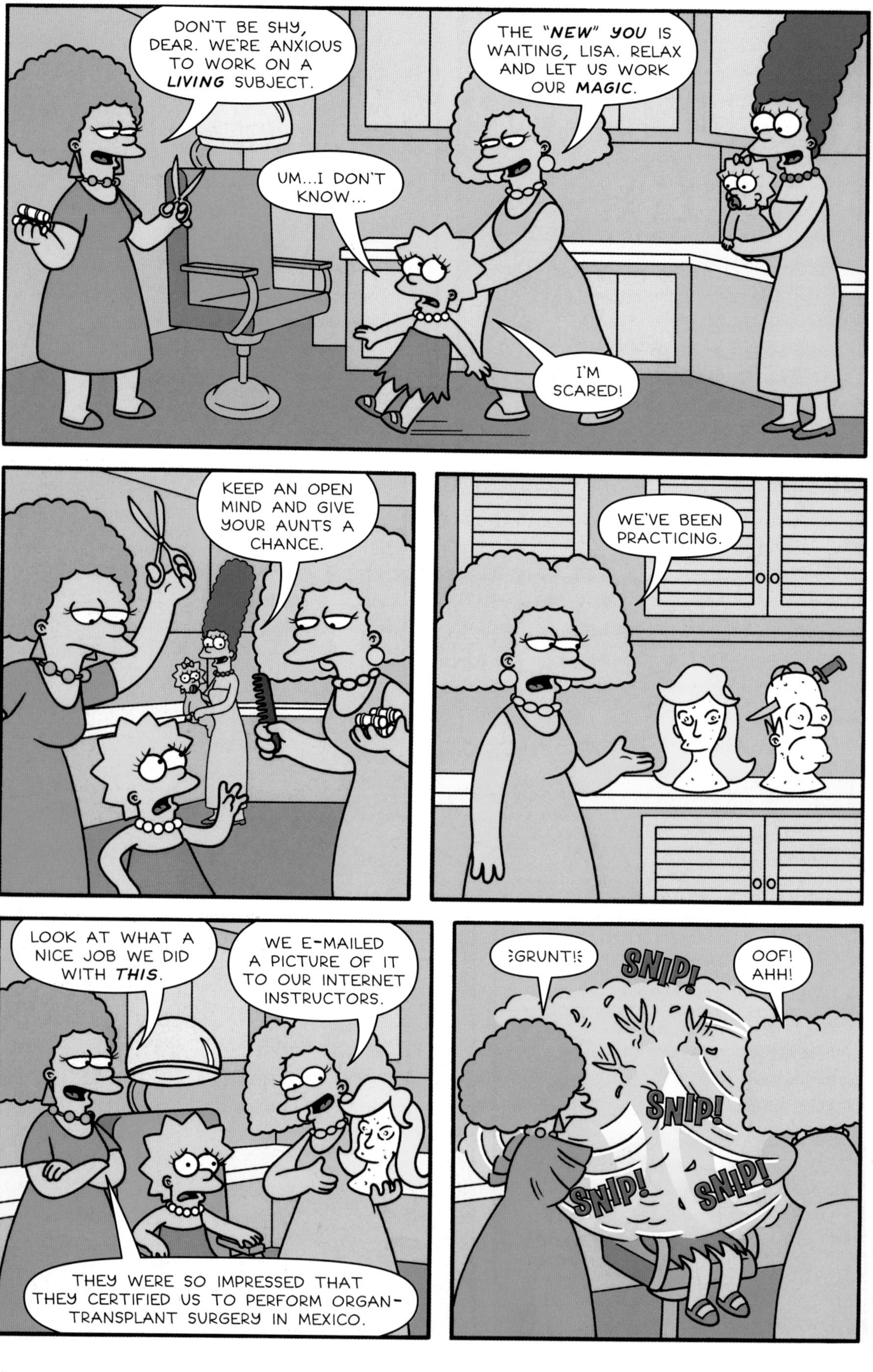
DON'T BE SHY, DEAR. WE'RE ANXIOUS TO WORK ON A *LIVING* SUBJECT.
THE "*NEW*" *YOU* IS WAITING, LISA. RELAX AND LET US WORK OUR *MAGIC*.
UM...I DON'T KNOW...
I'M SCARED!
KEEP AN OPEN MIND AND GIVE YOUR AUNTS A CHANCE.
WE'VE BEEN PRACTICING.
LOOK AT WHAT A NICE JOB WE DID WITH *THIS*.
WE E-MAILED A PICTURE OF IT TO OUR INTERNET INSTRUCTORS.
THEY WERE SO IMPRESSED THAT THEY CERTIFIED US TO PERFORM ORGAN-TRANSPLANT SURGERY IN MEXICO.
GRUNT!
SNIP!
OOF! AHH!
SNIP!
SNIP!
SNIP!

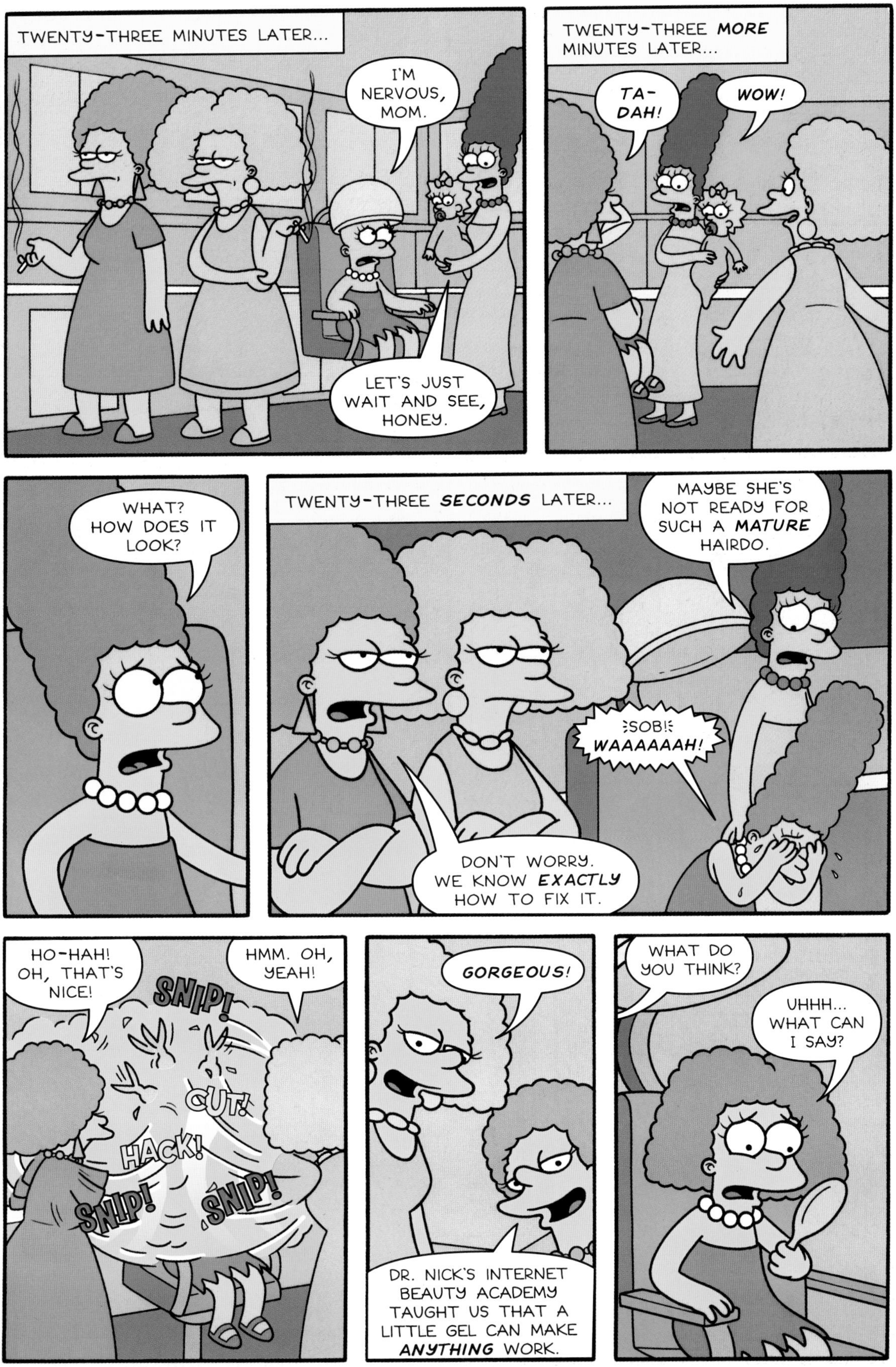
TWENTY-THREE MINUTES LATER...
I'M NERVOUS, MOM.
LET'S JUST WAIT AND SEE, HONEY.
TWENTY-THREE MORE MINUTES LATER...
TA-DAH!
WOW!
WHAT? HOW DOES IT LOOK?
TWENTY-THREE SECONDS LATER...
MAYBE SHE'S NOT READY FOR SUCH A MATURE HAIRDO.
SOB! WAAAAAAH!
DON'T WORRY. WE KNOW EXACTLY HOW TO FIX IT.
HO-HAH! OH, THAT'S NICE!
HMM. OH, YEAH!
SNIP!
CUT!
HACK!
SNIP!
SNIP!
GORGEOUS!
DR. NICK'S INTERNET BEAUTY ACADEMY TAUGHT US THAT A LITTLE GEL CAN MAKE ANYTHING WORK.
WHAT DO YOU THINK?
UHHH... WHAT CAN I SAY?

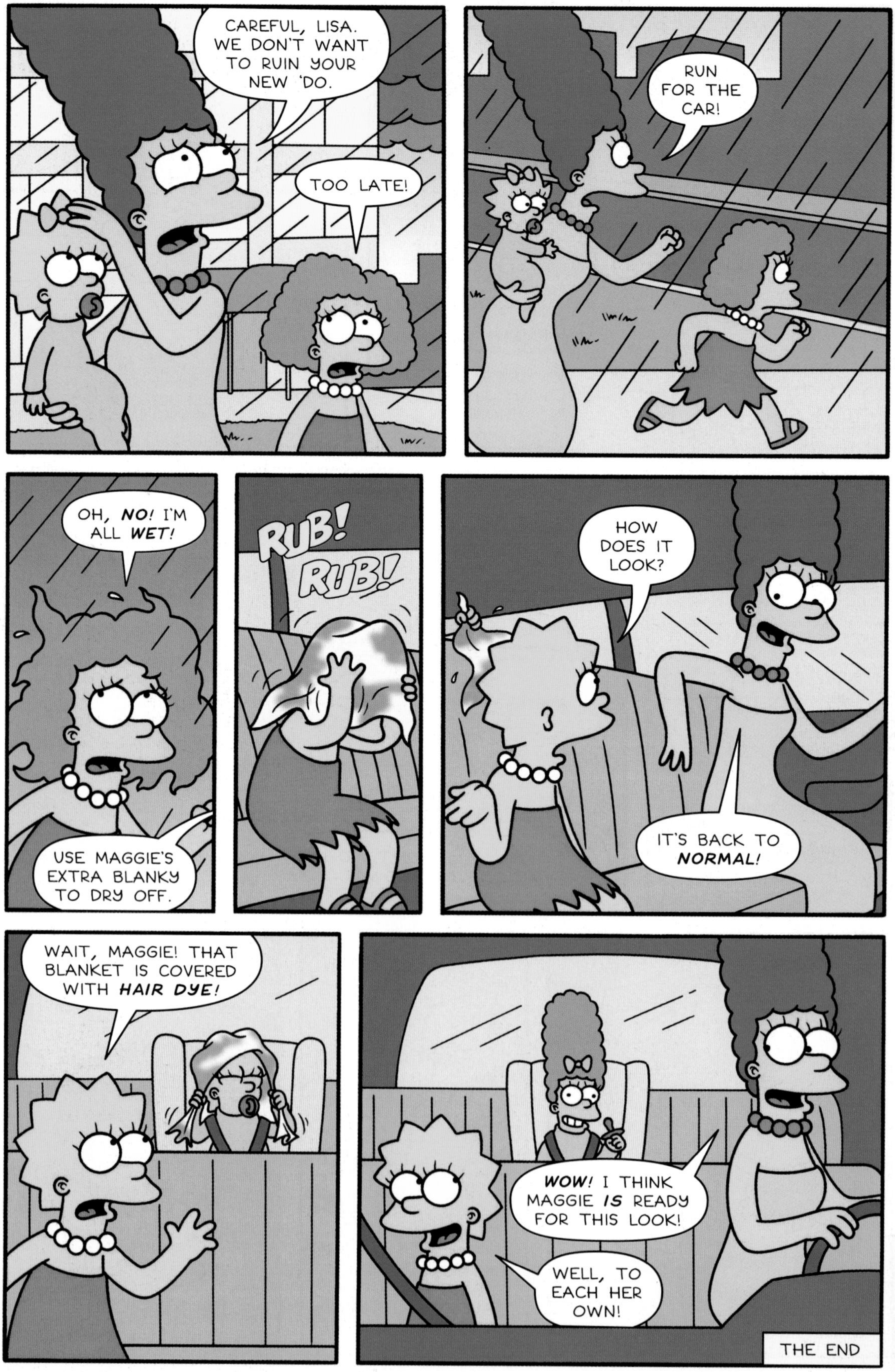
CAREFUL, LISA. WE DON'T WANT TO RUIN YOUR NEW 'DO.
TOO LATE!
RUN FOR THE CAR!
OH, ***NO***! I'M ALL ***WET***!
USE MAGGIE'S EXTRA BLANKY TO DRY OFF.
RUB!
RUB!
HOW DOES IT LOOK?
IT'S BACK TO ***NORMAL***!
WAIT, MAGGIE! THAT BLANKET IS COVERED WITH ***HAIR DYE***!
WOW! I THINK MAGGIE ***IS*** READY FOR THIS LOOK!
WELL, TO EACH HER OWN!
THE END

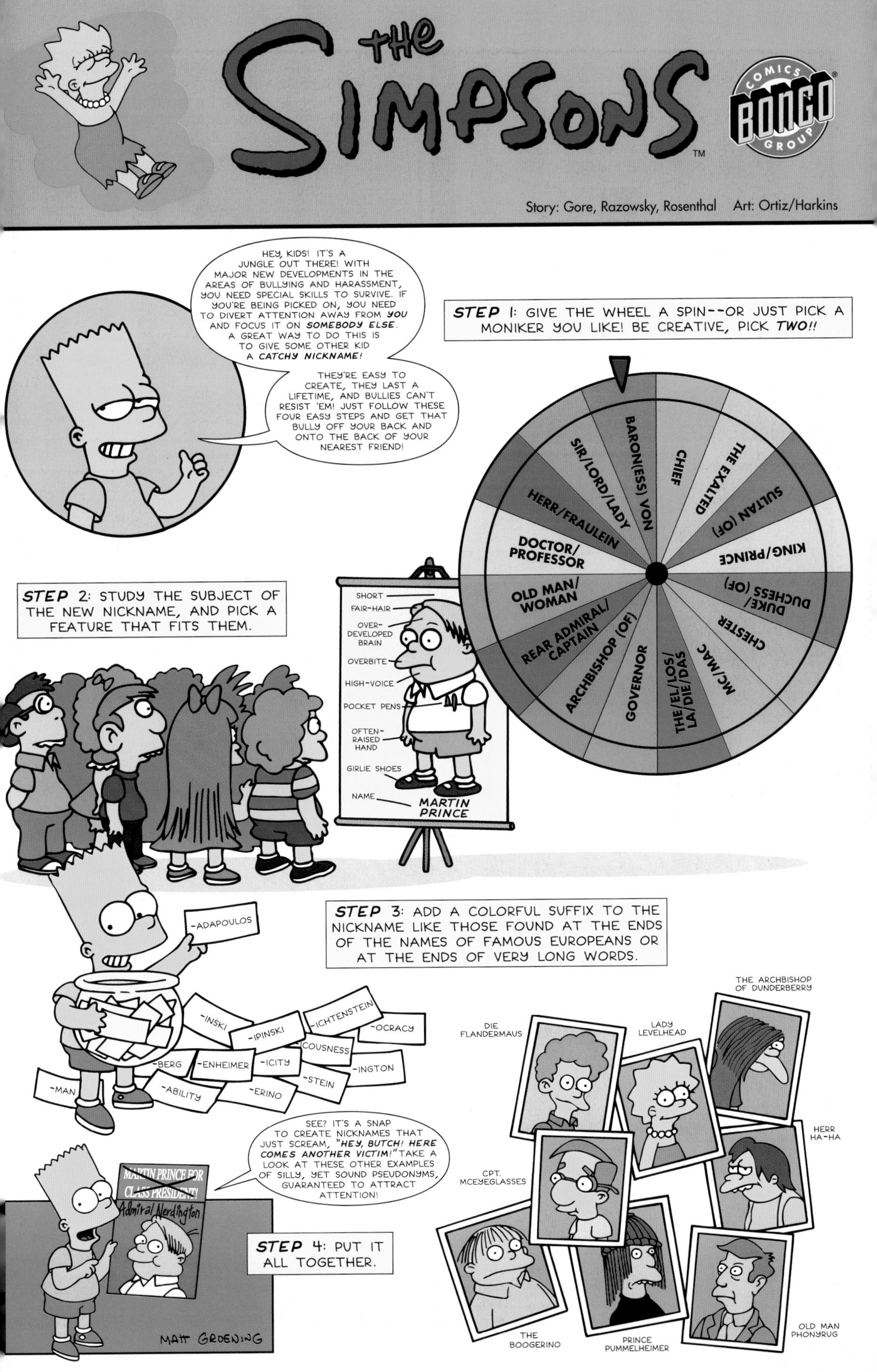
THE SIMPSONS™
BONGO COMICS GROUP
Story: Gore, Razowsky, Rosenthal Art: Ortiz/Harkins
HEY, KIDS! IT'S A JUNGLE OUT THERE! WITH MAJOR NEW DEVELOPMENTS IN THE AREAS OF BULLYING AND HARASSMENT, YOU NEED SPECIAL SKILLS TO SURVIVE. IF YOU'RE BEING PICKED ON, YOU NEED TO DIVERT ATTENTION AWAY FROM *YOU* AND FOCUS IT ON *SOMEBODY ELSE*. A GREAT WAY TO DO THIS IS TO GIVE SOME OTHER KID A *CATCHY NICKNAME!*
THEY'RE EASY TO CREATE, THEY LAST A LIFETIME, AND BULLIES CAN'T RESIST 'EM! JUST FOLLOW THESE FOUR EASY STEPS AND GET THAT BULLY OFF YOUR BACK AND ONTO THE BACK OF YOUR NEAREST FRIEND!
STEP 1: GIVE THE WHEEL A SPIN--OR JUST PICK A MONIKER YOU LIKE! BE CREATIVE, PICK *TWO!!*
CHIEF
THE EXALTED
SULTAN (OF)
KING/PRINCE
DUKE/DUCHESS (OF)
CHESTER
MC/MAC
THE/EL/LOS/LA/DIE/DAS
GOVERNOR
ARCHBISHOP (OF)
REAR ADMIRAL/CAPTAIN
OLD MAN/WOMAN
DOCTOR/PROFESSOR
HERR/FRAULEIN
SIR/LORD/LADY
BARON(ESS) VON
STEP 2: STUDY THE SUBJECT OF THE NEW NICKNAME, AND PICK A FEATURE THAT FITS THEM.
SHORT
FAIR-HAIR
OVER-DEVELOPED BRAIN
OVERBITE
HIGH-VOICE
POCKET PENS
OFTEN-RAISED HAND
GIRLIE SHOES
NAME
MARTIN PRINCE
STEP 3: ADD A COLORFUL SUFFIX TO THE NICKNAME LIKE THOSE FOUND AT THE ENDS OF THE NAMES OF FAMOUS EUROPEANS OR AT THE ENDS OF VERY LONG WORDS.
-ADAPOULOS
-INSKI
-IPINSKI
-ICHTENSTEIN
-OCRACY
COUSNESS
-BERG
-ENHEIMER
-ICITY
-INGTON
-MAN
-ABILITY
-ERINO
-STEIN
SEE? IT'S A SNAP TO CREATE NICKNAMES THAT JUST SCREAM, *"HEY, BUTCH! HERE COMES ANOTHER VICTIM!"* TAKE A LOOK AT THESE OTHER EXAMPLES OF SILLY, YET SOUND PSEUDONYMS, GUARANTEED TO ATTRACT ATTENTION!
MARTIN PRINCE FOR CLASS PRESIDENT!
Admiral Nerdington
STEP 4: PUT IT ALL TOGETHER.
MATT GROENING
THE ARCHBISHOP OF DUNDERBERRY
DIE FLANDERMAUS
LADY LEVELHEAD
HERR HA-HA
CPT. MCEYEGLASSES
THE BOOGERINO
PRINCE PUMMELHEIMER
OLD MAN PHONYRUG

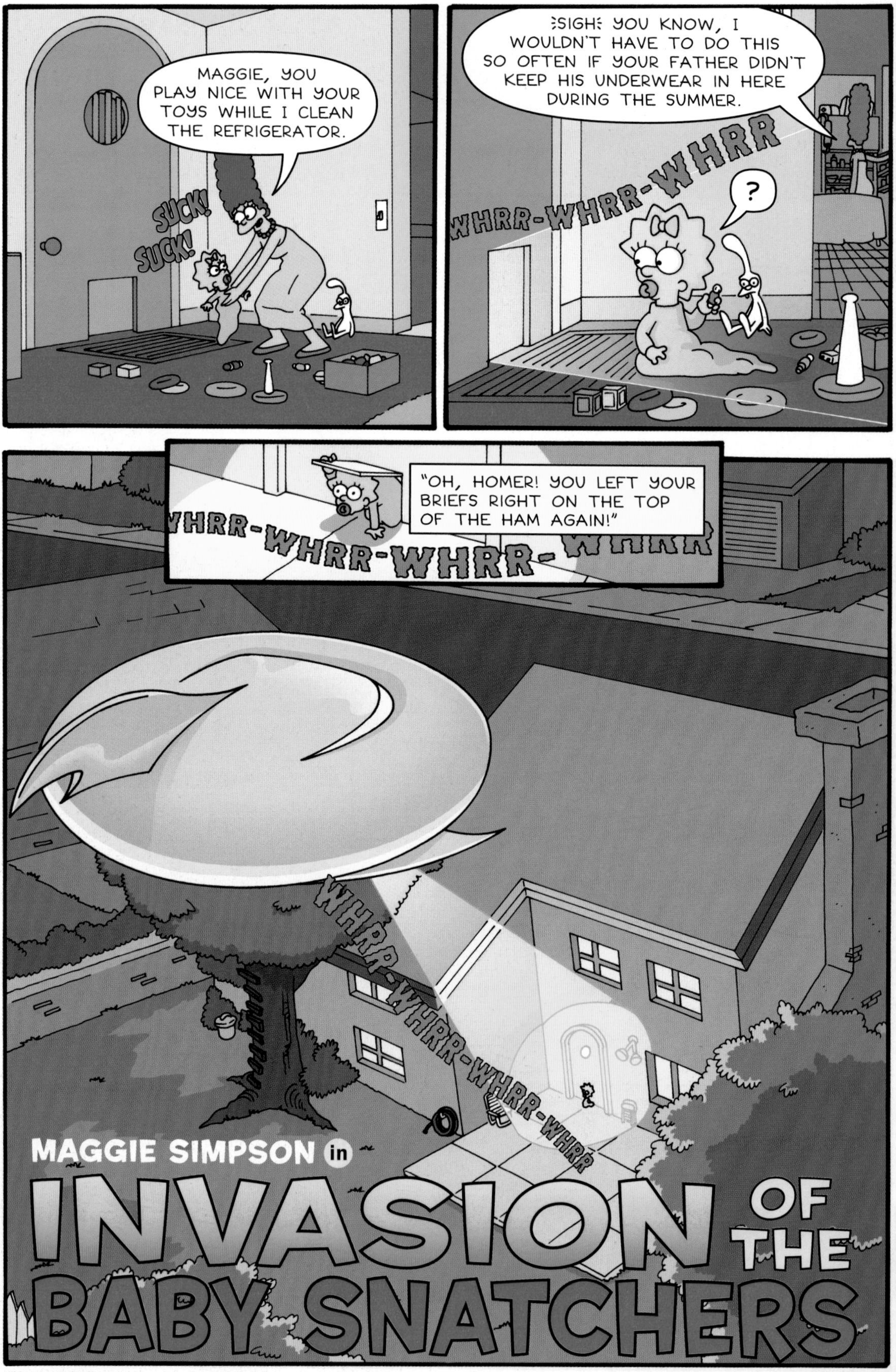
MAGGIE, YOU PLAY NICE WITH YOUR TOYS WHILE I CLEAN THE REFRIGERATOR.
SUCK! SUCK!
:SIGH: YOU KNOW, I WOULDN'T HAVE TO DO THIS SO OFTEN IF YOUR FATHER DIDN'T KEEP HIS UNDERWEAR IN HERE DURING THE SUMMER.
WHRR-WHRR-WHRR
?
"OH, HOMER! YOU LEFT YOUR BRIEFS RIGHT ON THE TOP OF THE HAM AGAIN!"
WHRR-WHRR-WHRR-WHRR
WHRR-WHRR-WHRR-WHRR
MAGGIE SIMPSON in
INVASION OF THE BABY SNATCHERS

TONY DIGEROLAMO STORY | *LUIS ESCOBAR* PENCILS | *PATRICK OWSLEY* INKS | *RICK REESE* COLORS | *KAREN BATES* LETTERS | *BILL MORRISON* EDITOR

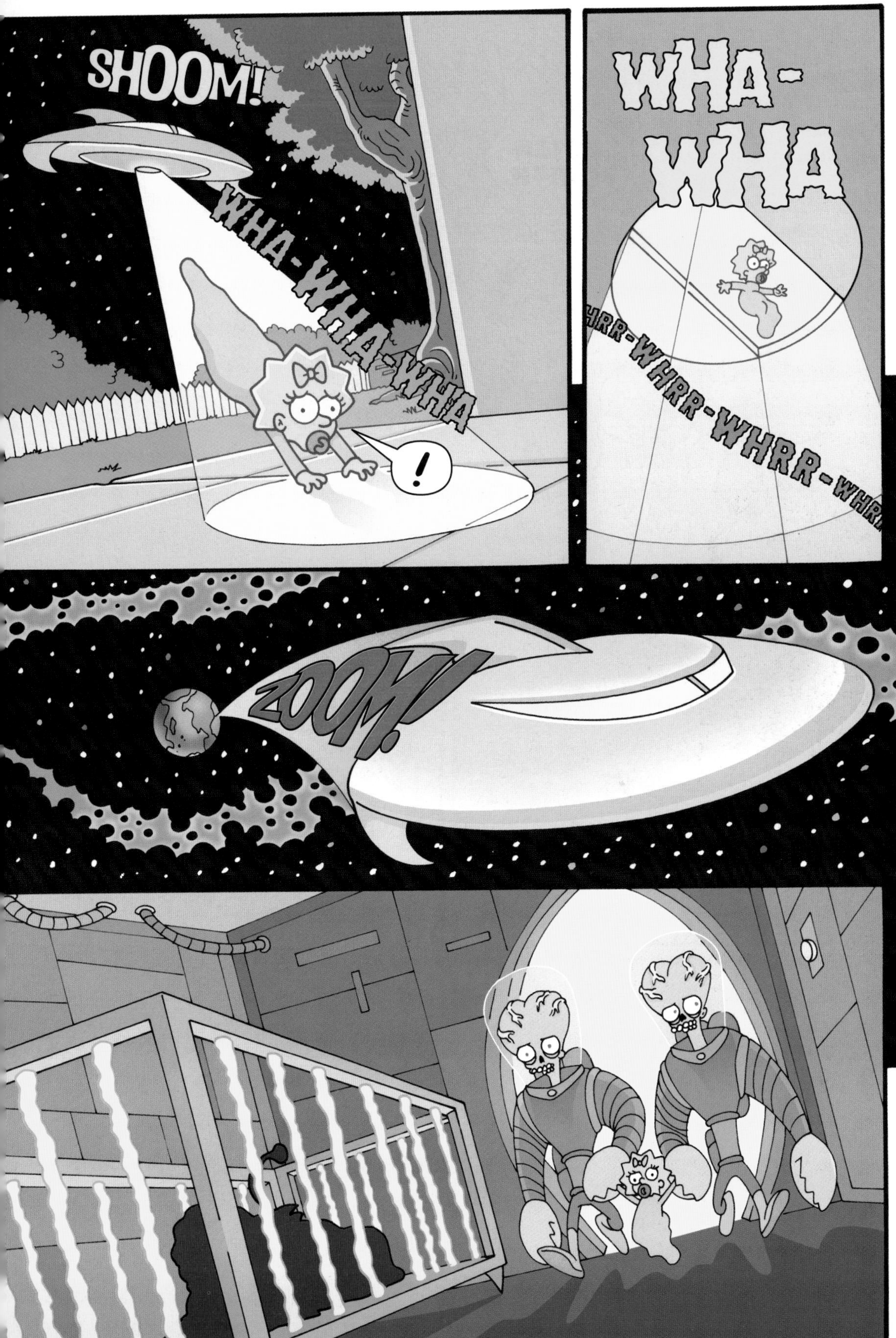

SHOOM!
WHA-WHA-WHA-WHA
!
WHA-WHA
HRR-WHRR-WHRR-WHRR-WHR
ZOOM!

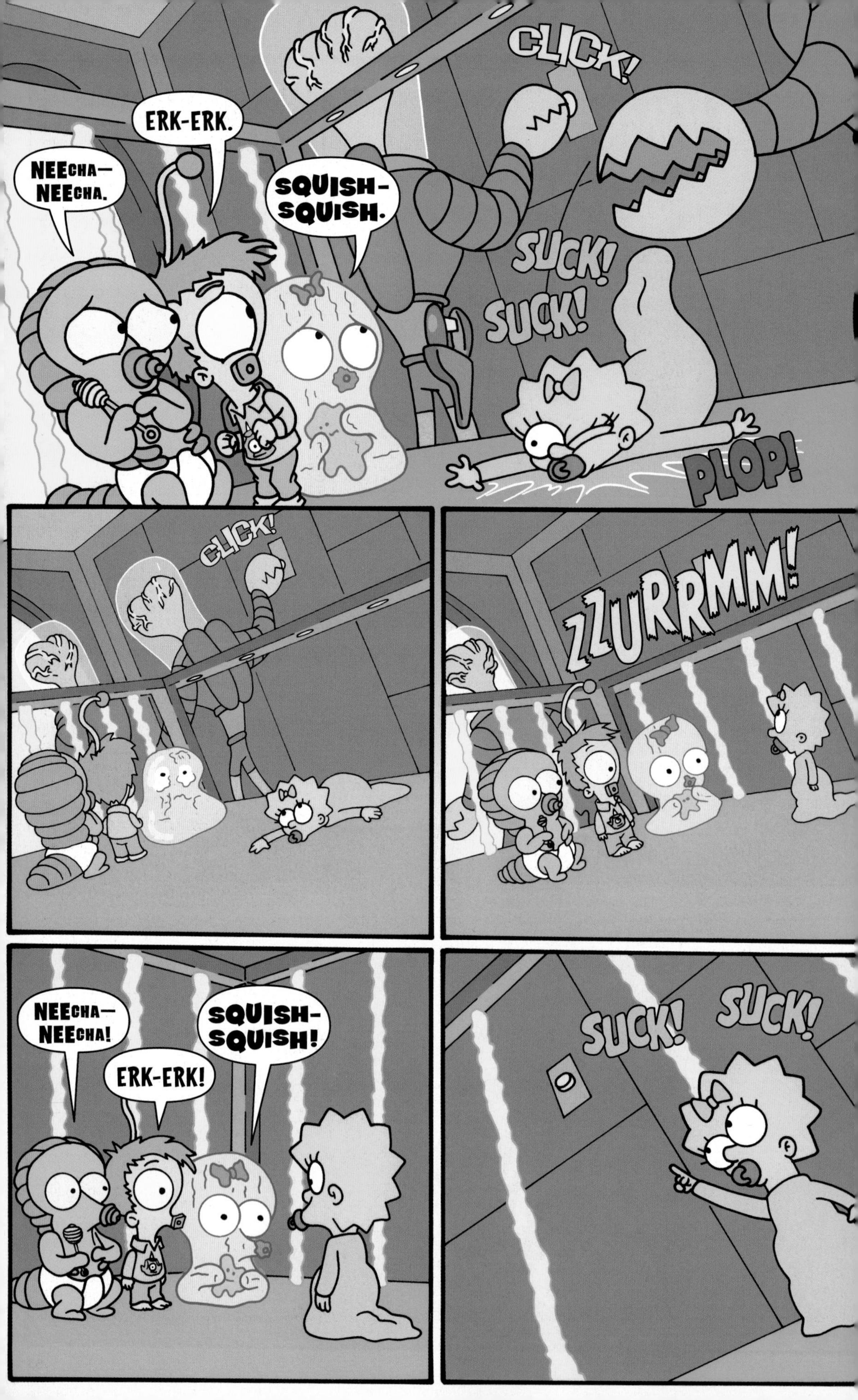
CLICK!
NEECHA—
NEECHA.
ERK-ERK.
SQUISH-
SQUISH.
SUCK!
SUCK!
PLOP!
CLICK!
ZZURRRMM!
NEECHA—
NEECHA!
ERK-ERK!
SQUISH-
SQUISH!
SUCK!
SUCK!

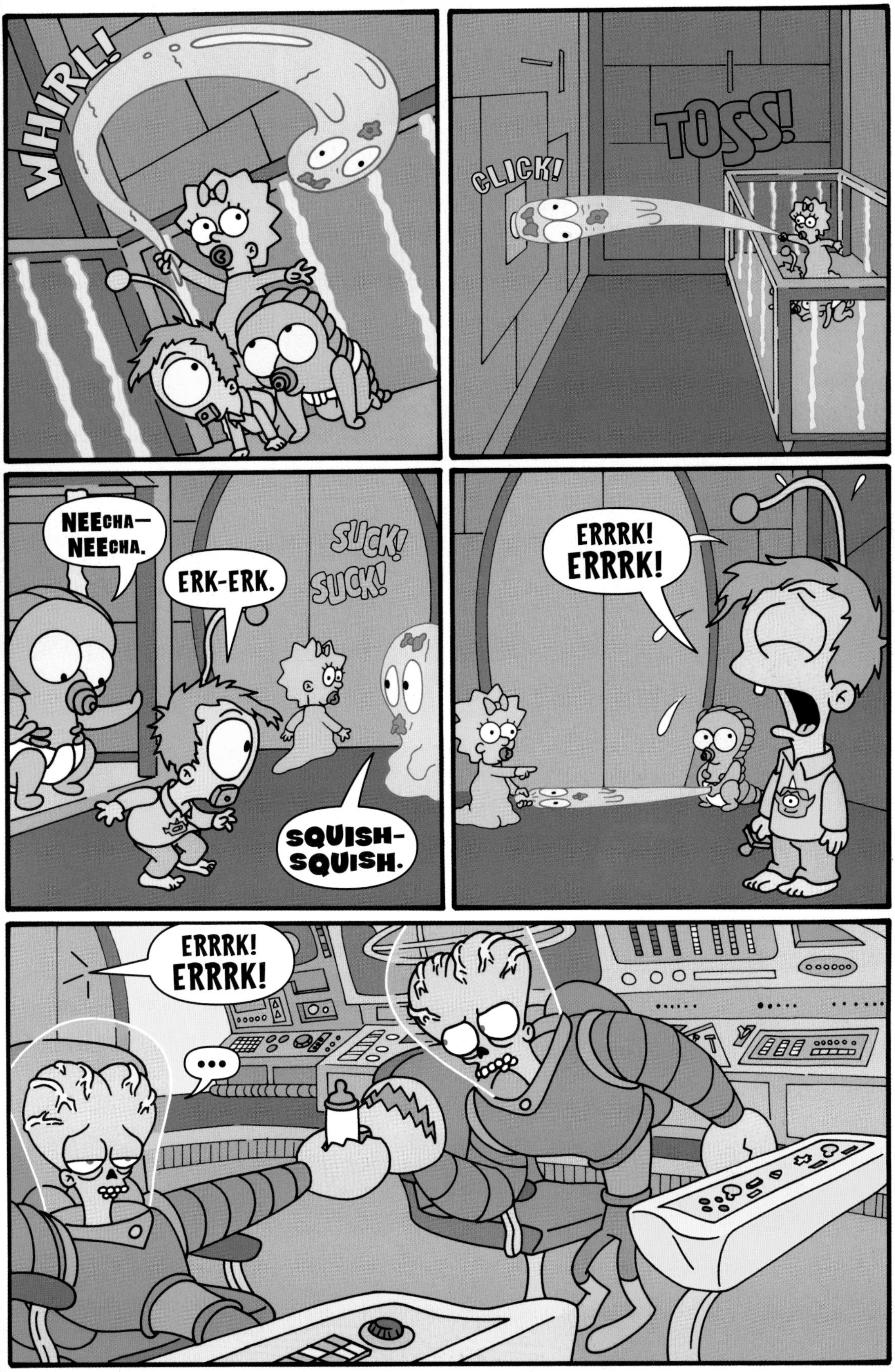
WHIRL!
CLICK!
TOSS!
NEECHA—
NEECHA.
ERK-ERK.
SUCK!
SUCK!
SQUISH-
SQUISH.
ERRRK!
ERRRK!
ERRRK!
ERRRK!
...

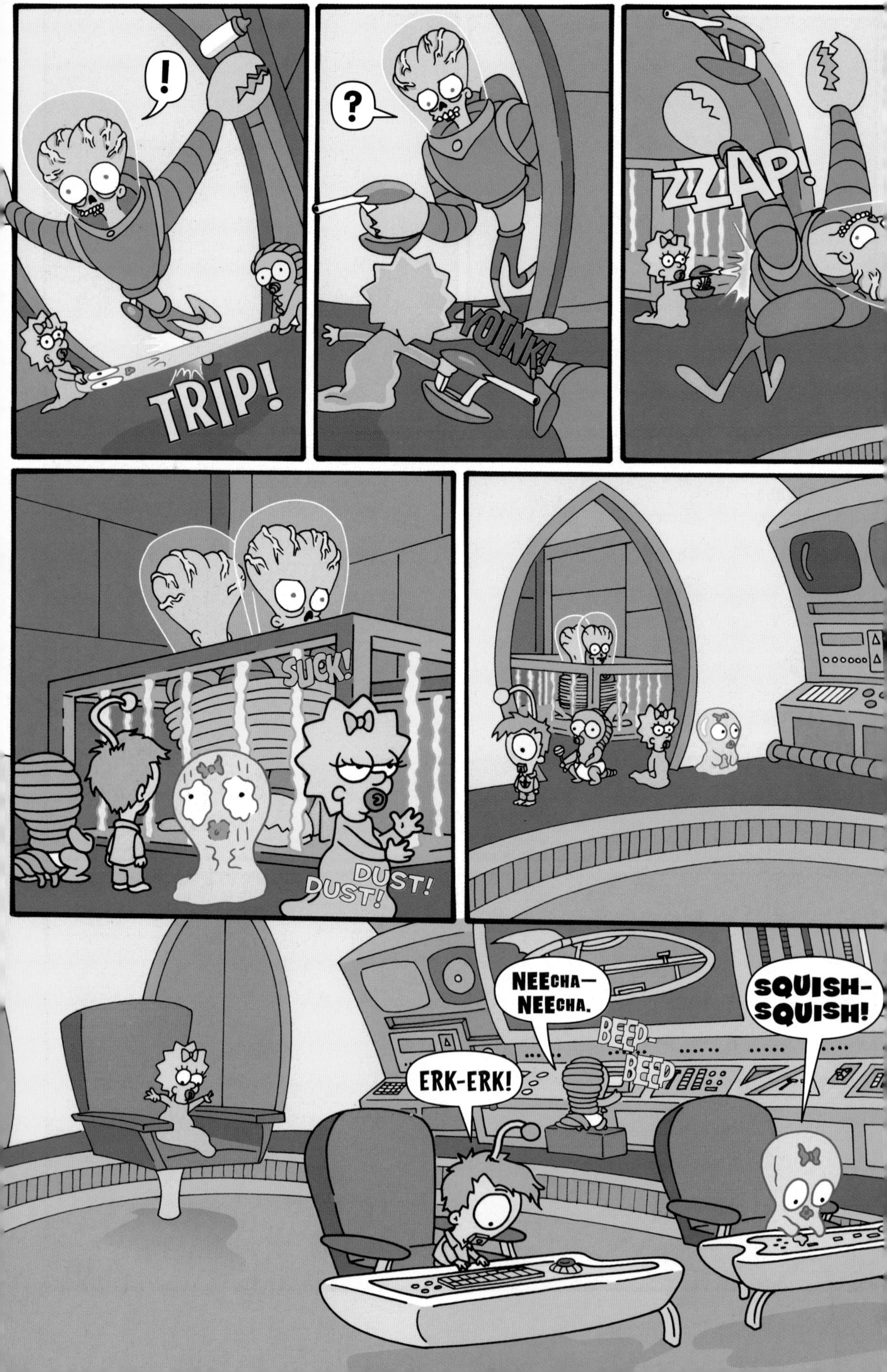
!
TRIP!
?
YOINK!
ZZAP!
SUCK!
DUST!
DUST!
NEECHA—
NEECHA.
BEEP-
BEEP
SQUISH-
SQUISH!
ERK-ERK!

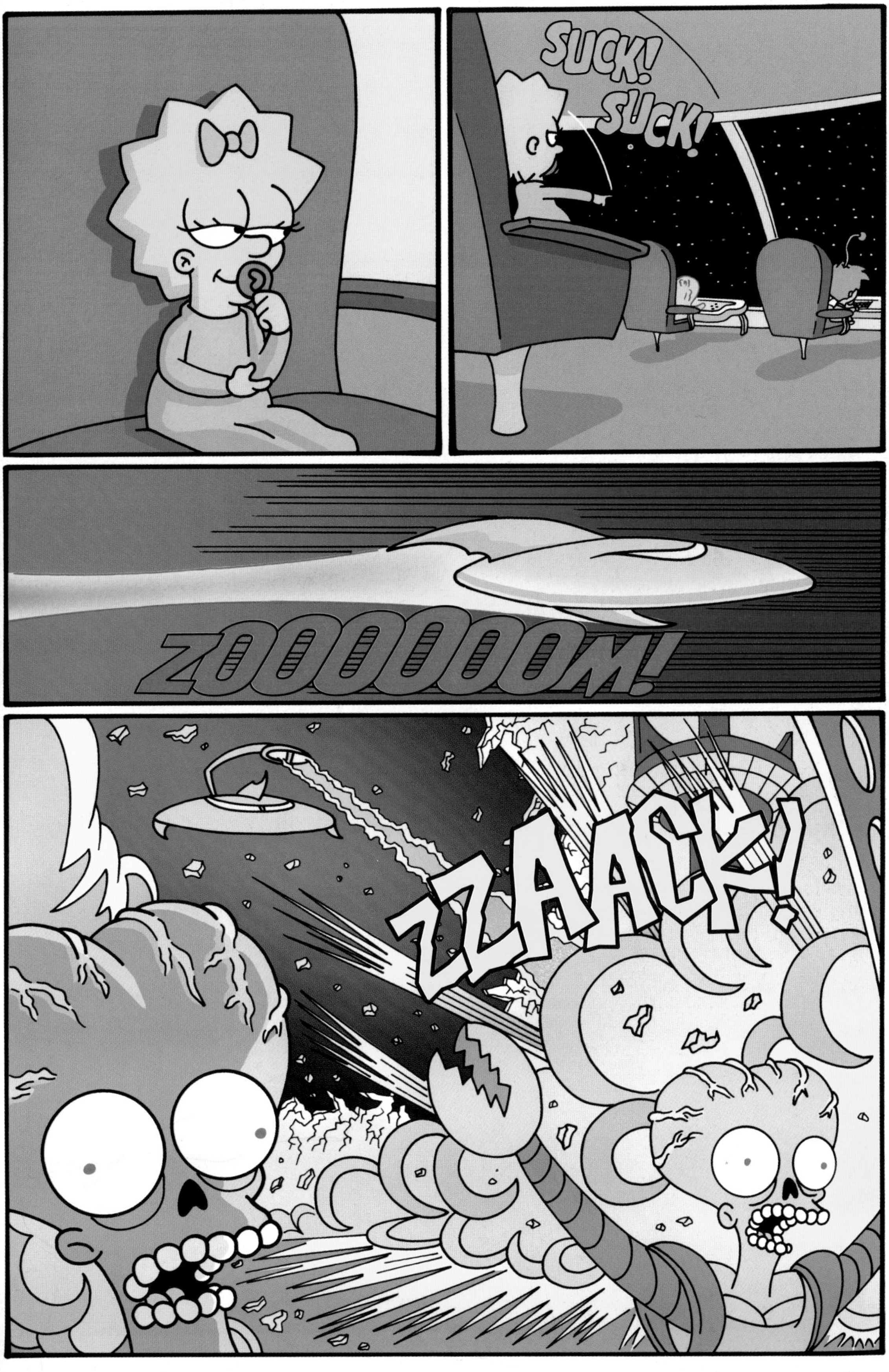
SUCK!
SUCK!
ZOOOOOOM!
ZZAACK!

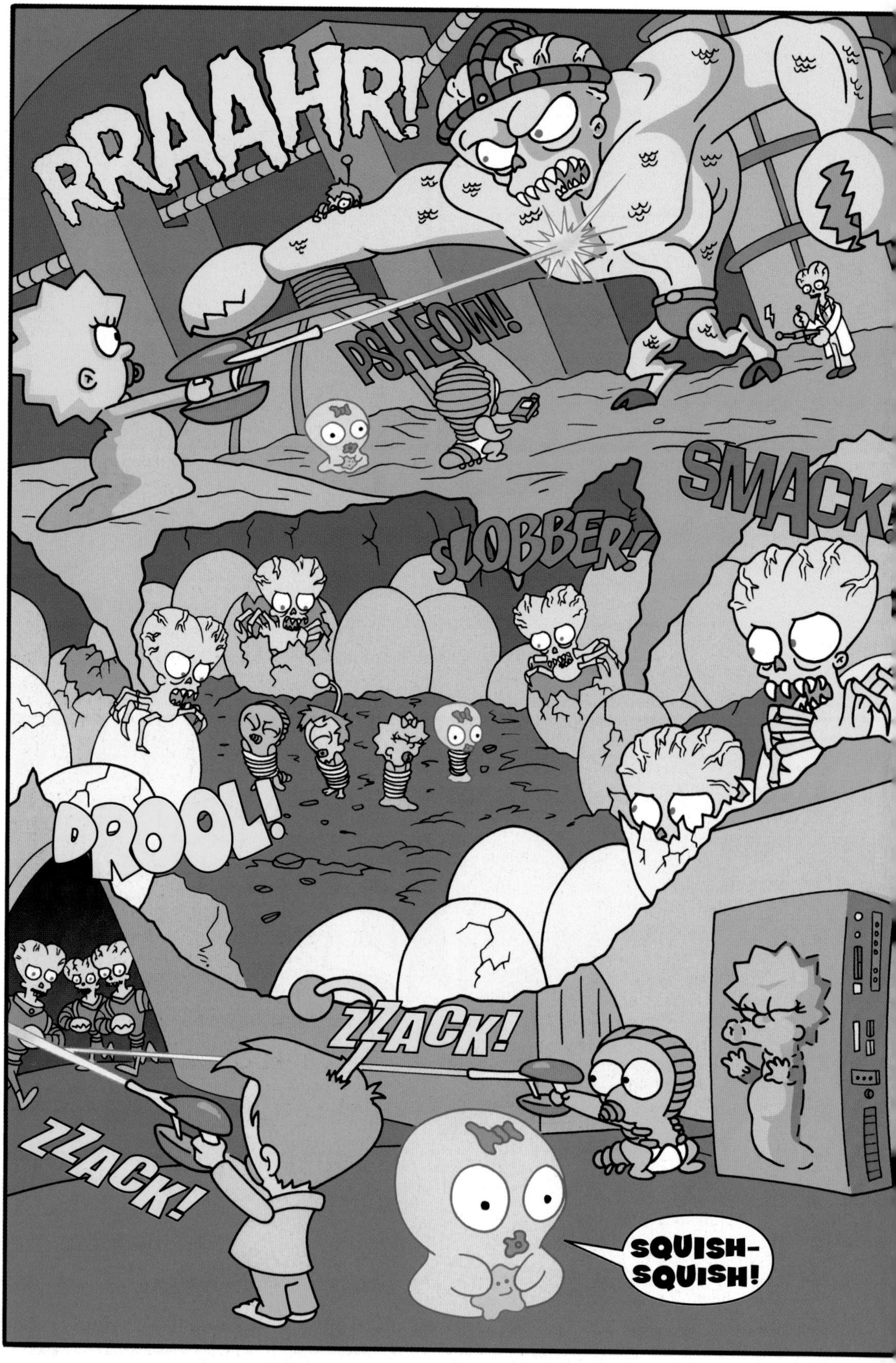
RRAAHR!
PSHEOW!
SMACK!
SLOBBER!
DROOL!
ZZACK!
ZZACK!
SQUISH-SQUISH!

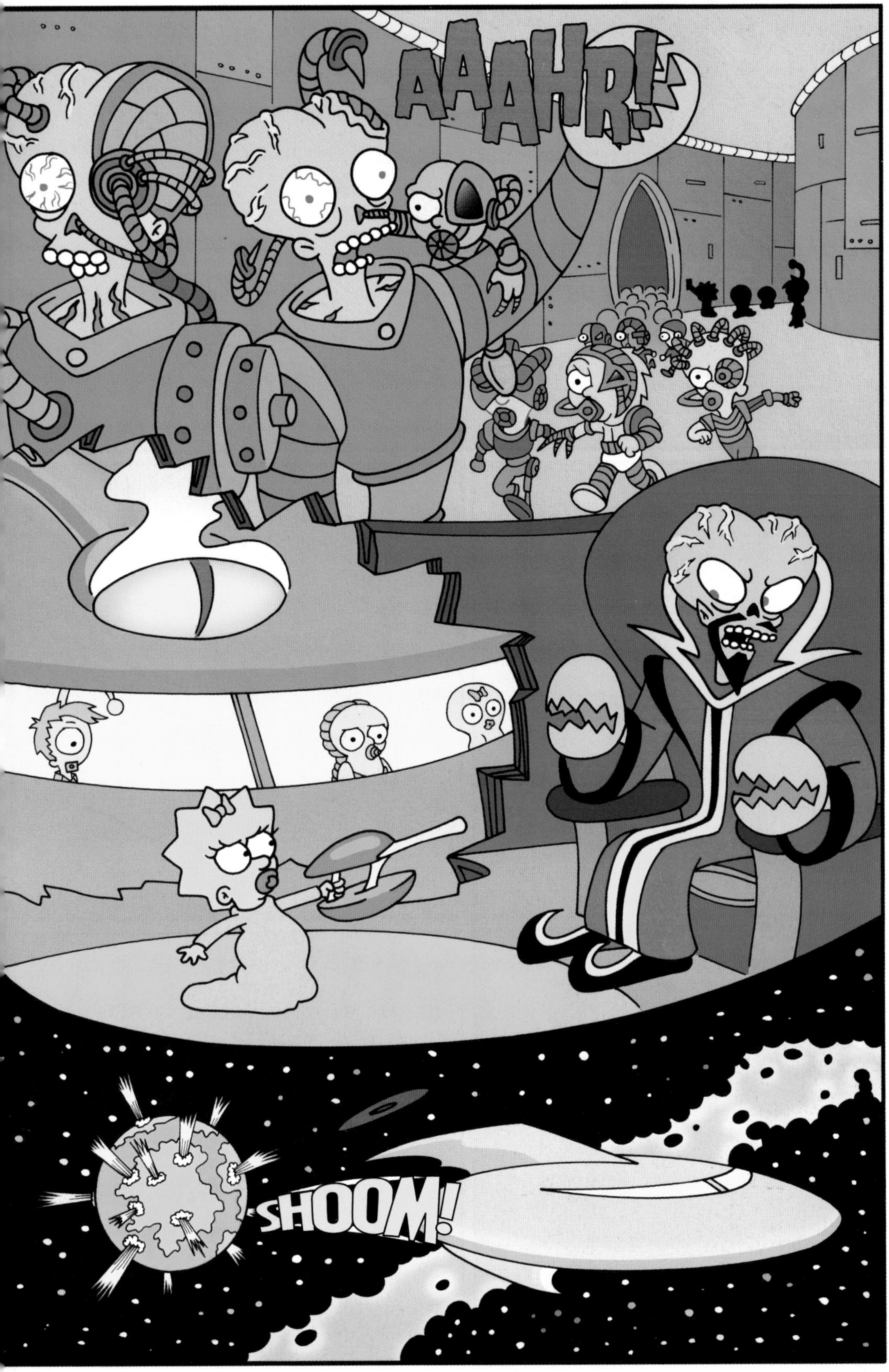
AAAHR!
SHOOM!

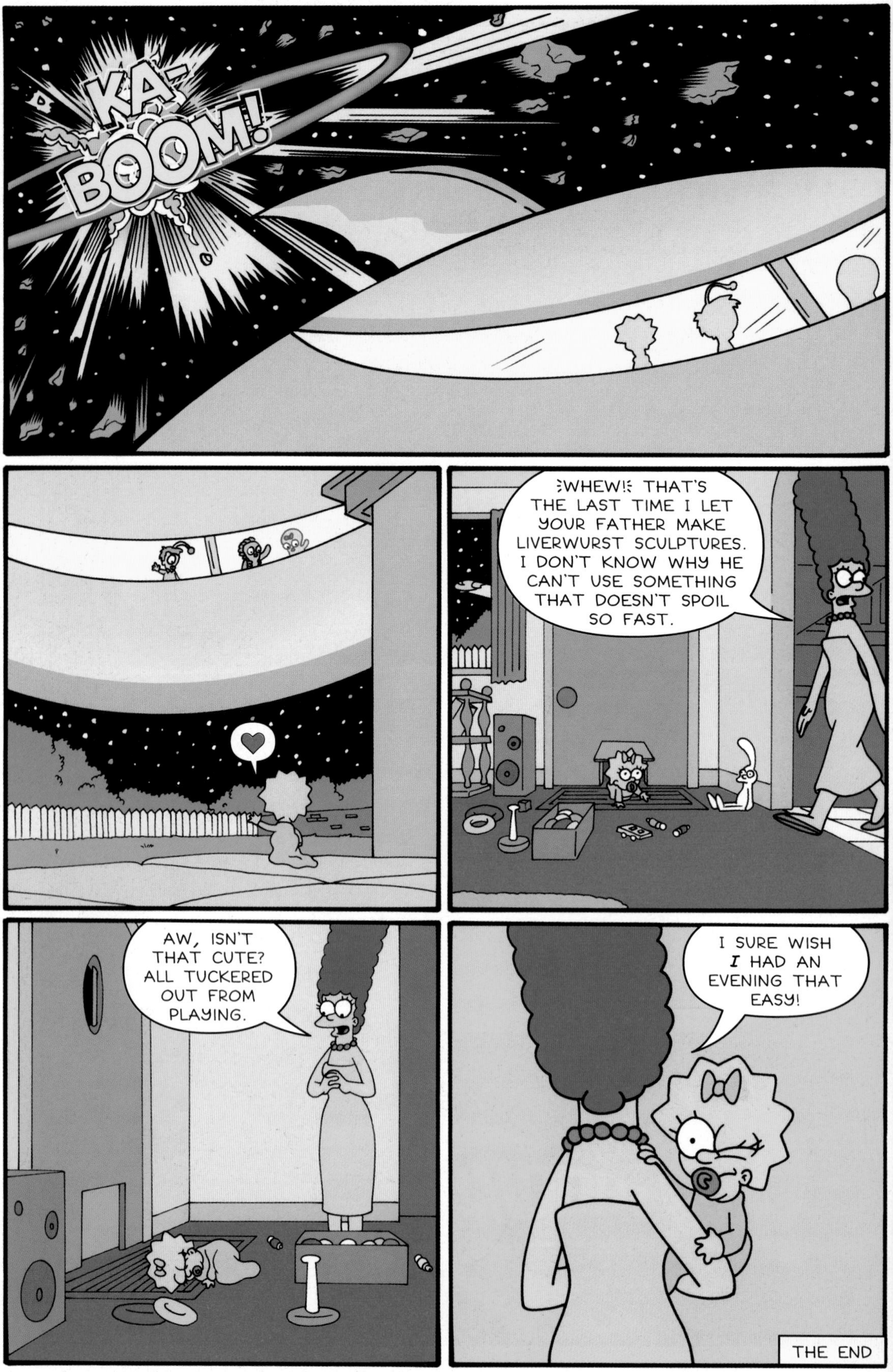
KA-BOOM!
WHEW! THAT'S THE LAST TIME I LET YOUR FATHER MAKE LIVERWURST SCULPTURES. I DON'T KNOW WHY HE CAN'T USE SOMETHING THAT DOESN'T SPOIL SO FAST.
AW, ISN'T THAT CUTE? ALL TUCKERED OUT FROM PLAYING.
I SURE WISH I HAD AN EVENING THAT EASY!
THE END

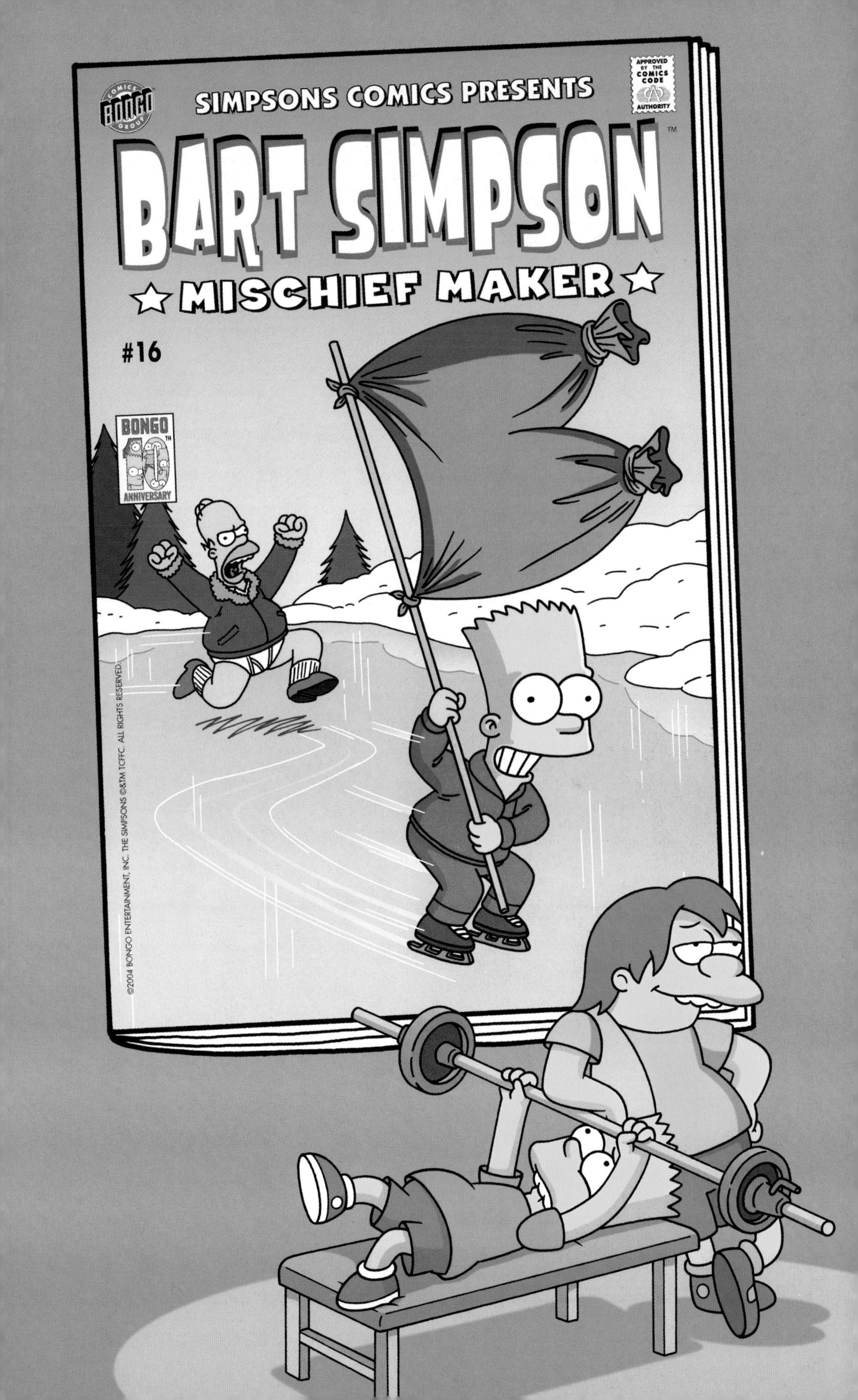
COMICS BONGO GROUP
SIMPSONS COMICS PRESENTS
APPROVED BY THE COMICS CODE AUTHORITY
BART SIMPSON™
MISCHIEF MAKER
#16
BONGO 10TH ANNIVERSARY
©2004 BONGO ENTERTAINMENT, INC. THE SIMPSONS ©&TM TCFFC. ALL RIGHTS RESERVED.

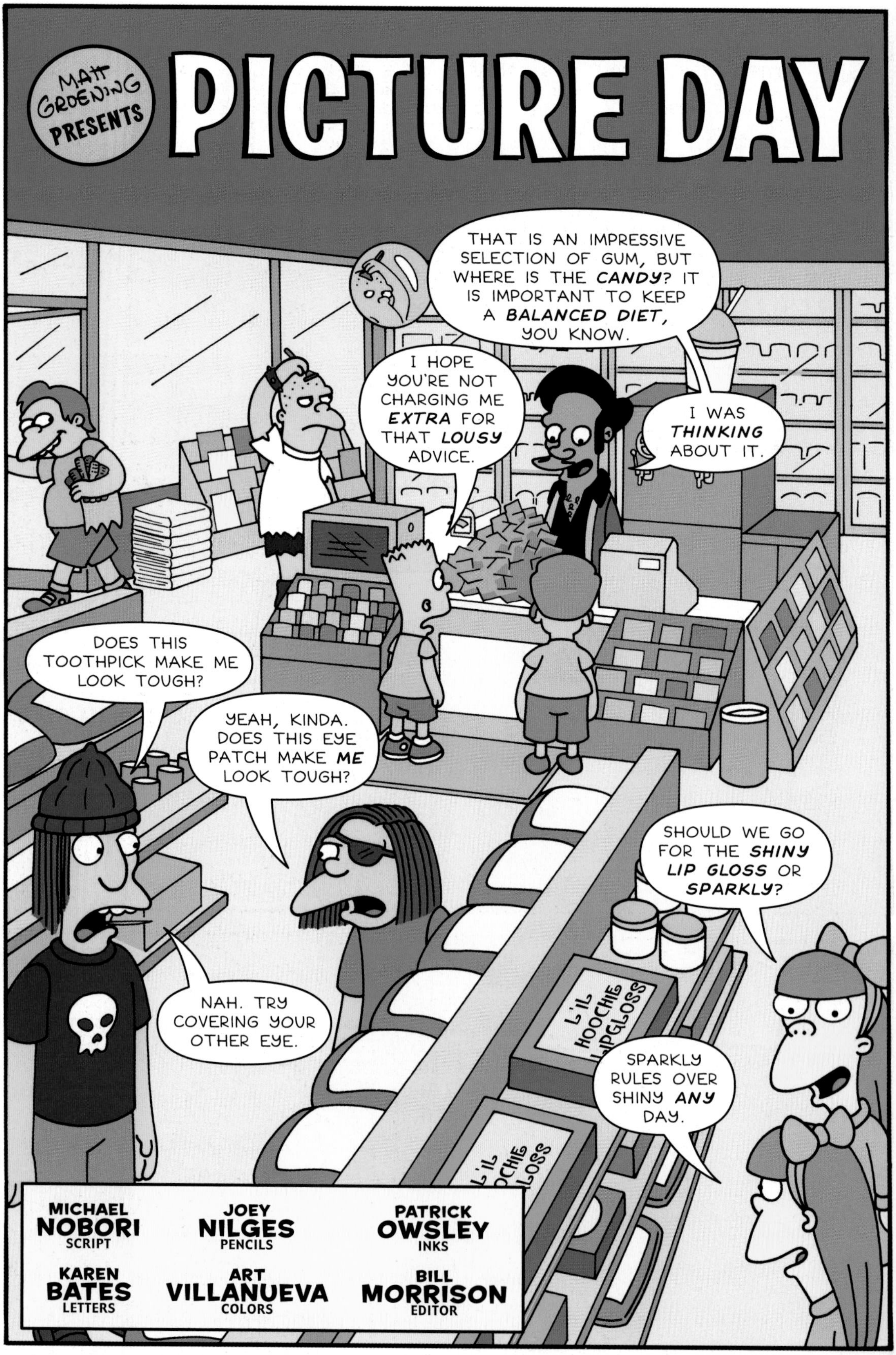
MATT GROENING PRESENTS
PICTURE DAY
THAT IS AN IMPRESSIVE SELECTION OF GUM, BUT WHERE IS THE CANDY? IT IS IMPORTANT TO KEEP A BALANCED DIET, YOU KNOW.
I HOPE YOU'RE NOT CHARGING ME EXTRA FOR THAT LOUSY ADVICE.
I WAS THINKING ABOUT IT.
DOES THIS TOOTHPICK MAKE ME LOOK TOUGH?
YEAH, KINDA. DOES THIS EYE PATCH MAKE ME LOOK TOUGH?
NAH. TRY COVERING YOUR OTHER EYE.
SHOULD WE GO FOR THE SHINY LIP GLOSS OR SPARKLY?
SPARKLY RULES OVER SHINY ANY DAY.
L'IL HOOCHIE LIPGLOSS
MICHAEL NOBORI SCRIPT
JOEY NILGES PENCILS
PATRICK OWSLEY INKS
KAREN BATES LETTERS
ART VILLANUEVA COLORS
BILL MORRISON EDITOR

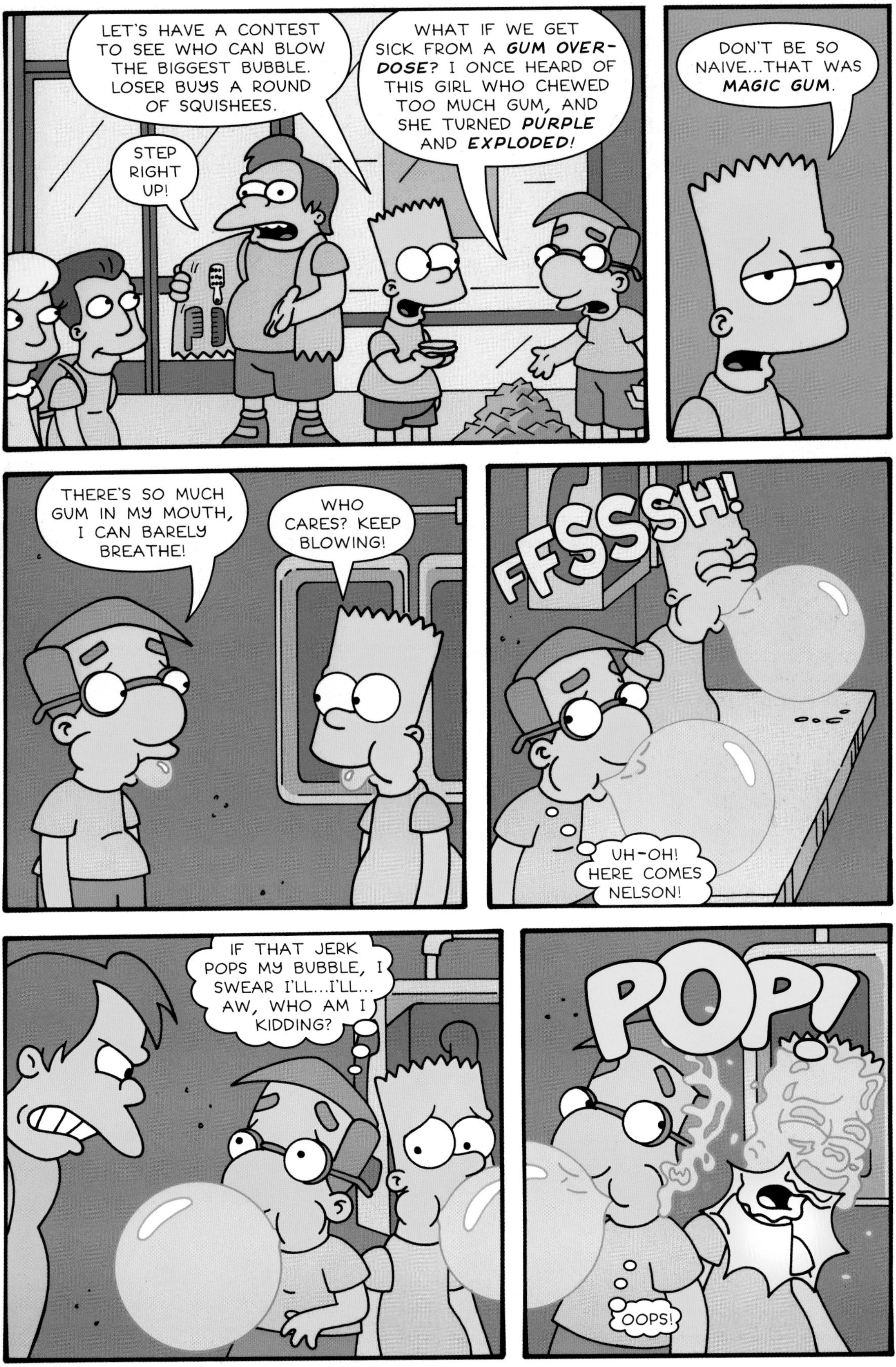
LET'S HAVE A CONTEST TO SEE WHO CAN BLOW THE BIGGEST BUBBLE. LOSER BUYS A ROUND OF SQUISHEES.
STEP RIGHT UP!
WHAT IF WE GET SICK FROM A **GUM OVER-DOSE**? I ONCE HEARD OF THIS GIRL WHO CHEWED TOO MUCH GUM, AND SHE TURNED **PURPLE** AND **EXPLODED**!
DON'T BE SO NAIVE...THAT WAS **MAGIC GUM**.
THERE'S SO MUCH GUM IN MY MOUTH, I CAN BARELY BREATHE!
WHO CARES? KEEP BLOWING!
FFSSSH!
UH-OH! HERE COMES NELSON!
IF THAT JERK POPS MY BUBBLE, I SWEAR I'LL...I'LL... AW, WHO AM I KIDDING?
POP!
OOPS!

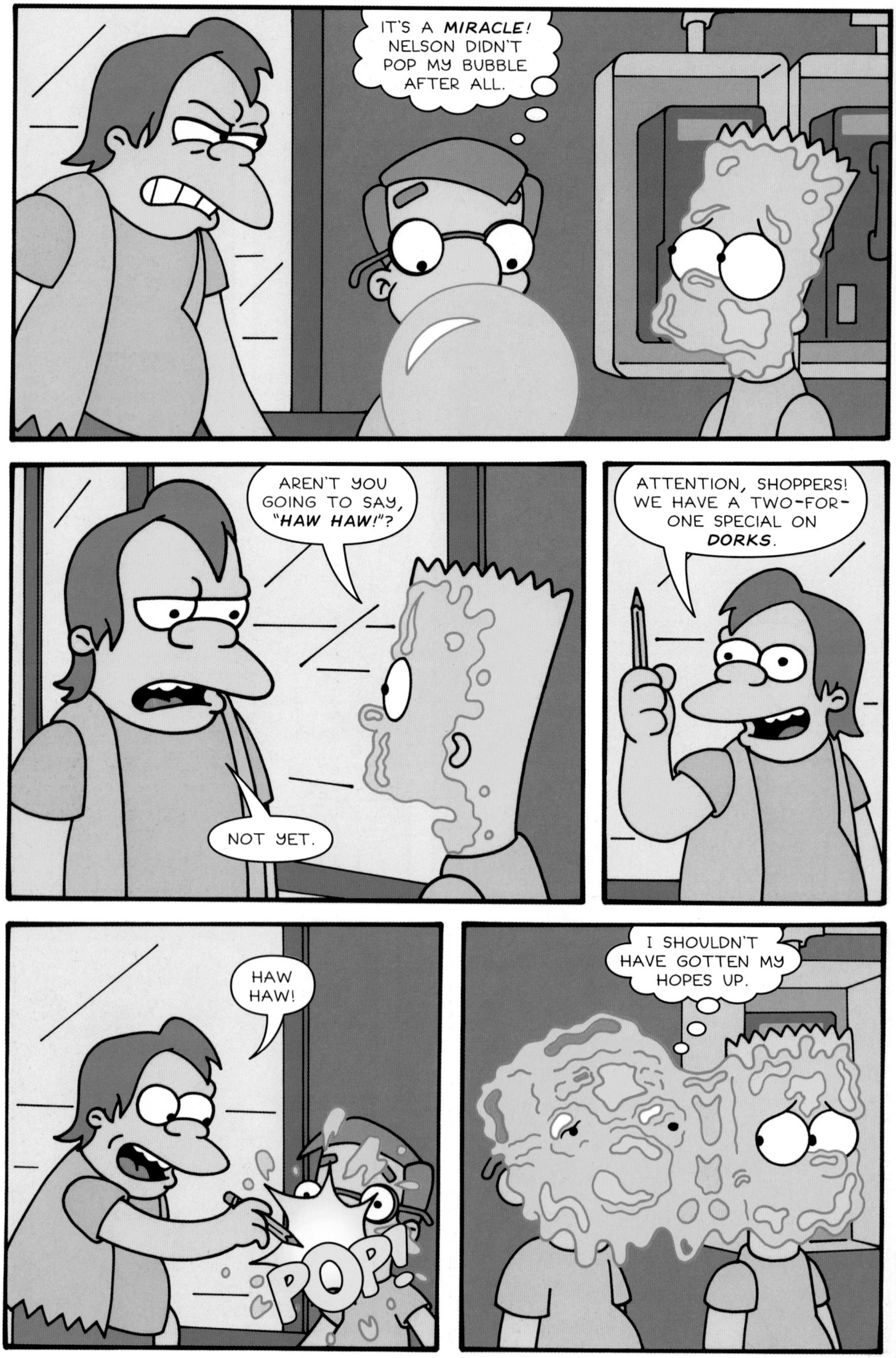

IT'S A ***MIRACLE!*** NELSON DIDN'T POP MY BUBBLE AFTER ALL.
AREN'T YOU GOING TO SAY, "***HAW HAW!***"?
NOT YET.
ATTENTION, SHOPPERS! WE HAVE A TWO-FOR-ONE SPECIAL ON ***DORKS***.
HAW HAW!
POP!
I SHOULDN'T HAVE GOTTEN MY HOPES UP.

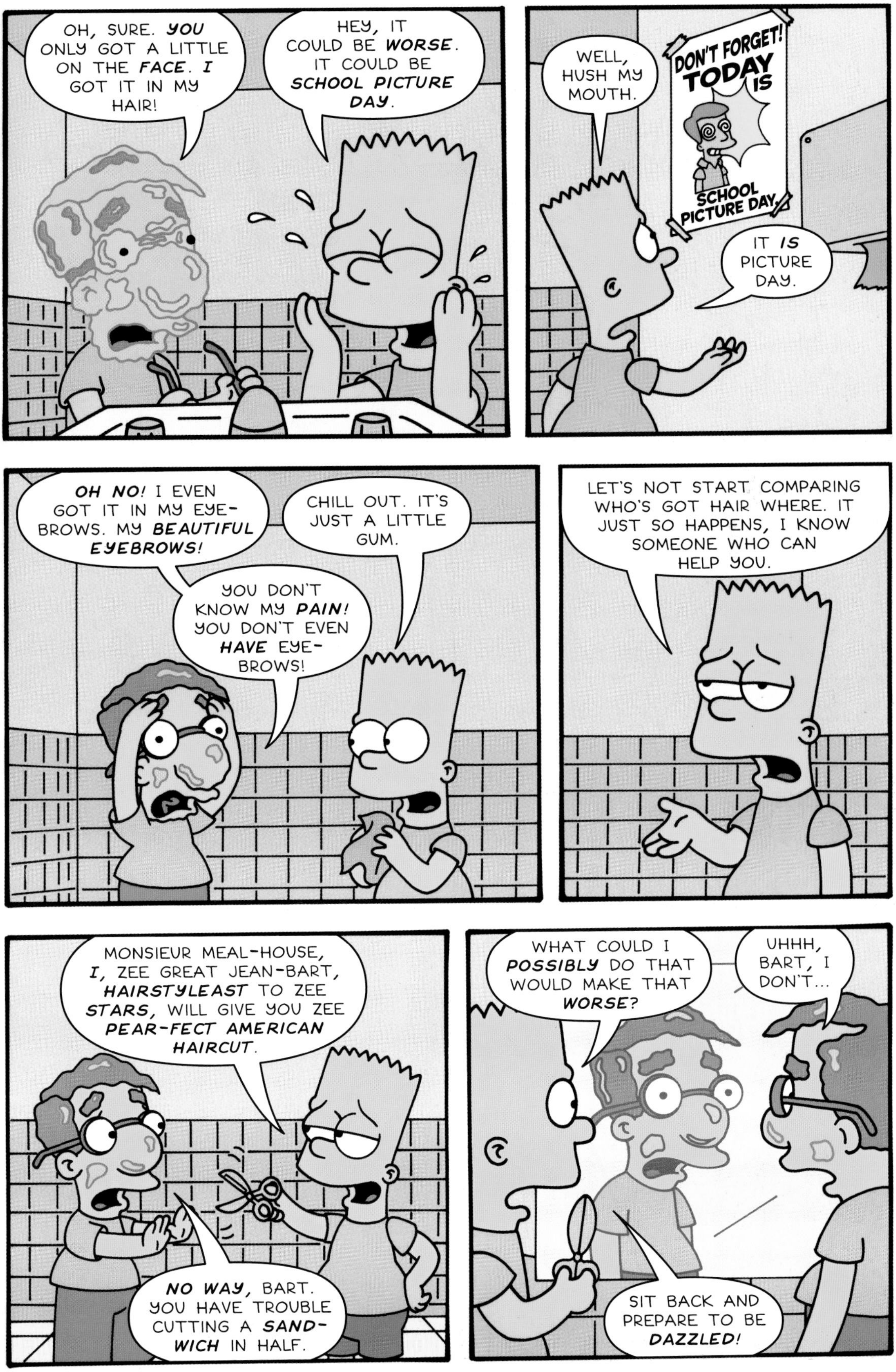

OH, SURE. YOU ONLY GOT A LITTLE ON THE FACE. I GOT IT IN MY HAIR!
HEY, IT COULD BE WORSE. IT COULD BE SCHOOL PICTURE DAY.
WELL, HUSH MY MOUTH.
DON'T FORGET! TODAY IS SCHOOL PICTURE DAY
IT IS PICTURE DAY.
OH NO! I EVEN GOT IT IN MY EYE-BROWS. MY BEAUTIFUL EYEBROWS!
CHILL OUT. IT'S JUST A LITTLE GUM.
YOU DON'T KNOW MY PAIN! YOU DON'T EVEN HAVE EYE-BROWS!
LET'S NOT START COMPARING WHO'S GOT HAIR WHERE. IT JUST SO HAPPENS, I KNOW SOMEONE WHO CAN HELP YOU.
MONSIEUR MEAL-HOUSE, I, ZEE GREAT JEAN-BART, HAIRSTYLEAST TO ZEE STARS, WILL GIVE YOU ZEE PEAR-FECT AMERICAN HAIRCUT.
NO WAY, BART. YOU HAVE TROUBLE CUTTING A SAND-WICH IN HALF.
WHAT COULD I POSSIBLY DO THAT WOULD MAKE THAT WORSE?
UHHH, BART, I DON'T...
SIT BACK AND PREPARE TO BE DAZZLED!

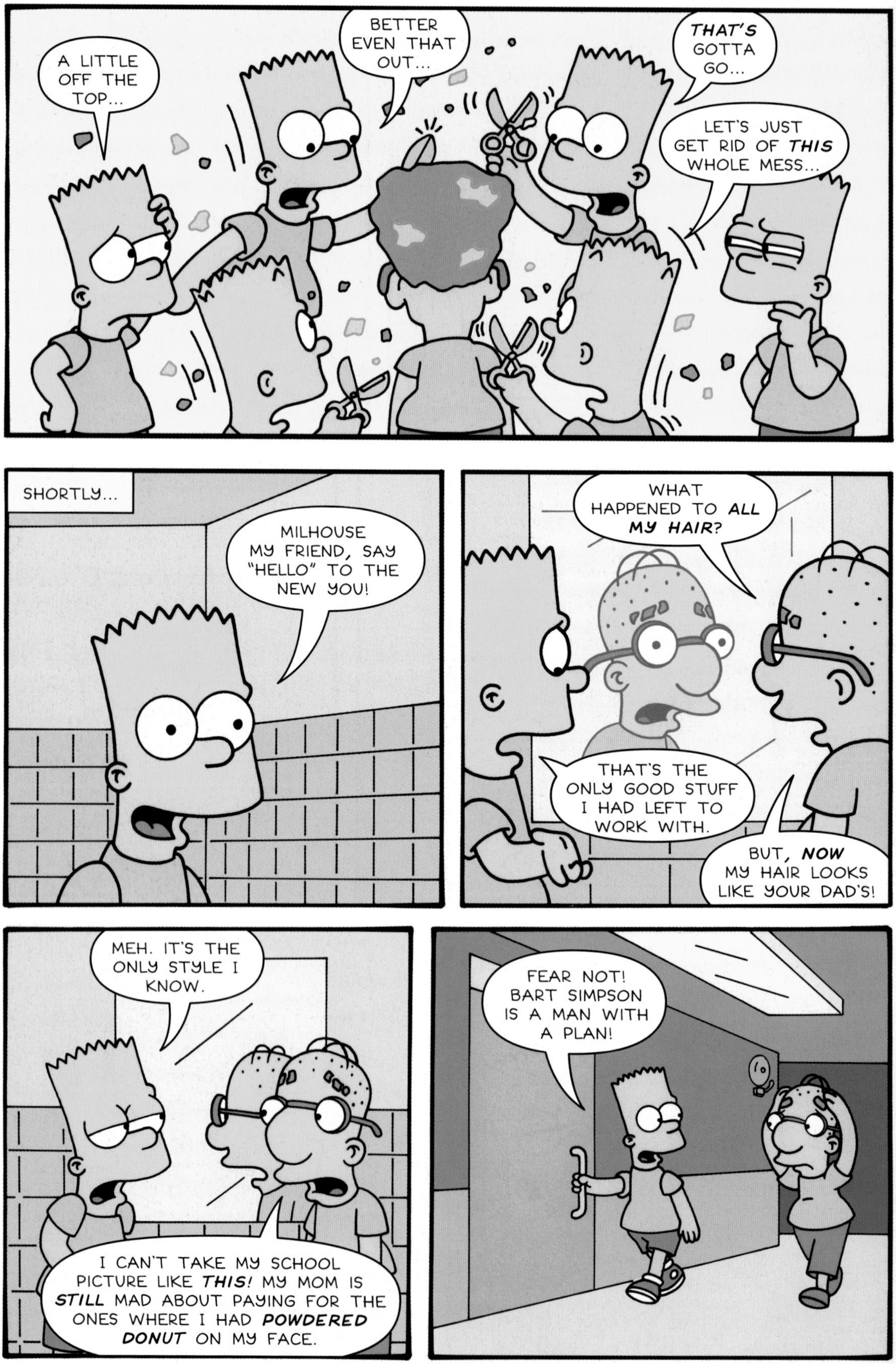
A LITTLE OFF THE TOP...
BETTER EVEN THAT OUT...
THAT'S GOTTA GO...
LET'S JUST GET RID OF THIS WHOLE MESS...
SHORTLY...
MILHOUSE MY FRIEND, SAY "HELLO" TO THE NEW YOU!
WHAT HAPPENED TO ALL MY HAIR?
THAT'S THE ONLY GOOD STUFF I HAD LEFT TO WORK WITH.
BUT, NOW MY HAIR LOOKS LIKE YOUR DAD'S!
MEH. IT'S THE ONLY STYLE I KNOW.
I CAN'T TAKE MY SCHOOL PICTURE LIKE THIS! MY MOM IS STILL MAD ABOUT PAYING FOR THE ONES WHERE I HAD POWDERED DONUT ON MY FACE.
FEAR NOT! BART SIMPSON IS A MAN WITH A PLAN!

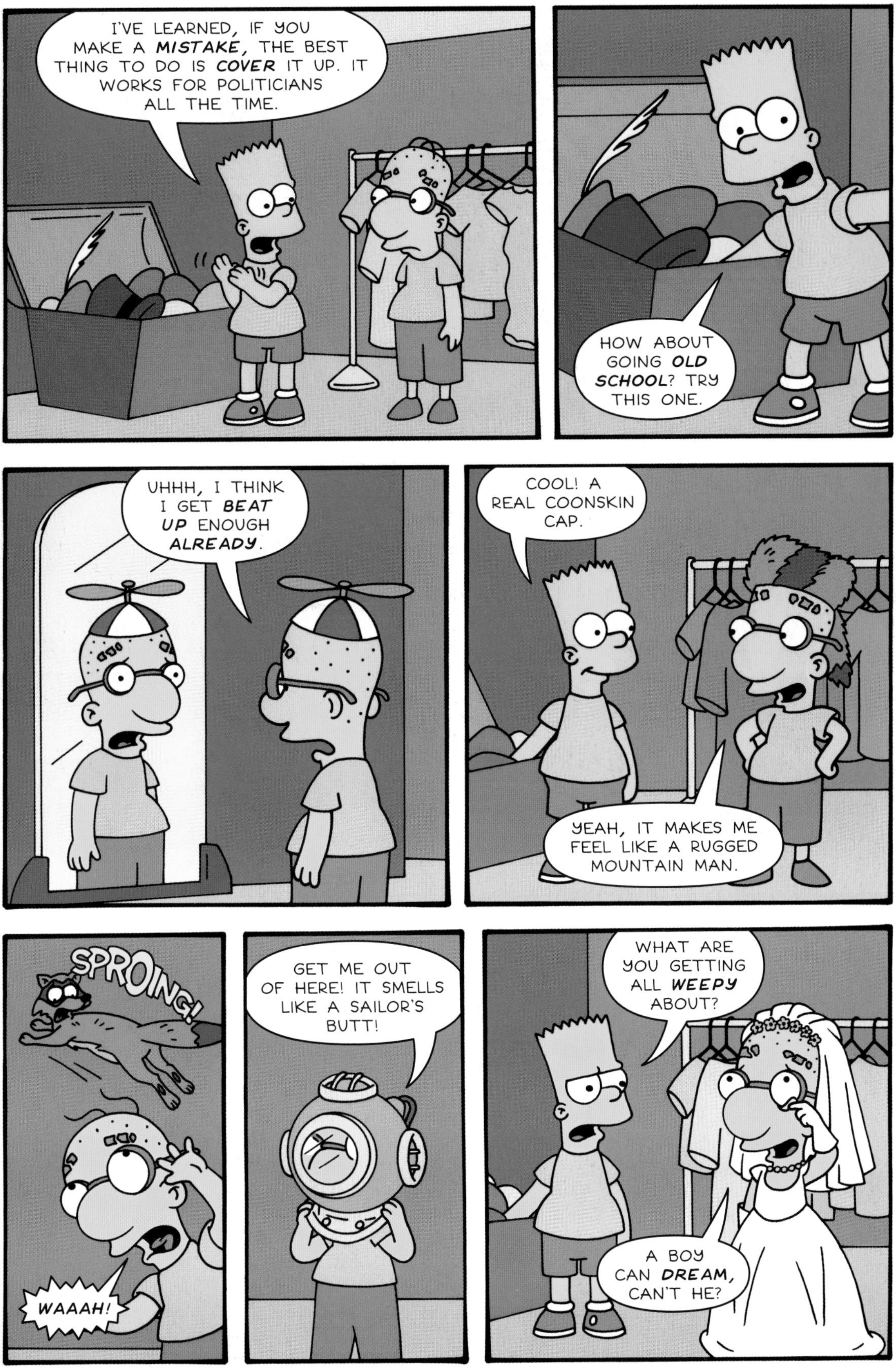
I'VE LEARNED, IF YOU MAKE A MISTAKE, THE BEST THING TO DO IS COVER IT UP. IT WORKS FOR POLITICIANS ALL THE TIME.
HOW ABOUT GOING OLD SCHOOL? TRY THIS ONE.
UHHH, I THINK I GET BEAT UP ENOUGH ALREADY.
COOL! A REAL COONSKIN CAP.
YEAH, IT MAKES ME FEEL LIKE A RUGGED MOUNTAIN MAN.
SPROING!
WAAAH!
GET ME OUT OF HERE! IT SMELLS LIKE A SAILOR'S BUTT!
WHAT ARE YOU GETTING ALL WEEPY ABOUT?
A BOY CAN DREAM, CAN'T HE?

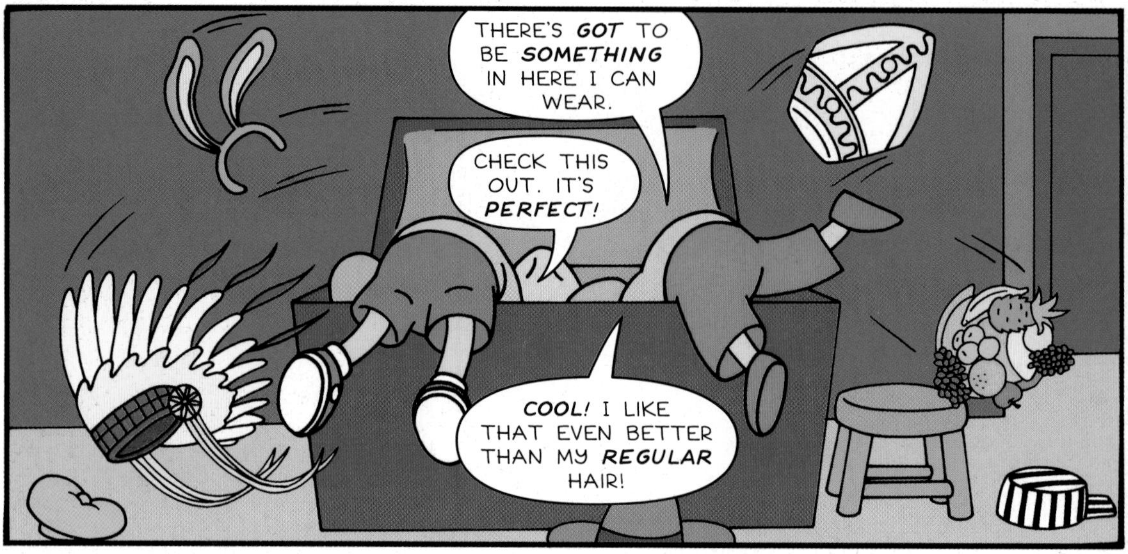
THERE'S *GOT* TO BE *SOMETHING* IN HERE I CAN WEAR.
CHECK THIS OUT. IT'S *PERFECT!*
COOL! I LIKE THAT EVEN BETTER THAN MY *REGULAR* HAIR!

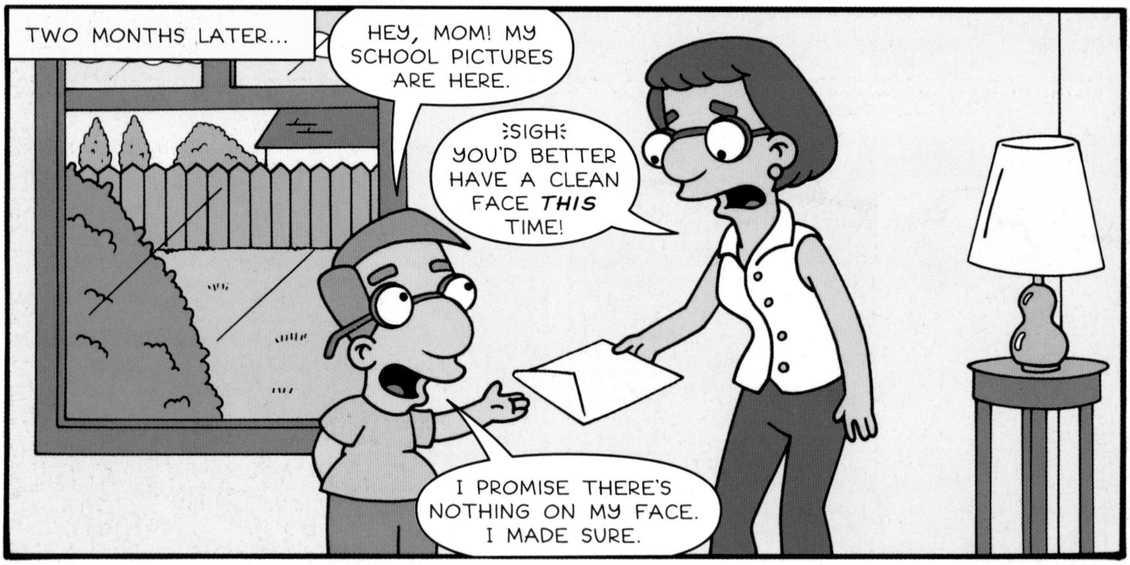
TWO MONTHS LATER...
HEY, MOM! MY SCHOOL PICTURES ARE HERE.
⁝SIGH⁝ YOU'D BETTER HAVE A CLEAN FACE *THIS* TIME!
I PROMISE THERE'S NOTHING ON MY FACE. I MADE SURE.

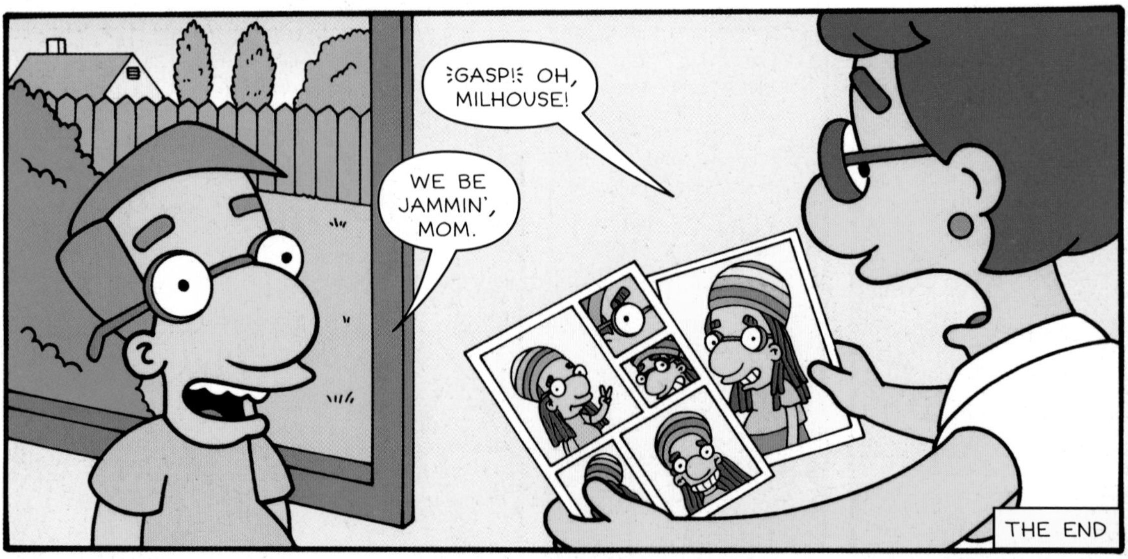
⁝GASP!⁝ OH, MILHOUSE!
WE BE JAMMIN', MOM.
THE END

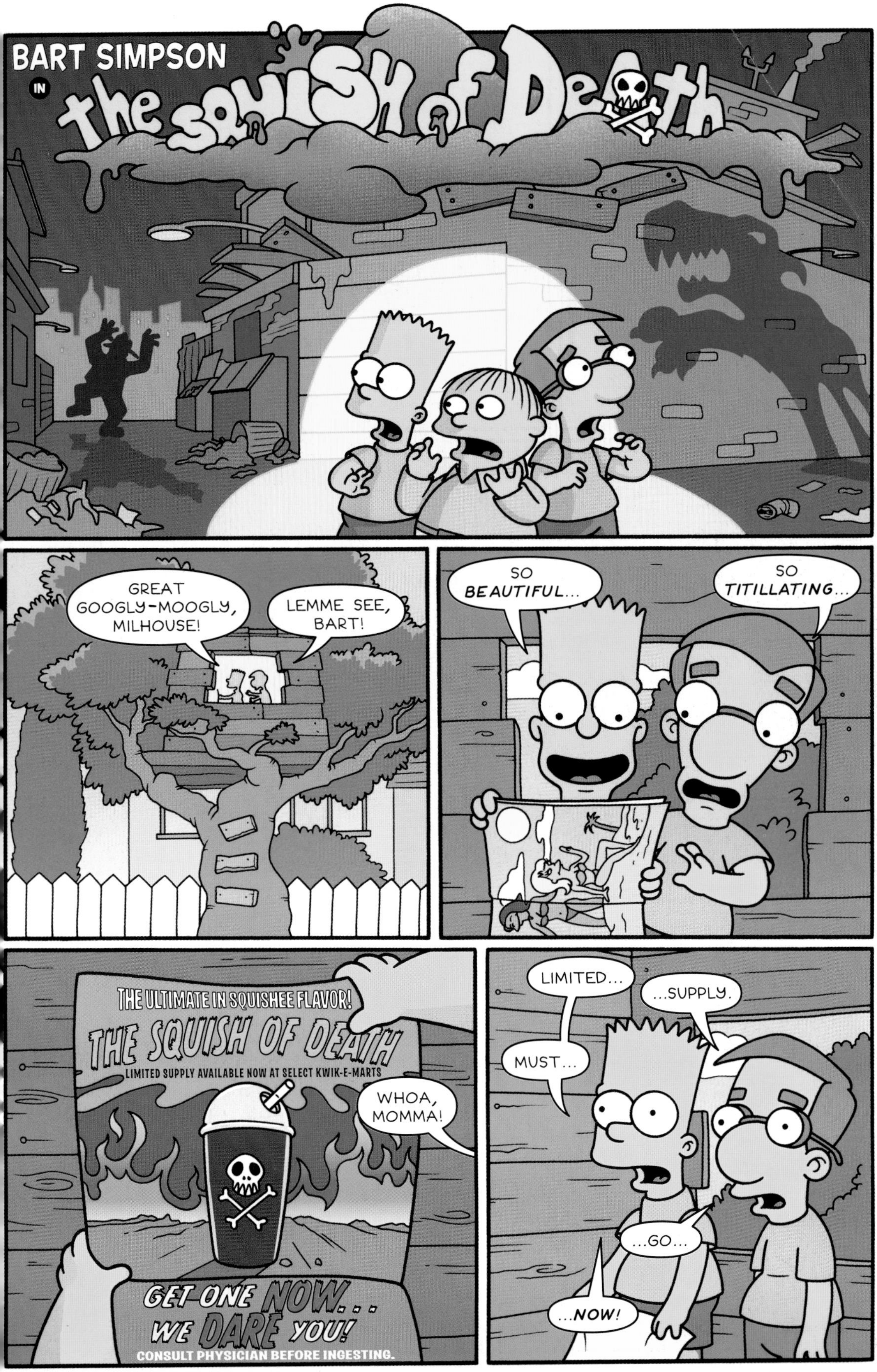
BART SIMPSON
IN
the SQUISH of DEATH
GREAT GOOGLY-MOOGLY, MILHOUSE!
LEMME SEE, BART!
SO *BEAUTIFUL*...
SO *TITILLATING*...
THE ULTIMATE IN SQUISHEE FLAVOR!
THE SQUISH OF DEATH
LIMITED SUPPLY AVAILABLE NOW AT SELECT KWIK-E-MARTS
GET ONE NOW... WE DARE YOU!
CONSULT PHYSICIAN BEFORE INGESTING.
WHOA, MOMMA!
LIMITED...
...SUPPLY.
MUST...
...GO...
...*NOW!*

JAMES BATES SCRIPT · RYAN RIVETTE PENCILS · MIKE ROTE INKS · RICK REESE COLORS · KAREN BATES LETTERS · BILL MORRISON EDITOR

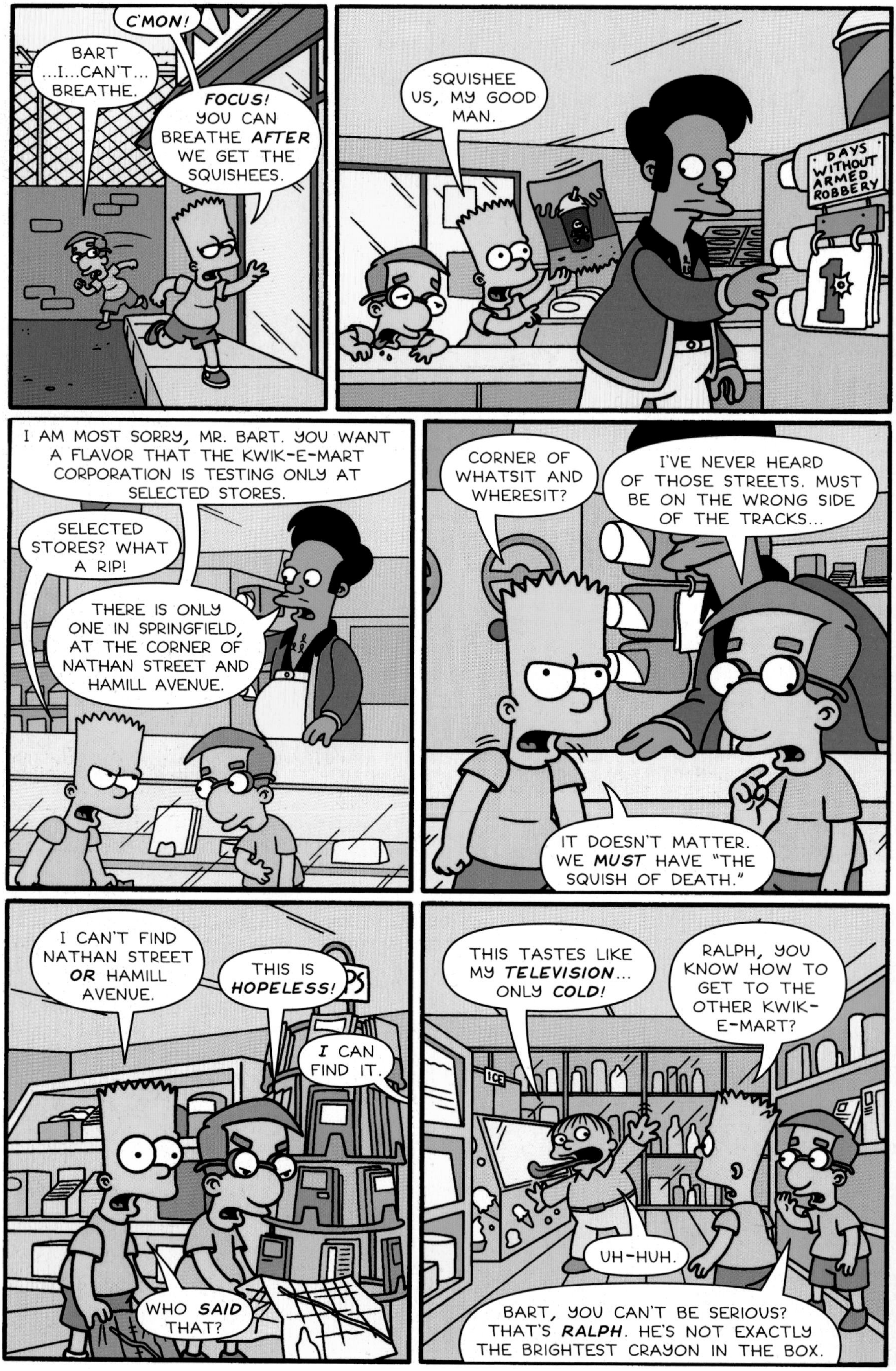

C'MON!
BART ...I...CAN'T... BREATHE.
FOCUS! YOU CAN BREATHE AFTER WE GET THE SQUISHEES.
SQUISHEE US, MY GOOD MAN.
DAYS WITHOUT ARMED ROBBERY
1
I AM MOST SORRY, MR. BART. YOU WANT A FLAVOR THAT THE KWIK-E-MART CORPORATION IS TESTING ONLY AT SELECTED STORES.
SELECTED STORES? WHAT A RIP!
THERE IS ONLY ONE IN SPRINGFIELD, AT THE CORNER OF NATHAN STREET AND HAMILL AVENUE.
CORNER OF WHATSIT AND WHERESIT?
I'VE NEVER HEARD OF THOSE STREETS. MUST BE ON THE WRONG SIDE OF THE TRACKS...
IT DOESN'T MATTER. WE MUST HAVE "THE SQUISH OF DEATH."
I CAN'T FIND NATHAN STREET OR HAMILL AVENUE.
THIS IS HOPELESS!
I CAN FIND IT.
WHO SAID THAT?
THIS TASTES LIKE MY TELEVISION... ONLY COLD!
RALPH, YOU KNOW HOW TO GET TO THE OTHER KWIK-E-MART?
ICE
UH-HUH.
BART, YOU CAN'T BE SERIOUS? THAT'S RALPH. HE'S NOT EXACTLY THE BRIGHTEST CRAYON IN THE BOX.

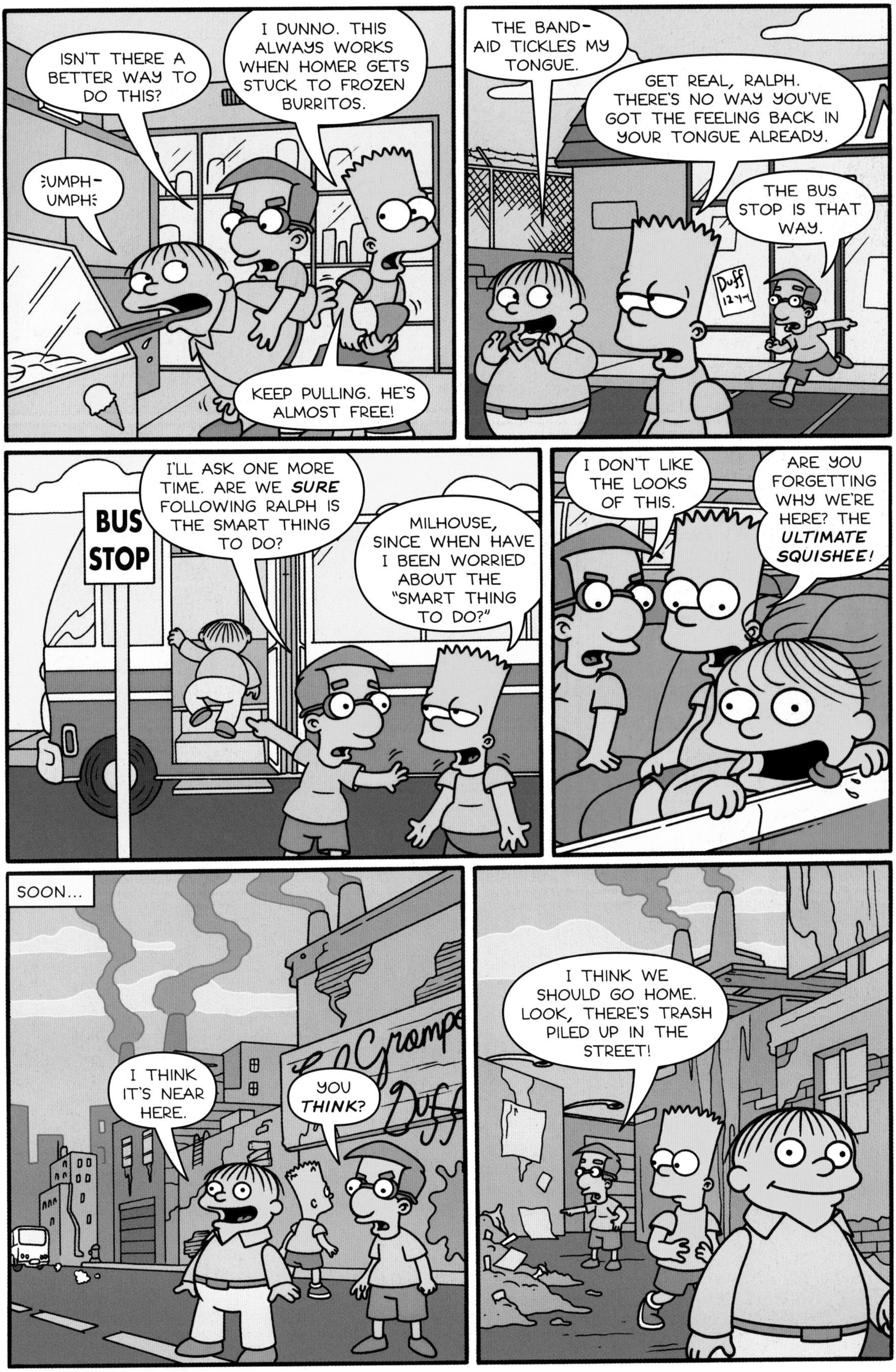
ISN'T THERE A BETTER WAY TO DO THIS?
I DUNNO. THIS ALWAYS WORKS WHEN HOMER GETS STUCK TO FROZEN BURRITOS.
UMPH-UMPH
KEEP PULLING. HE'S ALMOST FREE!
THE BAND-AID TICKLES MY TONGUE.
GET REAL, RALPH. THERE'S NO WAY YOU'VE GOT THE FEELING BACK IN YOUR TONGUE ALREADY.
THE BUS STOP IS THAT WAY.
Duff
BUS STOP
I'LL ASK ONE MORE TIME. ARE WE *SURE* FOLLOWING RALPH IS THE SMART THING TO DO?
MILHOUSE, SINCE WHEN HAVE I BEEN WORRIED ABOUT THE "SMART THING TO DO?"
I DON'T LIKE THE LOOKS OF THIS.
ARE YOU FORGETTING WHY WE'RE HERE? THE *ULTIMATE SQUISHEE!*
SOON...
I THINK IT'S NEAR HERE.
YOU *THINK*?
I THINK WE SHOULD GO HOME. LOOK, THERE'S TRASH PILED UP IN THE STREET!

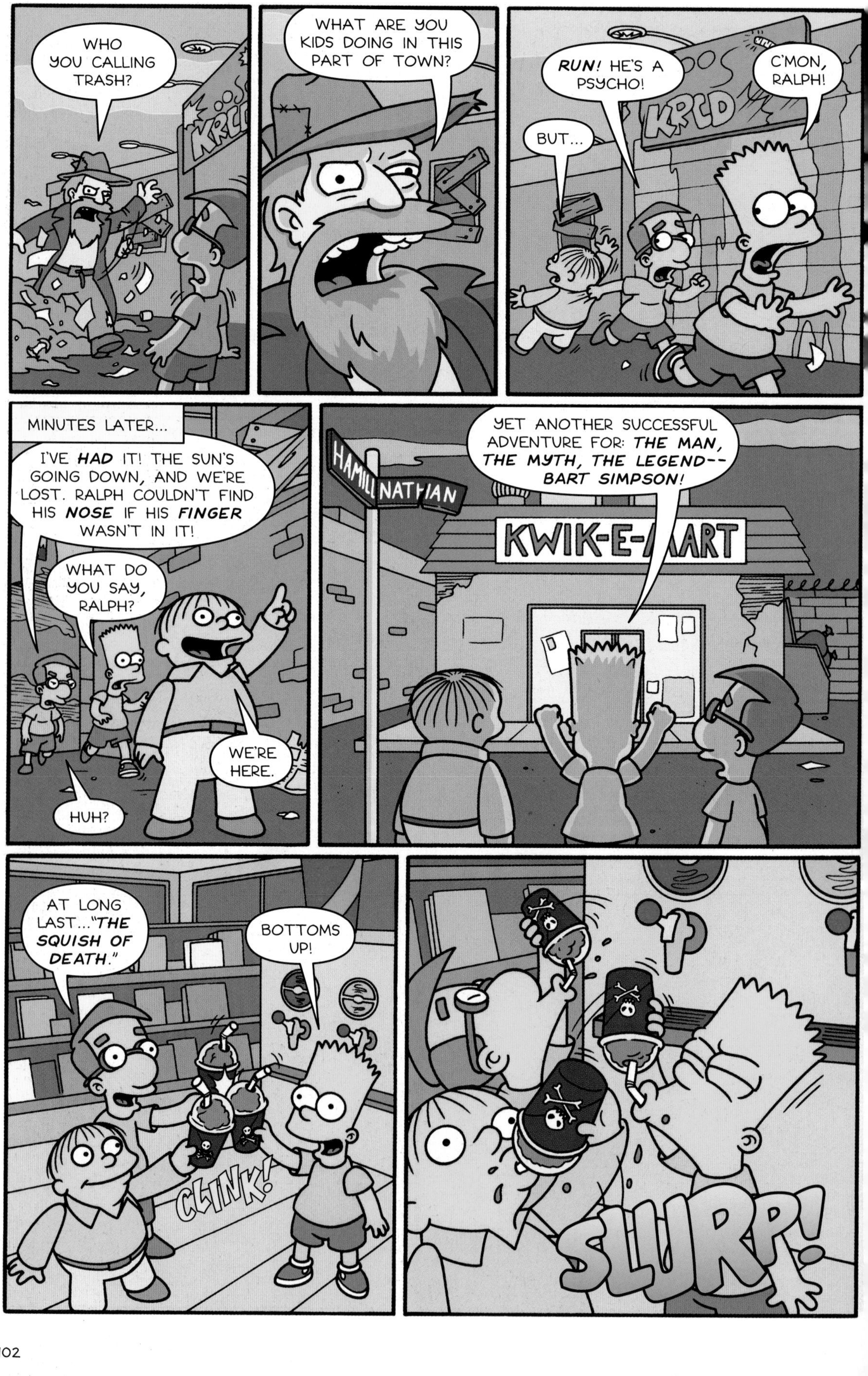
WHO YOU CALLING TRASH?
KRCD
WHAT ARE YOU KIDS DOING IN THIS PART OF TOWN?
BUT...
RUN! HE'S A PSYCHO!
C'MON, RALPH!
KRCD
MINUTES LATER...
I'VE HAD IT! THE SUN'S GOING DOWN, AND WE'RE LOST. RALPH COULDN'T FIND HIS NOSE IF HIS FINGER WASN'T IN IT!
WHAT DO YOU SAY, RALPH?
WE'RE HERE.
HUH?
YET ANOTHER SUCCESSFUL ADVENTURE FOR: THE MAN, THE MYTH, THE LEGEND--BART SIMPSON!
KWIK-E-MART
AT LONG LAST..."THE SQUISH OF DEATH."
BOTTOMS UP!
CLINK!
SLURP!

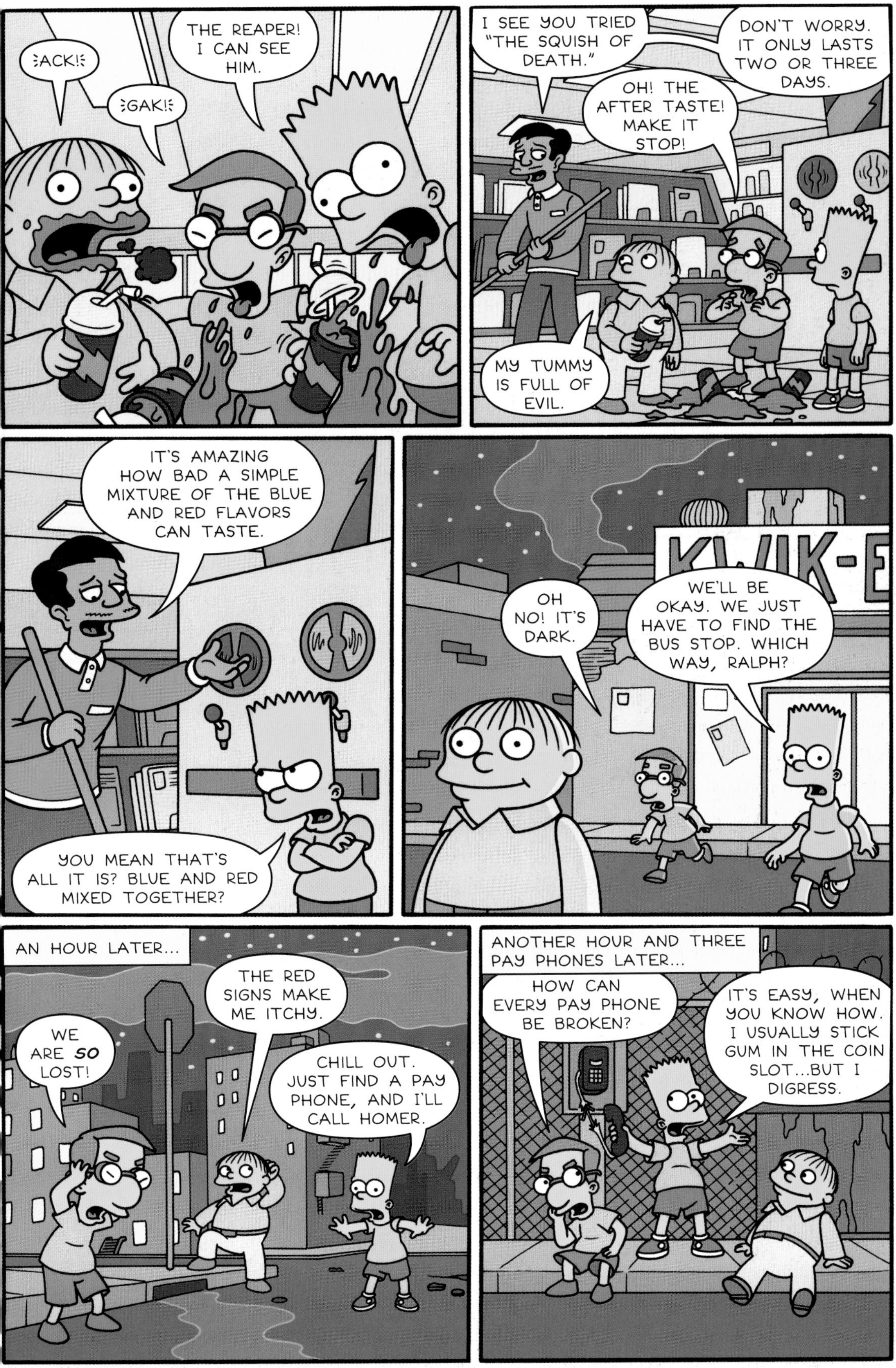
ACK!
GAK!
THE REAPER! I CAN SEE HIM.
I SEE YOU TRIED "THE SQUISH OF DEATH."
DON'T WORRY. IT ONLY LASTS TWO OR THREE DAYS.
OH! THE AFTER TASTE! MAKE IT STOP!
MY TUMMY IS FULL OF EVIL.
IT'S AMAZING HOW BAD A SIMPLE MIXTURE OF THE BLUE AND RED FLAVORS CAN TASTE.
YOU MEAN THAT'S ALL IT IS? BLUE AND RED MIXED TOGETHER?
KWIK-E
OH NO! IT'S DARK.
WE'LL BE OKAY. WE JUST HAVE TO FIND THE BUS STOP. WHICH WAY, RALPH?
AN HOUR LATER...
WE ARE *SO* LOST!
THE RED SIGNS MAKE ME ITCHY.
CHILL OUT. JUST FIND A PAY PHONE, AND I'LL CALL HOMER.
ANOTHER HOUR AND THREE PAY PHONES LATER...
HOW CAN EVERY PAY PHONE BE BROKEN?
IT'S EASY, WHEN YOU KNOW HOW. I USUALLY STICK GUM IN THE COIN SLOT...BUT I DIGRESS.

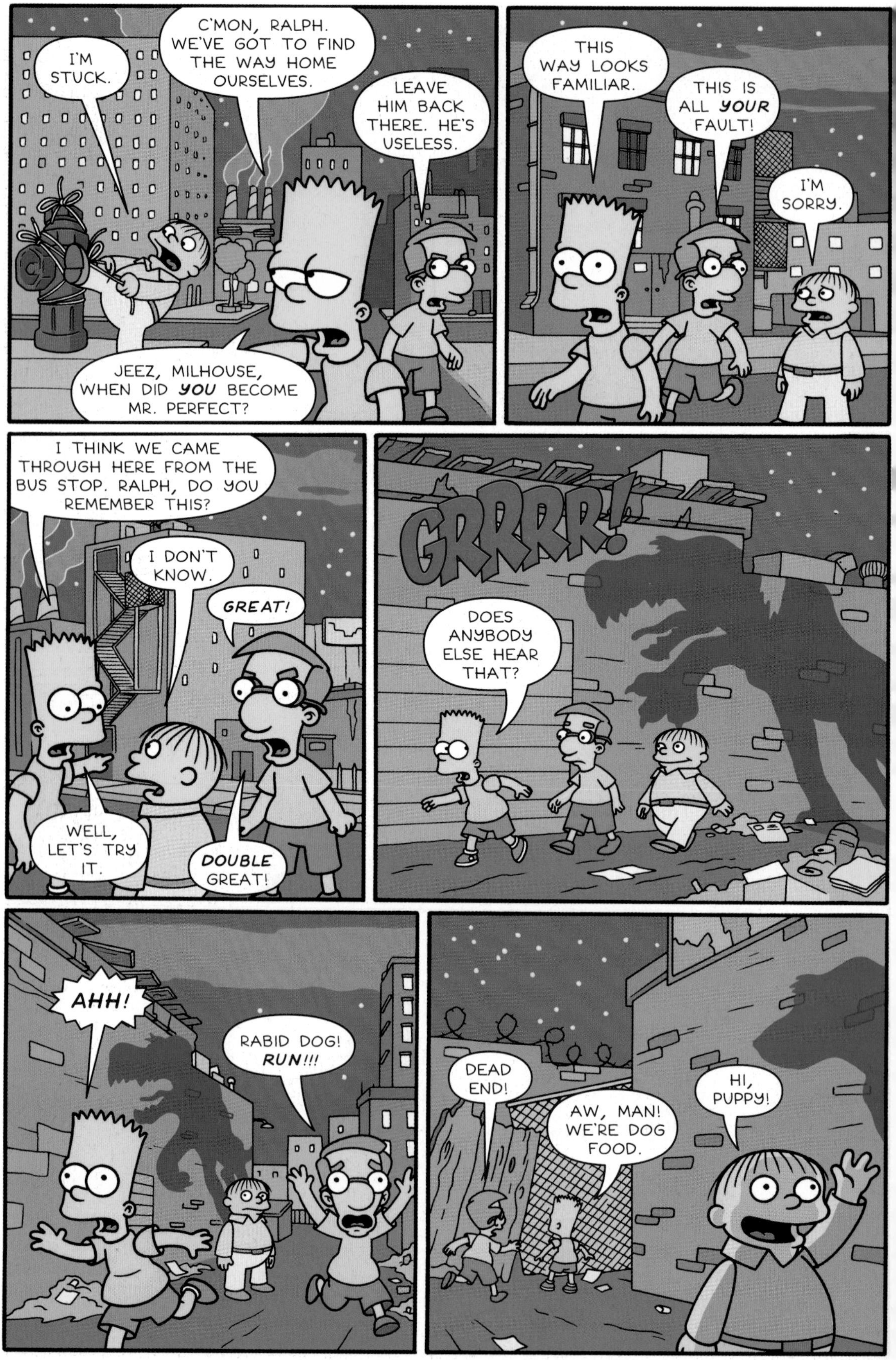
I'M STUCK.
C'MON, RALPH. WE'VE GOT TO FIND THE WAY HOME OURSELVES.
LEAVE HIM BACK THERE. HE'S USELESS.
JEEZ, MILHOUSE, WHEN DID **YOU** BECOME MR. PERFECT?
THIS WAY LOOKS FAMILIAR.
THIS IS ALL **YOUR** FAULT!
I'M SORRY.
I THINK WE CAME THROUGH HERE FROM THE BUS STOP. RALPH, DO YOU REMEMBER THIS?
I DON'T KNOW.
GREAT!
WELL, LET'S TRY IT.
DOUBLE GREAT!
GRRRR!
DOES ANYBODY ELSE HEAR THAT?
AHH!
RABID DOG! **RUN!!!**
DEAD END!
AW, MAN! WE'RE DOG FOOD.
HI, PUPPY!

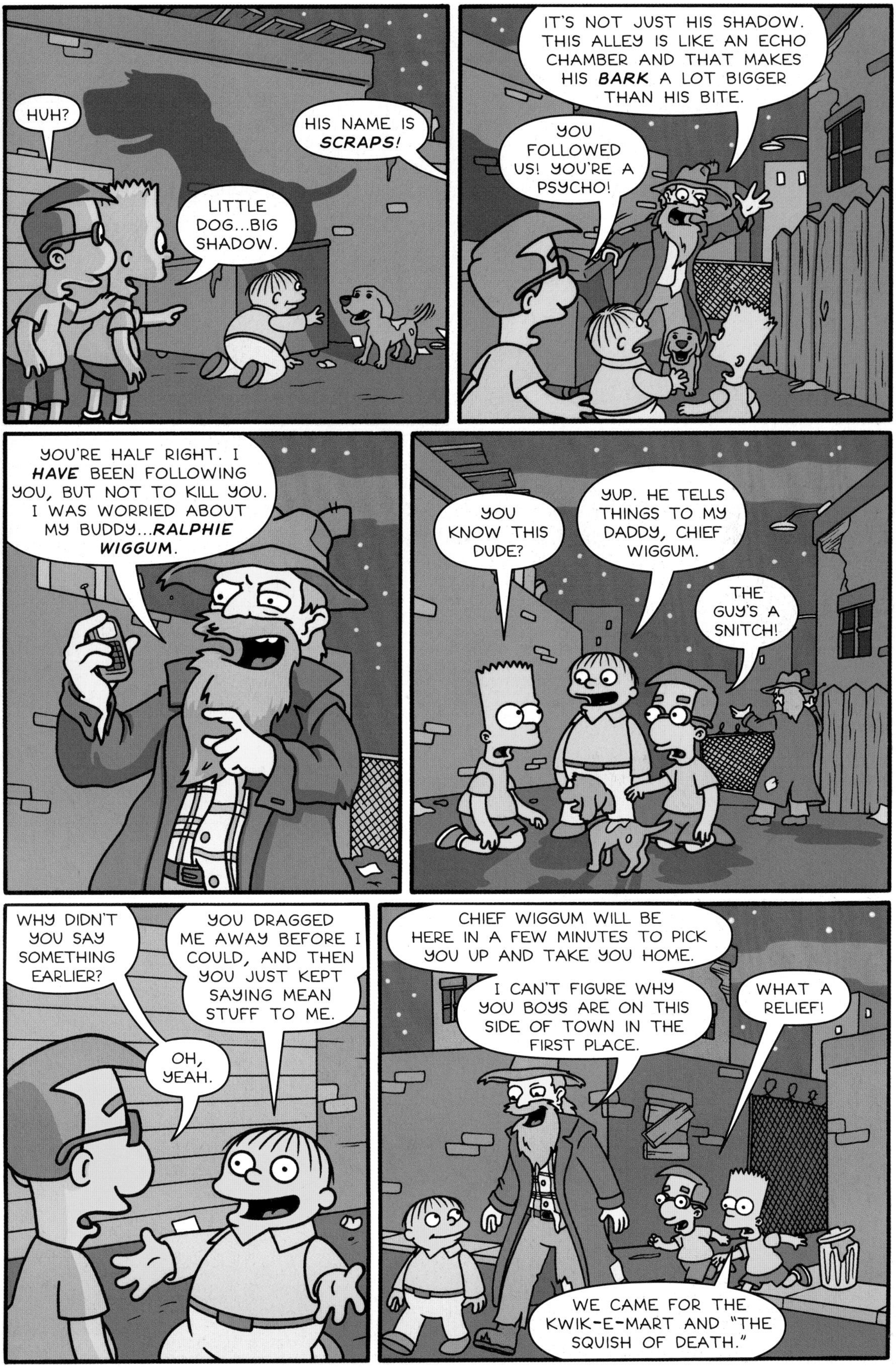
HUH?
HIS NAME IS *SCRAPS!*
LITTLE DOG...BIG SHADOW.
IT'S NOT JUST HIS SHADOW. THIS ALLEY IS LIKE AN ECHO CHAMBER AND THAT MAKES HIS *BARK* A LOT BIGGER THAN HIS BITE.
YOU FOLLOWED US! YOU'RE A PSYCHO!
YOU'RE HALF RIGHT. I *HAVE* BEEN FOLLOWING YOU, BUT NOT TO KILL YOU. I WAS WORRIED ABOUT MY BUDDY...*RALPHIE WIGGUM*.
YOU KNOW THIS DUDE?
YUP. HE TELLS THINGS TO MY DADDY, CHIEF WIGGUM.
THE GUY'S A SNITCH!
WHY DIDN'T YOU SAY SOMETHING EARLIER?
YOU DRAGGED ME AWAY BEFORE I COULD, AND THEN YOU JUST KEPT SAYING MEAN STUFF TO ME.
OH, YEAH.
CHIEF WIGGUM WILL BE HERE IN A FEW MINUTES TO PICK YOU UP AND TAKE YOU HOME.
I CAN'T FIGURE WHY YOU BOYS ARE ON THIS SIDE OF TOWN IN THE FIRST PLACE.
WHAT A RELIEF!
WE CAME FOR THE KWIK-E-MART AND "THE SQUISH OF DEATH."

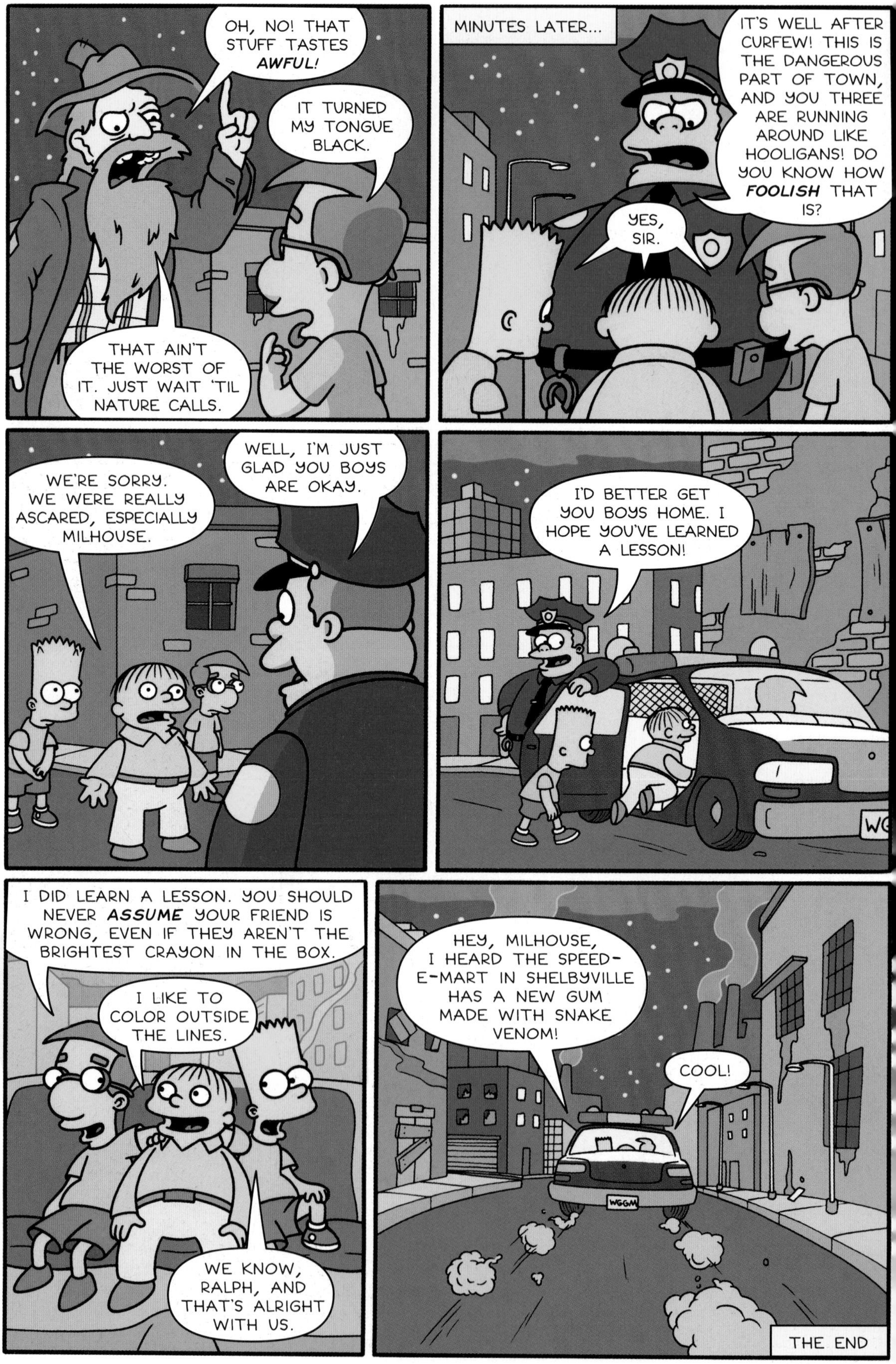

OH, NO! THAT STUFF TASTES AWFUL!
IT TURNED MY TONGUE BLACK.
THAT AIN'T THE WORST OF IT. JUST WAIT 'TIL NATURE CALLS.
MINUTES LATER...
IT'S WELL AFTER CURFEW! THIS IS THE DANGEROUS PART OF TOWN, AND YOU THREE ARE RUNNING AROUND LIKE HOOLIGANS! DO YOU KNOW HOW FOOLISH THAT IS?
YES, SIR.
WE'RE SORRY. WE WERE REALLY ASCARED, ESPECIALLY MILHOUSE.
WELL, I'M JUST GLAD YOU BOYS ARE OKAY.
I'D BETTER GET YOU BOYS HOME. I HOPE YOU'VE LEARNED A LESSON!
I DID LEARN A LESSON. YOU SHOULD NEVER ASSUME YOUR FRIEND IS WRONG, EVEN IF THEY AREN'T THE BRIGHTEST CRAYON IN THE BOX.
I LIKE TO COLOR OUTSIDE THE LINES.
WE KNOW, RALPH, AND THAT'S ALRIGHT WITH US.
HEY, MILHOUSE, I HEARD THE SPEED-E-MART IN SHELBYVILLE HAS A NEW GUM MADE WITH SNAKE VENOM!
COOL!
WGGM
THE END

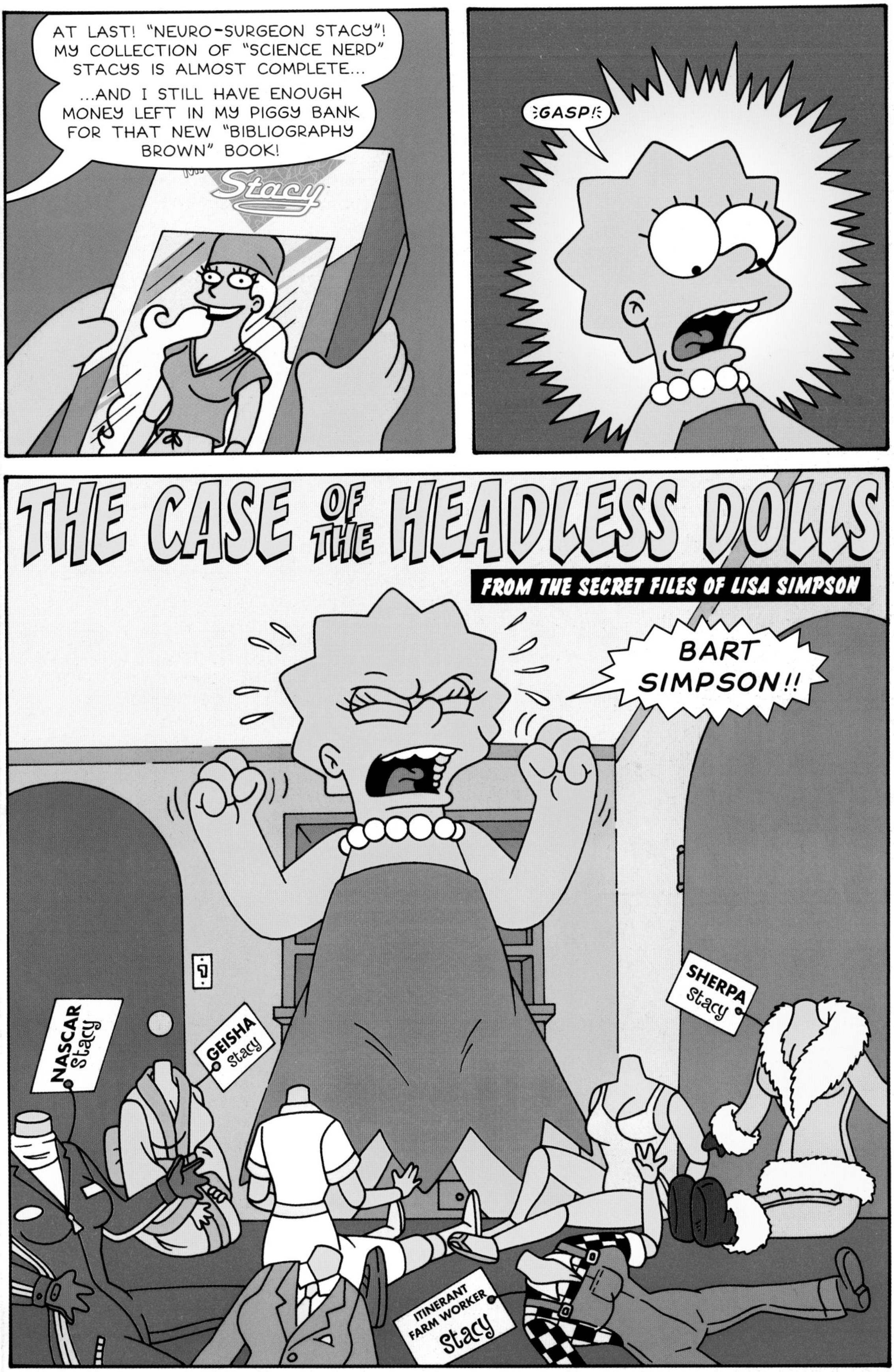
AT LAST! "NEURO-SURGEON STACY"! MY COLLECTION OF "SCIENCE NERD" STACYS IS ALMOST COMPLETE...
...AND I STILL HAVE ENOUGH MONEY LEFT IN MY PIGGY BANK FOR THAT NEW "BIBLIOGRAPHY BROWN" BOOK!
Stacy
GASP!
THE CASE OF THE HEADLESS DOLLS
FROM THE SECRET FILES OF LISA SIMPSON
BART SIMPSON!!
NASCAR Stacy
GEISHA Stacy
SHERPA Stacy
ITINERANT FARM WORKER Stacy

EARL KRESS
TERRY DELEGEANE
SCRIPT

PHIL ORTIZ
PENCILS

PATRICK OWSLEY
INKS

ART VILLANUEVA
COLORS

KAREN BATES
LETTERS

BILL MORRISON
EDITOR

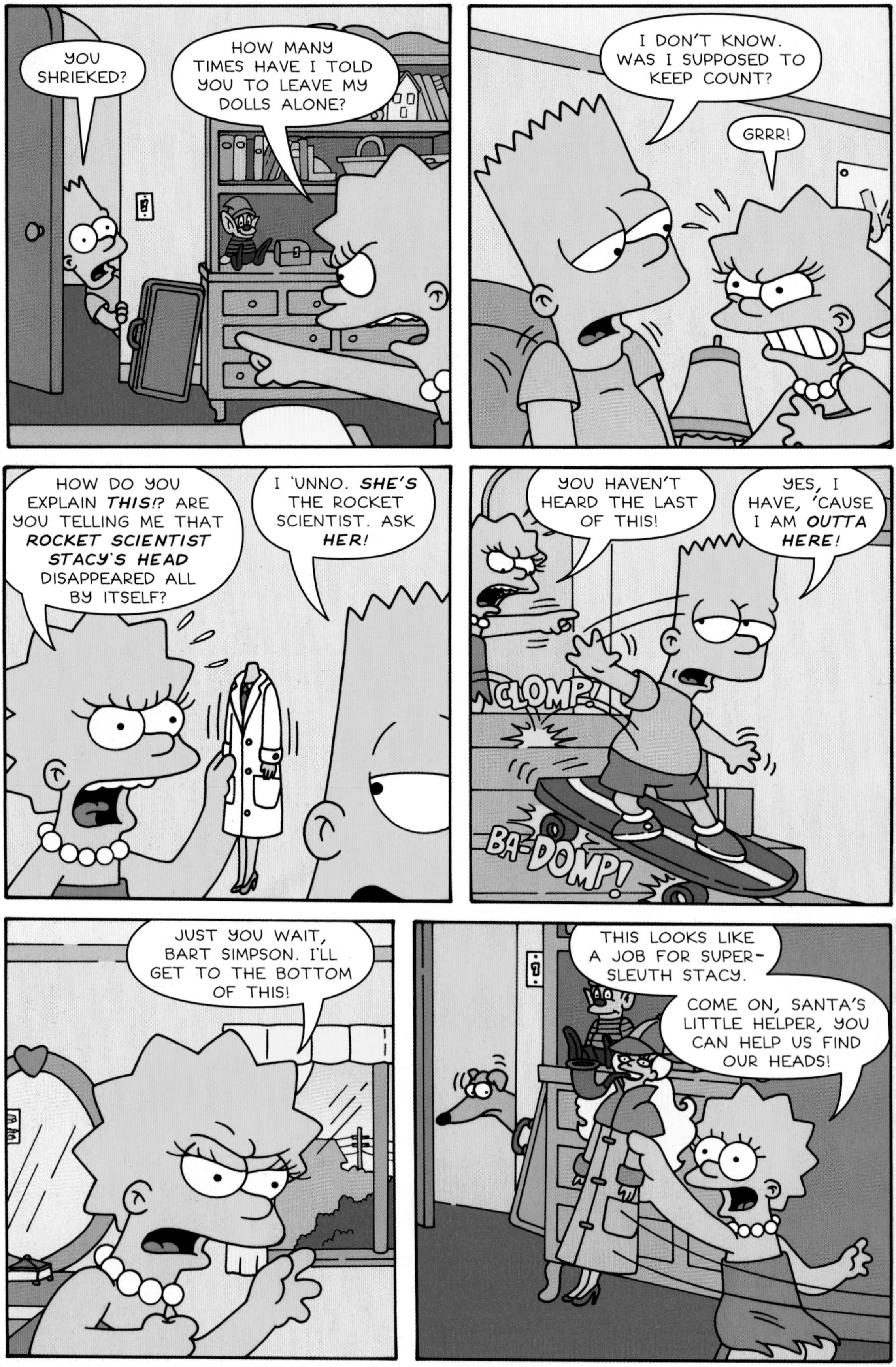
YOU SHRIEKED?
HOW MANY TIMES HAVE I TOLD YOU TO LEAVE MY DOLLS ALONE?
I DON'T KNOW. WAS I SUPPOSED TO KEEP COUNT?
GRRR!
HOW DO YOU EXPLAIN THIS!? ARE YOU TELLING ME THAT ROCKET SCIENTIST STACY'S HEAD DISAPPEARED ALL BY ITSELF?
I 'UNNO. SHE'S THE ROCKET SCIENTIST. ASK HER!
YOU HAVEN'T HEARD THE LAST OF THIS!
YES, I HAVE, 'CAUSE I AM OUTTA HERE!
CLOMP!
BA-DOMP!
JUST YOU WAIT, BART SIMPSON. I'LL GET TO THE BOTTOM OF THIS!
THIS LOOKS LIKE A JOB FOR SUPER-SLEUTH STACY.
COME ON, SANTA'S LITTLE HELPER, YOU CAN HELP US FIND OUR HEADS!

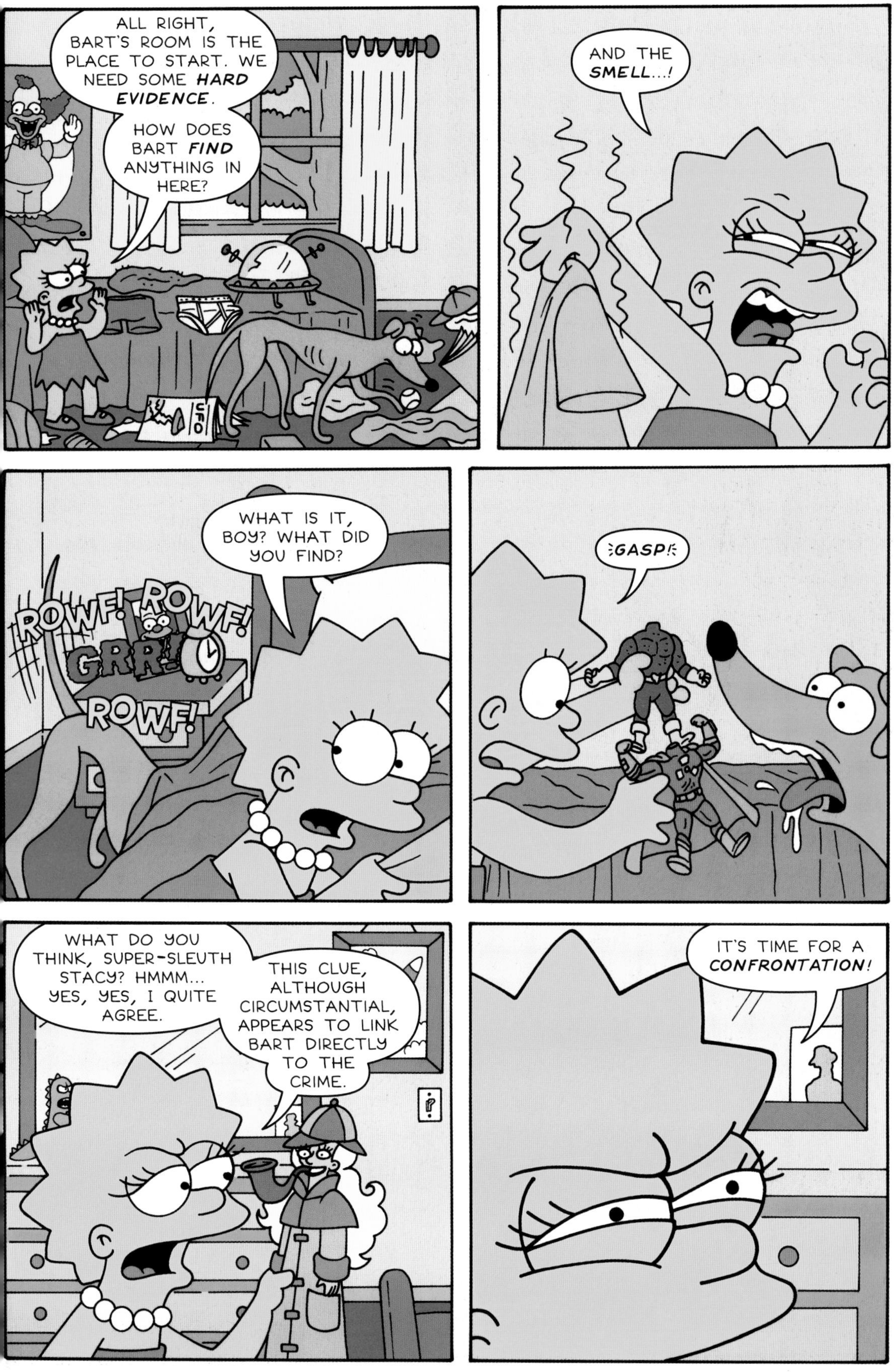
ALL RIGHT, BART'S ROOM IS THE PLACE TO START. WE NEED SOME HARD EVIDENCE.
HOW DOES BART FIND ANYTHING IN HERE?
UFO
AND THE SMELL...!
WHAT IS IT, BOY? WHAT DID YOU FIND?
ROWF! ROWF!
GRR!
ROWF!
GASP!
WHAT DO YOU THINK, SUPER-SLEUTH STACY? HMMM... YES, YES, I QUITE AGREE.
THIS CLUE, ALTHOUGH CIRCUMSTANTIAL, APPEARS TO LINK BART DIRECTLY TO THE CRIME.
IT'S TIME FOR A CONFRONTATION!

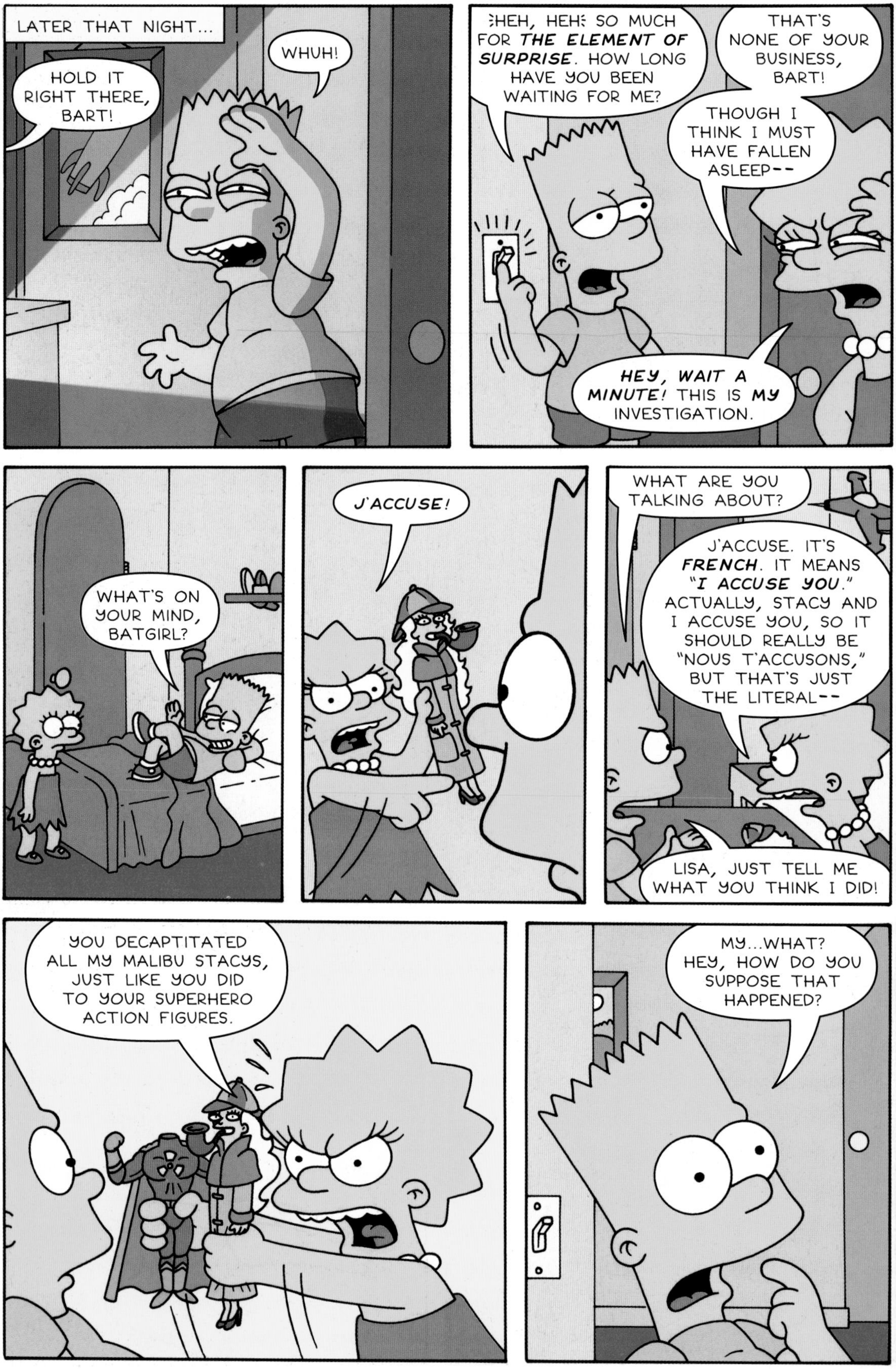
LATER THAT NIGHT...
HOLD IT RIGHT THERE, BART!
WHUH!
:HEH, HEH: SO MUCH FOR THE ELEMENT OF SURPRISE. HOW LONG HAVE YOU BEEN WAITING FOR ME?
THAT'S NONE OF YOUR BUSINESS, BART!
THOUGH I THINK I MUST HAVE FALLEN ASLEEP--
HEY, WAIT A MINUTE! THIS IS MY INVESTIGATION.
WHAT'S ON YOUR MIND, BATGIRL?
J'ACCUSE!
WHAT ARE YOU TALKING ABOUT?
J'ACCUSE. IT'S FRENCH. IT MEANS "I ACCUSE YOU." ACTUALLY, STACY AND I ACCUSE YOU, SO IT SHOULD REALLY BE "NOUS T'ACCUSONS," BUT THAT'S JUST THE LITERAL--
LISA, JUST TELL ME WHAT YOU THINK I DID!
YOU DECAPTITATED ALL MY MALIBU STACYS, JUST LIKE YOU DID TO YOUR SUPERHERO ACTION FIGURES.
MY...WHAT? HEY, HOW DO YOU SUPPOSE THAT HAPPENED?

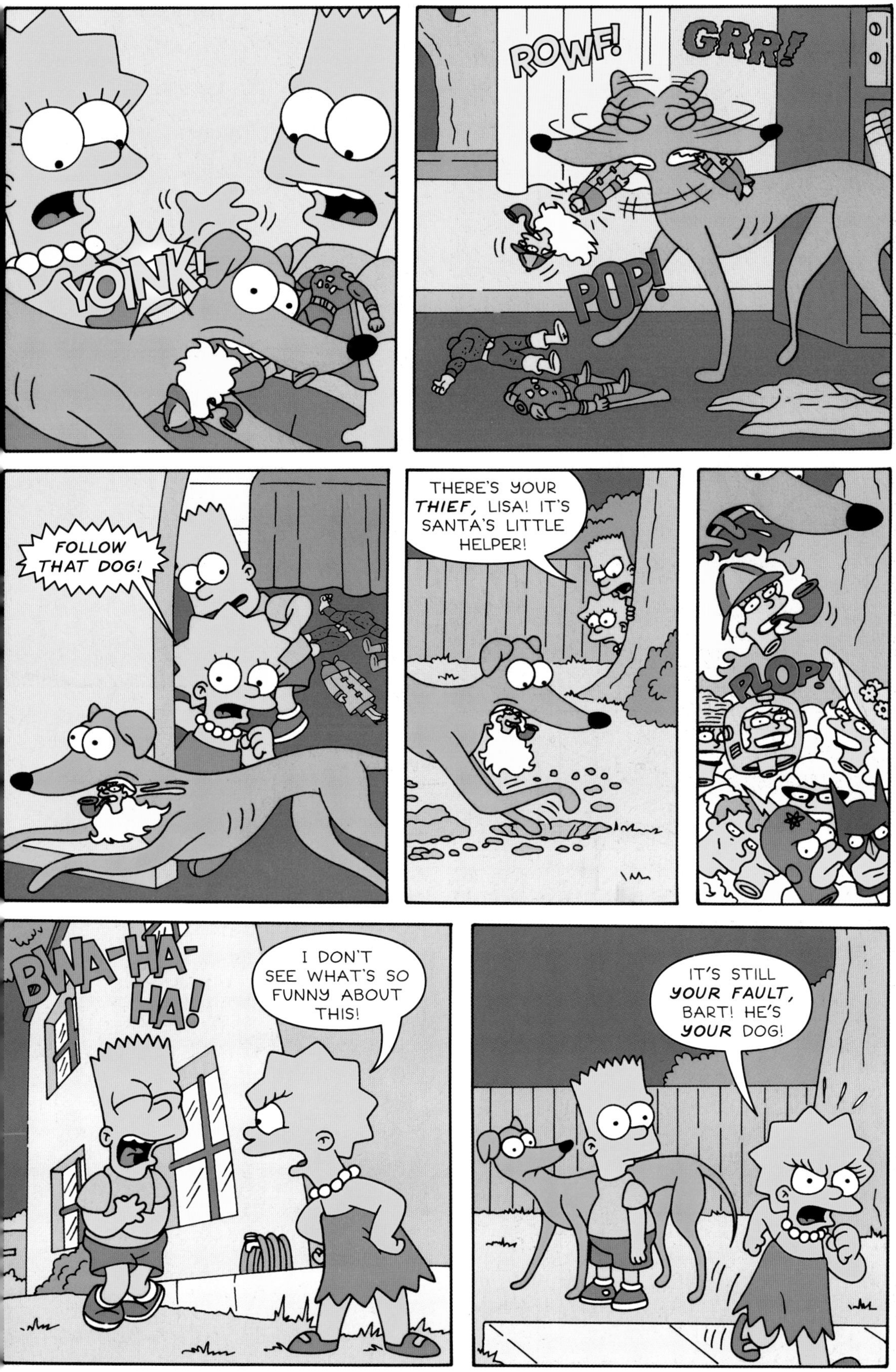
YOINK!
ROWF!
GRR!
POP!
FOLLOW THAT DOG!
THERE'S YOUR *THIEF,* LISA! IT'S SANTA'S LITTLE HELPER!
PLOP!
BWA-HA-HA!
I DON'T SEE WHAT'S SO FUNNY ABOUT THIS!
IT'S STILL *YOUR FAULT,* BART! HE'S *YOUR* DOG!

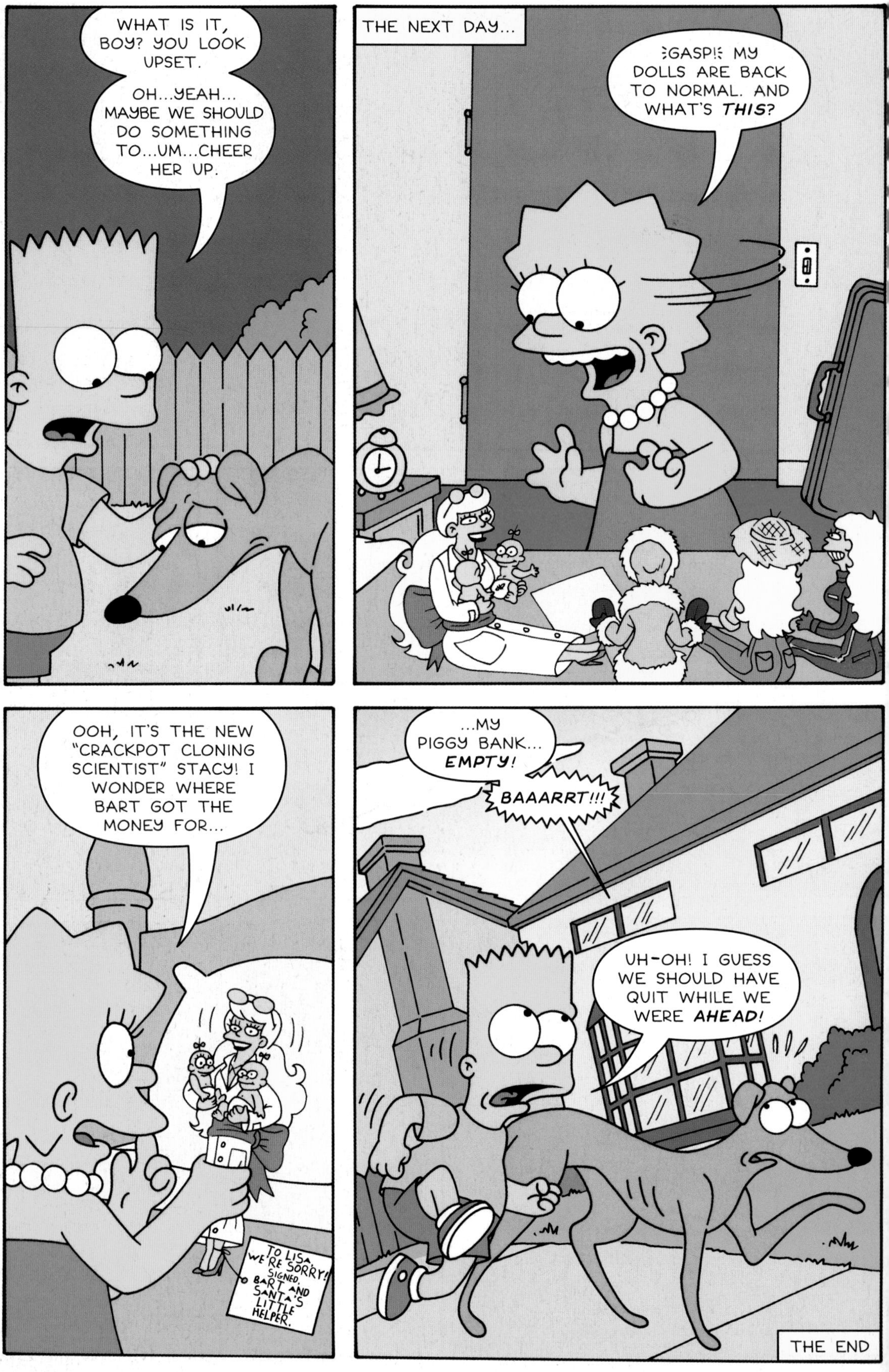
WHAT IS IT, BOY? YOU LOOK UPSET.
OH...YEAH... MAYBE WE SHOULD DO SOMETHING TO...UM...CHEER HER UP.
THE NEXT DAY...
GASP! MY DOLLS ARE BACK TO NORMAL. AND WHAT'S *THIS*?
OOH, IT'S THE NEW "CRACKPOT CLONING SCIENTIST" STACY! I WONDER WHERE BART GOT THE MONEY FOR...
TO LISA, WE'RE SORRY! SIGNED, BART AND SANTA'S LITTLE HELPER.
...MY PIGGY BANK... **EMPTY!**
BAAARRT!!!
UH-OH! I GUESS WE SHOULD HAVE QUIT WHILE WE WERE **AHEAD!**
THE END

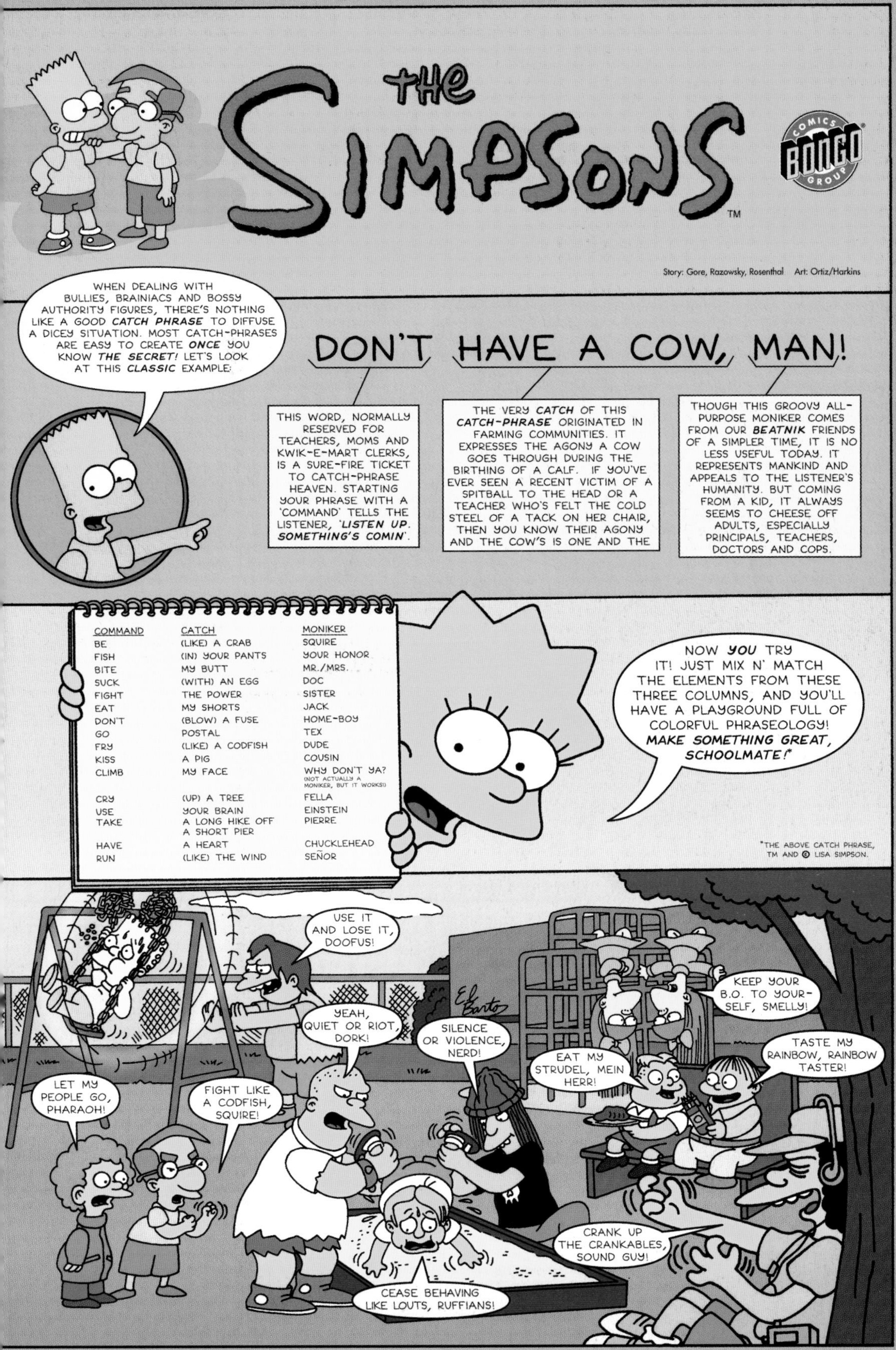

THE SIMPSONS TM
COMICS BONGO GROUP
Story: Gore, Razowsky, Rosenthal Art: Ortiz/Harkins
WHEN DEALING WITH BULLIES, BRAINIACS AND BOSSY AUTHORITY FIGURES, THERE'S NOTHING LIKE A GOOD **CATCH PHRASE** TO DIFFUSE A DICEY SITUATION. MOST CATCH-PHRASES ARE EASY TO CREATE **ONCE** YOU KNOW **THE SECRET!** LET'S LOOK AT THIS **CLASSIC** EXAMPLE:
DON'T HAVE A COW, MAN!
THIS WORD, NORMALLY RESERVED FOR TEACHERS, MOMS AND KWIK-E-MART CLERKS, IS A SURE-FIRE TICKET TO CATCH-PHRASE HEAVEN. STARTING YOUR PHRASE WITH A 'COMMAND' TELLS THE LISTENER, '**LISTEN UP. SOMETHING'S COMIN**'.
THE VERY **CATCH** OF THIS **CATCH-PHRASE** ORIGINATED IN FARMING COMMUNITIES. IT EXPRESSES THE AGONY A COW GOES THROUGH DURING THE BIRTHING OF A CALF. IF YOU'VE EVER SEEN A RECENT VICTIM OF A SPITBALL TO THE HEAD OR A TEACHER WHO'S FELT THE COLD STEEL OF A TACK ON HER CHAIR, THEN YOU KNOW THEIR AGONY AND THE COW'S IS ONE AND THE
THOUGH THIS GROOVY ALL-PURPOSE MONIKER COMES FROM OUR **BEATNIK** FRIENDS OF A SIMPLER TIME, IT IS NO LESS USEFUL TODAY. IT REPRESENTS MANKIND AND APPEALS TO THE LISTENER'S HUMANITY. BUT COMING FROM A KID, IT ALWAYS SEEMS TO CHEESE OFF ADULTS, ESPECIALLY PRINCIPALS, TEACHERS, DOCTORS AND COPS.
COMMAND: BE, FISH, BITE, SUCK, FIGHT, EAT, DON'T, GO, FRY, KISS, CLIMB, CRY, USE, TAKE, HAVE, RUN
CATCH: (LIKE) A CRAB, (IN) YOUR PANTS, MY BUTT, (WITH) AN EGG, THE POWER, MY SHORTS, (BLOW) A FUSE, POSTAL, (LIKE) A CODFISH, A PIG, MY FACE, (UP) A TREE, YOUR BRAIN, A LONG HIKE OFF A SHORT PIER, A HEART, (LIKE) THE WIND
MONIKER: SQUIRE, YOUR HONOR, MR./MRS., DOC, SISTER, JACK, HOME-BOY, TEX, DUDE, COUSIN, WHY DON'T YA? (NOT ACTUALLY A MONIKER, BUT IT WORKS!), FELLA, EINSTEIN, PIERRE, CHUCKLEHEAD, SEÑOR
NOW **YOU** TRY IT! JUST MIX N' MATCH THE ELEMENTS FROM THESE THREE COLUMNS, AND YOU'LL HAVE A PLAYGROUND FULL OF COLORFUL PHRASEOLOGY! **MAKE SOMETHING GREAT, SCHOOLMATE!***
*THE ABOVE CATCH PHRASE, TM AND © LISA SIMPSON.
USE IT AND LOSE IT, DOOFUS!
El Barto
YEAH, QUIET OR RIOT, DORK!
SILENCE OR VIOLENCE, NERD!
KEEP YOUR B.O. TO YOURSELF, SMELLY!
EAT MY STRUDEL, MEIN HERR!
TASTE MY RAINBOW, RAINBOW TASTER!
LET MY PEOPLE GO, PHARAOH!
FIGHT LIKE A CODFISH, SQUIRE!
CRANK UP THE CRANKABLES, SOUND GUY!
CEASE BEHAVING LIKE LOUTS, RUFFIANS!

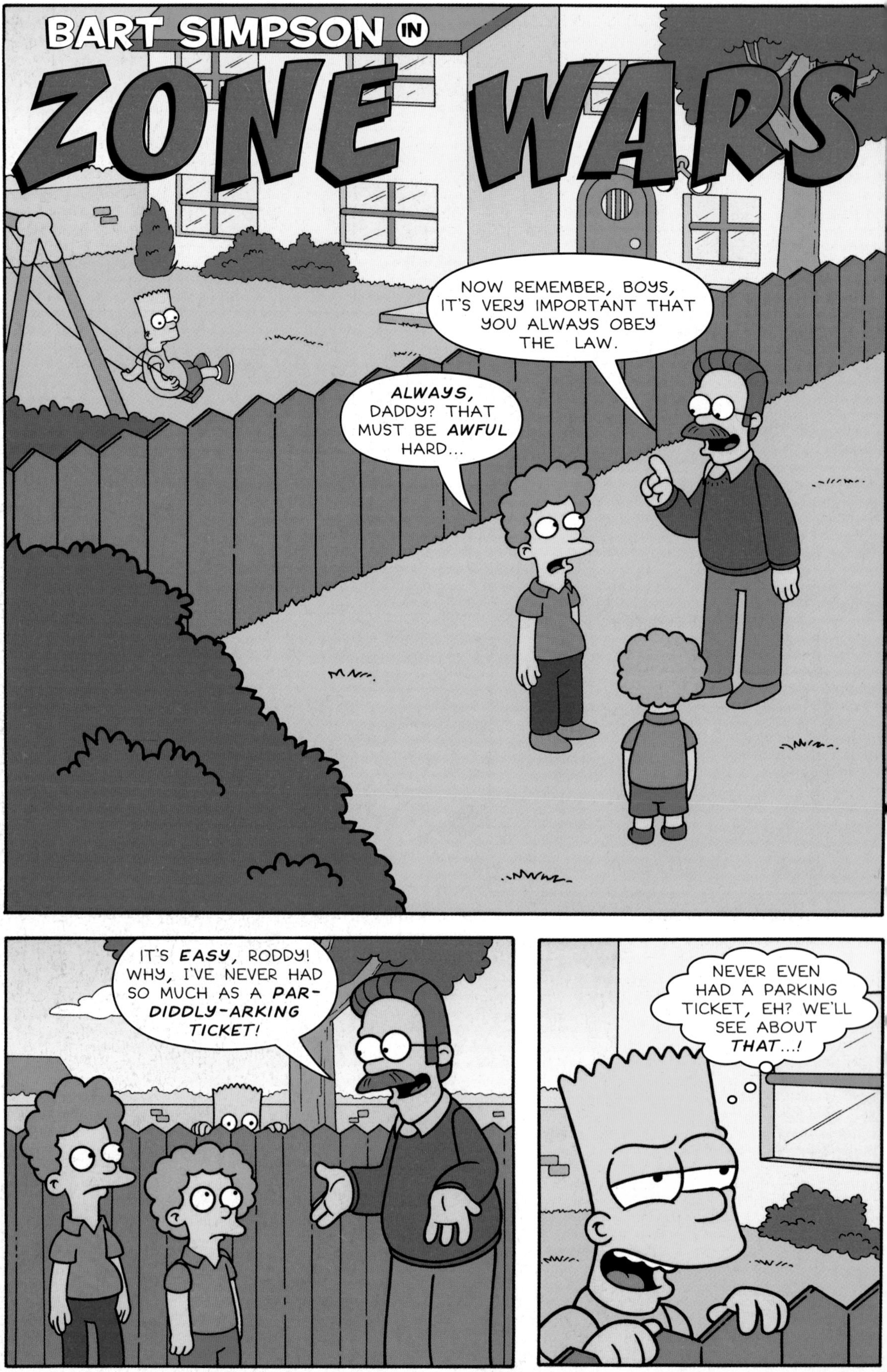
BART SIMPSON IN
ZONE WARS
NOW REMEMBER, BOYS, IT'S VERY IMPORTANT THAT YOU ALWAYS OBEY THE LAW.
ALWAYS, DADDY? THAT MUST BE AWFUL HARD...
IT'S EASY, RODDY! WHY, I'VE NEVER HAD SO MUCH AS A PAR-DIDDLY-ARKING TICKET!
NEVER EVEN HAD A PARKING TICKET, EH? WE'LL SEE ABOUT THAT...!

BRYAN UHLENBROCK SCRIPT · JOEY NILGES PENCILS · PHYLLIS NOVIN INKS · ART VILLANUEVA COLORS · KAREN BATES LETTERS · BILL MORRISON EDITOR

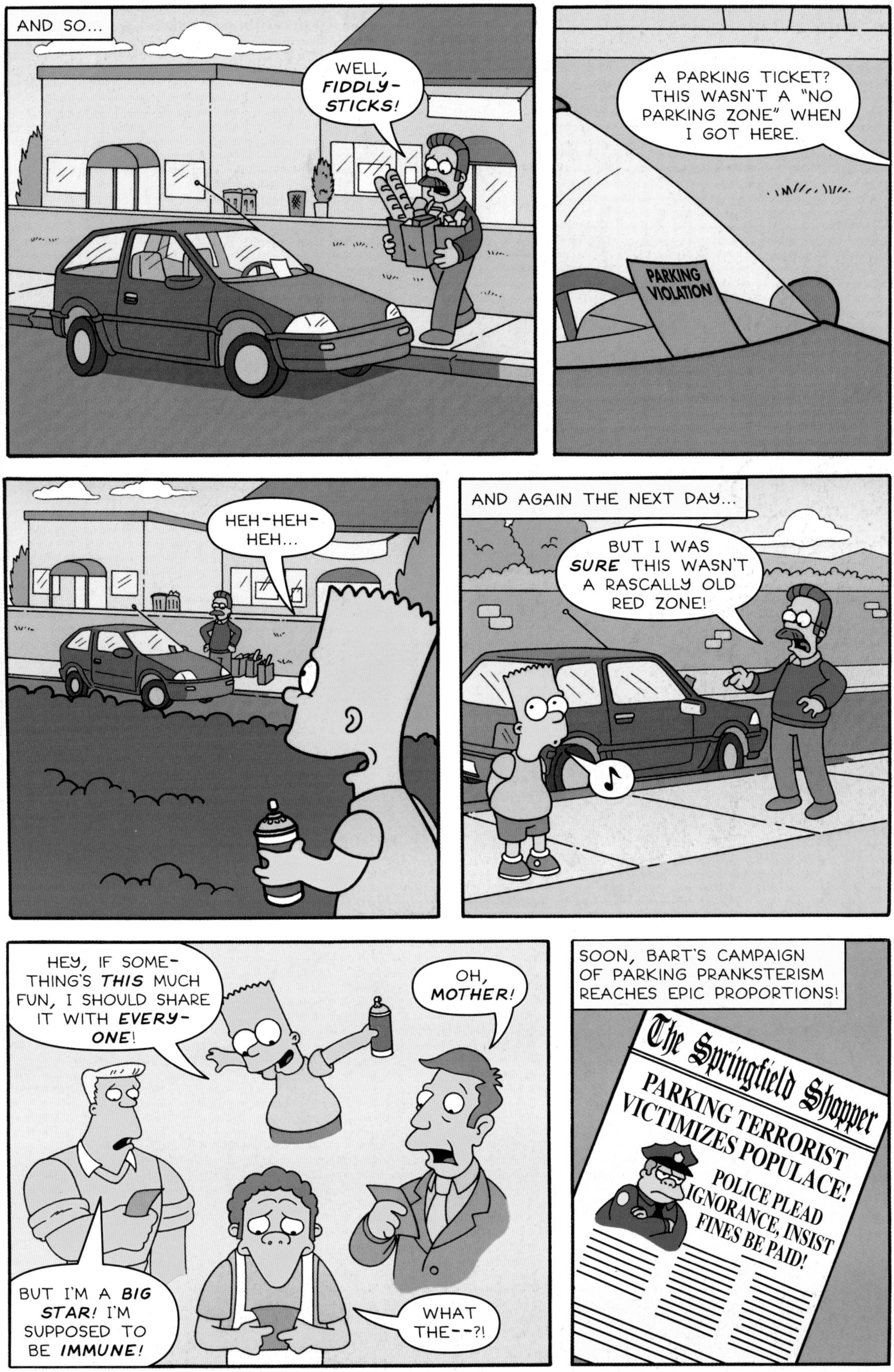
AND SO...
WELL, FIDDLY-STICKS!
A PARKING TICKET? THIS WASN'T A "NO PARKING ZONE" WHEN I GOT HERE.
PARKING VIOLATION
HEH-HEH-HEH...
AND AGAIN THE NEXT DAY...
BUT I WAS SURE THIS WASN'T A RASCALLY OLD RED ZONE!
♪
HEY, IF SOMETHING'S THIS MUCH FUN, I SHOULD SHARE IT WITH EVERYONE!
OH, MOTHER!
BUT I'M A BIG STAR! I'M SUPPOSED TO BE IMMUNE!
WHAT THE--?!
SOON, BART'S CAMPAIGN OF PARKING PRANKSTERISM REACHES EPIC PROPORTIONS!
The Springfield Shopper
PARKING TERRORIST VICTIMIZES POPULACE!
POLICE PLEAD IGNORANCE, INSIST FINES BE PAID!

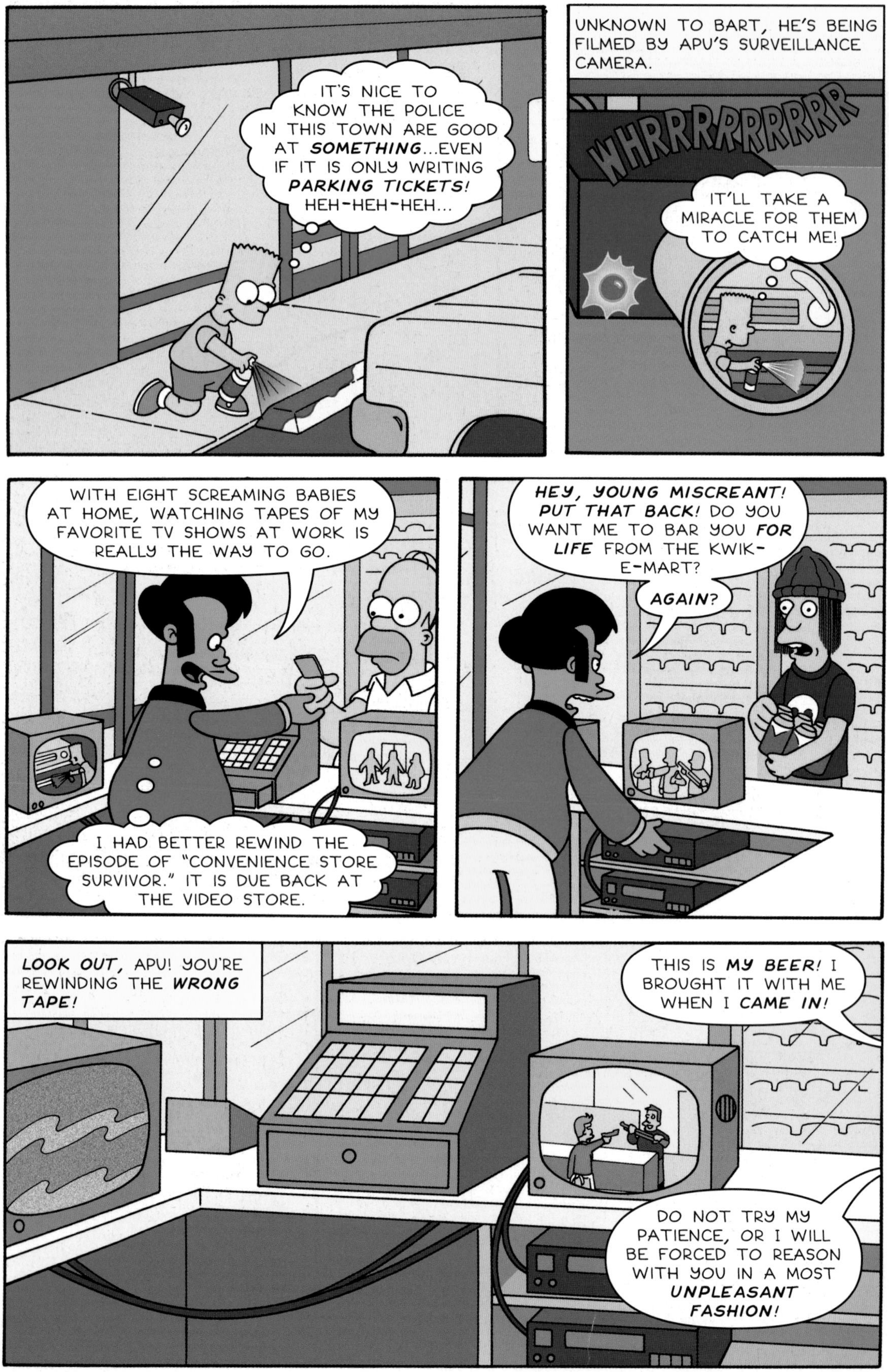
IT'S NICE TO KNOW THE POLICE IN THIS TOWN ARE GOOD AT SOMETHING...EVEN IF IT IS ONLY WRITING PARKING TICKETS! HEH-HEH-HEH...
UNKNOWN TO BART, HE'S BEING FILMED BY APU'S SURVEILLANCE CAMERA.
WHRRRRRRRRR
IT'LL TAKE A MIRACLE FOR THEM TO CATCH ME!
WITH EIGHT SCREAMING BABIES AT HOME, WATCHING TAPES OF MY FAVORITE TV SHOWS AT WORK IS REALLY THE WAY TO GO.
I HAD BETTER REWIND THE EPISODE OF "CONVENIENCE STORE SURVIVOR." IT IS DUE BACK AT THE VIDEO STORE.
HEY, YOUNG MISCREANT! PUT THAT BACK! DO YOU WANT ME TO BAR YOU FOR LIFE FROM THE KWIK-E-MART?
AGAIN?
LOOK OUT, APU! YOU'RE REWINDING THE WRONG TAPE!
THIS IS MY BEER! I BROUGHT IT WITH ME WHEN I CAME IN!
DO NOT TRY MY PATIENCE, OR I WILL BE FORCED TO REASON WITH YOU IN A MOST UNPLEASANT FASHION!

AND BECAUSE *GREAT MINDS* THINK ALIKE...

A LITTLE VIDEO SHOULD BE A FINE WAY TO RELAX TONIGHT! OOOH! "CONVENIENCE STORE SURVIVOR!" I LOVE THIS SHOW!

COVENIENCE STORE SURVIVOR

MAN, WHAT A RIP-OFF! WHERE'S THE VIOLENCE? WHERE ARE ALL THE ROBBERIES?

THERE'S NOTHING ON THIS VIDEO BUT THAT SIMPSON KID SPRAY-PAINTING A CURB.

HEY, WAIT A MINUTE! NO WONDER I'VE BEEN GETTING *WRITER'S CRAMP* FROM WRITING ALL THOSE *EXTRA* PARKING TICKETS! IT'S ALL THAT *KID'S FAULT!*

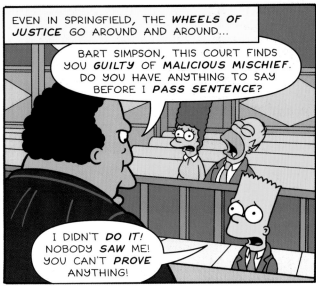

EVEN IN SPRINGFIELD, THE *WHEELS OF JUSTICE* GO AROUND AND AROUND...

BART SIMPSON, THIS COURT FINDS YOU *GUILTY* OF *MALICIOUS MISCHIEF.* DO YOU HAVE ANYTHING TO SAY BEFORE I *PASS SENTENCE?*

I DIDN'T *DO IT!* NOBODY *SAW* ME! YOU CAN'T *PROVE* ANYTHING!

YES, YOU *DID* DO IT! WE'VE *ALL* SEEN YOU, AND YOUR *GUILT* IS *PROVEN!*

I HEREBY SENTENCE YOU TO *HARD LABOR* SCRUBBING ALL THE *PAINT* OFF THOSE *PHONY RED ZONES!*

OH MAN, WHAT AM I GONNA *DO?* I'M SUPPOSED TO START CLEANING UP ALL THOSE RED ZONES *TOMORROW!* MY REP AS THIS TOWN'S NUMBER ONE SCOFFLAW WILL BE *TOAST!*

AH-HA! I'VE *GOT IT!*

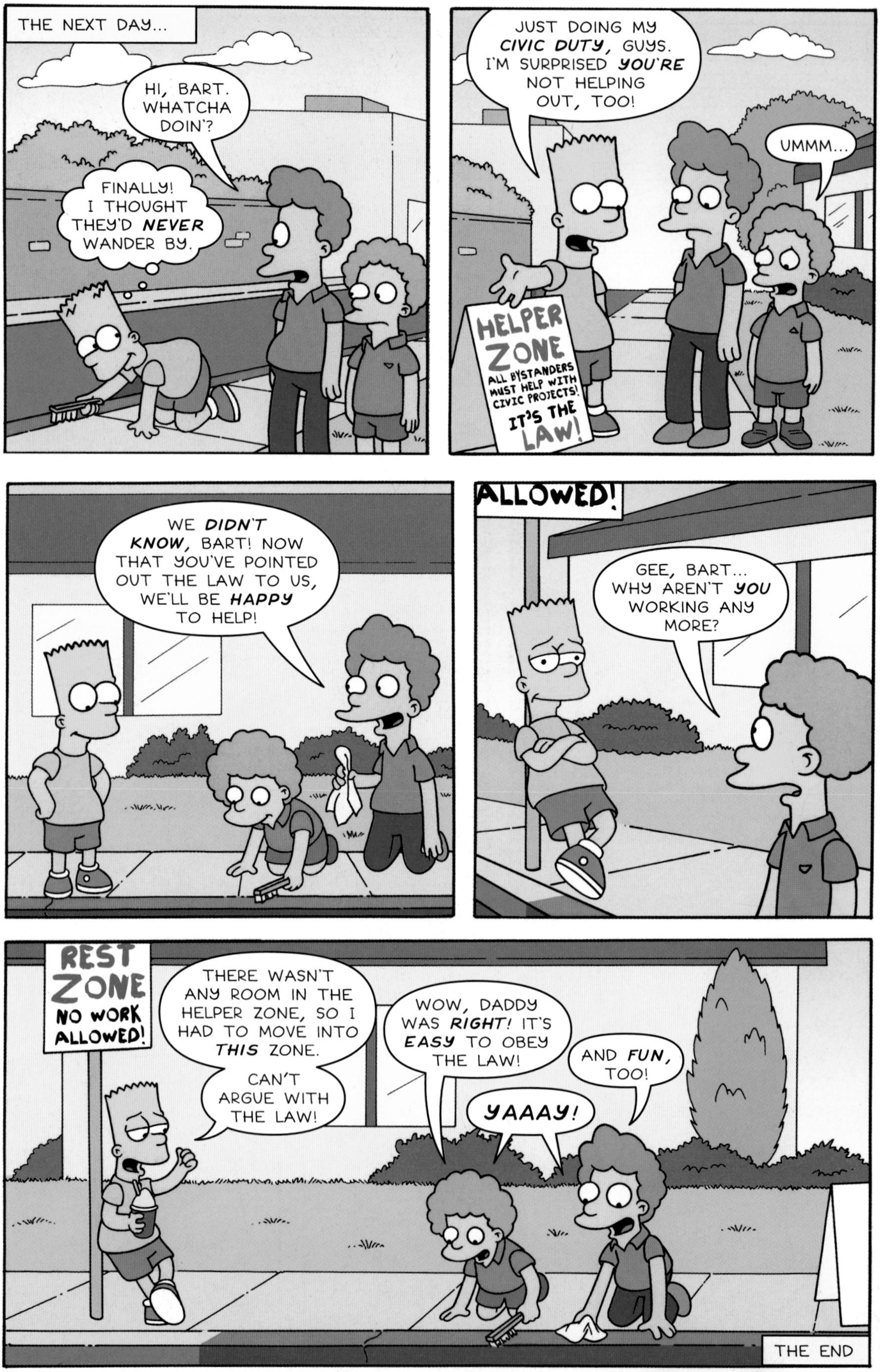
THE NEXT DAY...
HI, BART. WHATCHA DOIN'?
FINALLY! I THOUGHT THEY'D NEVER WANDER BY.
JUST DOING MY CIVIC DUTY, GUYS. I'M SURPRISED YOU'RE NOT HELPING OUT, TOO!
HELPER ZONE ALL BYSTANDERS MUST HELP WITH CIVIC PROJECTS! IT'S THE LAW!
UMMM...
WE DIDN'T KNOW, BART! NOW THAT YOU'VE POINTED OUT THE LAW TO US, WE'LL BE HAPPY TO HELP!
ALLOWED!
GEE, BART... WHY AREN'T YOU WORKING ANY MORE?
REST ZONE NO WORK ALLOWED!
THERE WASN'T ANY ROOM IN THE HELPER ZONE, SO I HAD TO MOVE INTO THIS ZONE.
CAN'T ARGUE WITH THE LAW!
WOW, DADDY WAS RIGHT! IT'S EASY TO OBEY THE LAW!
AND FUN, TOO!
YAAAY!
THE END

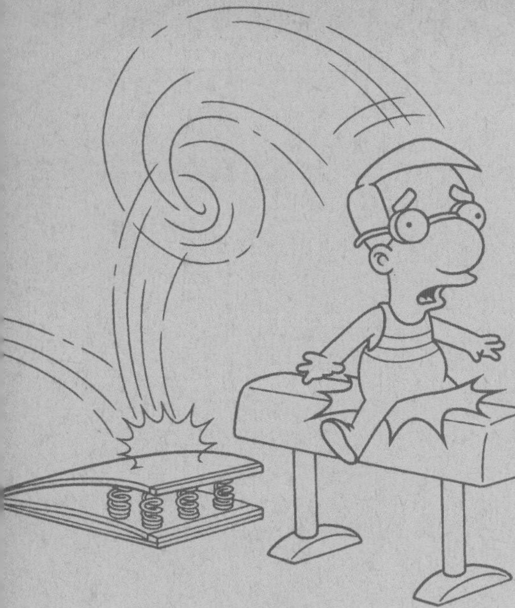
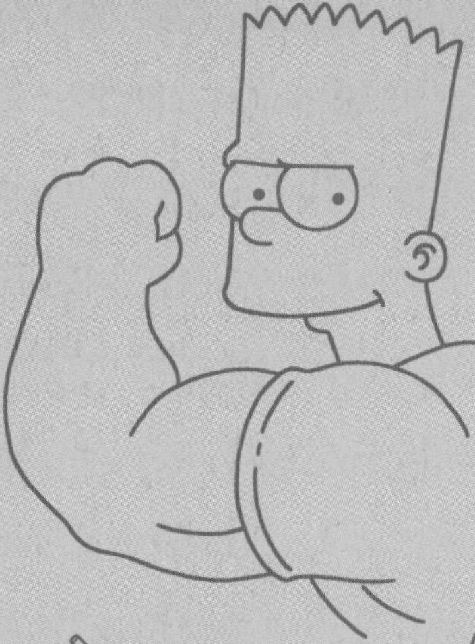
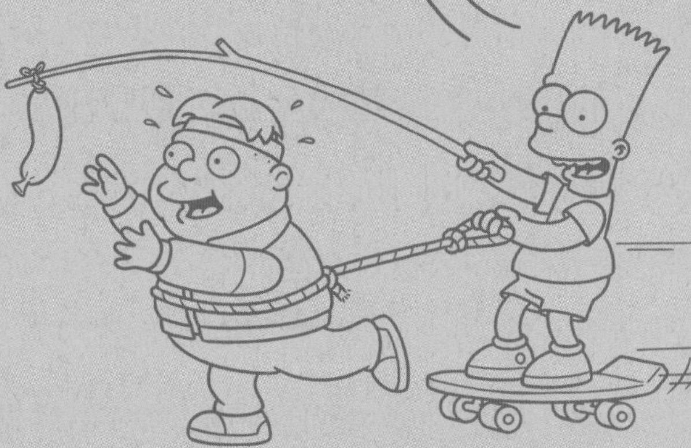
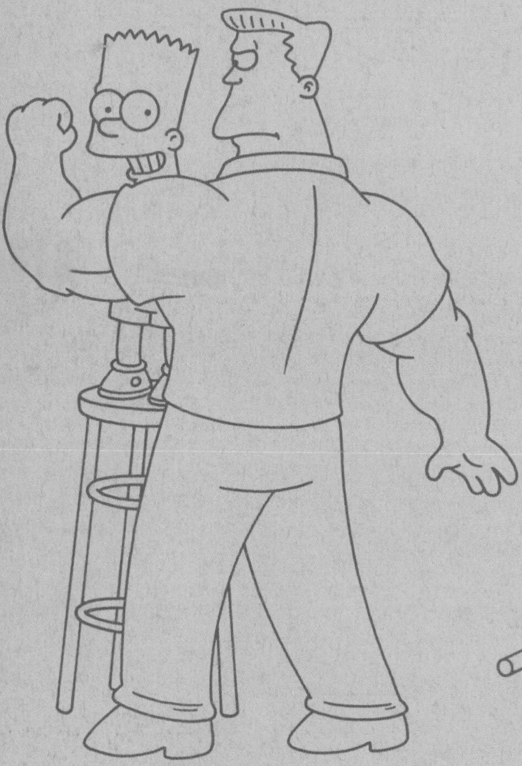
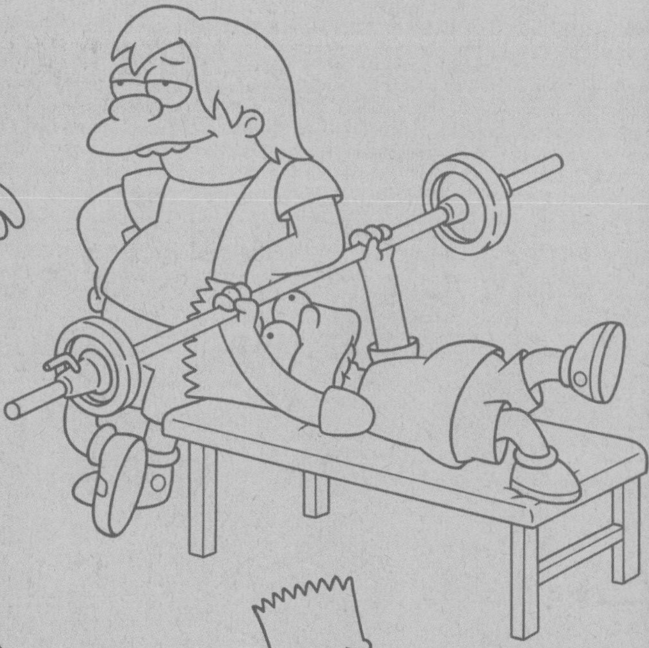
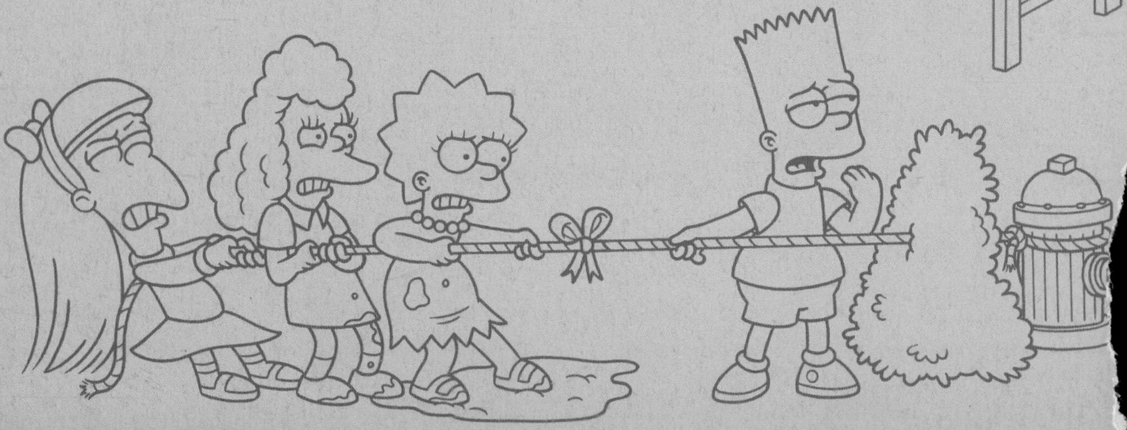